Dr Ramesh Manocha  medical practitioner, educatoi his medical training at the Un. and Liverpool Hospital. His PhD focused on the scientific evaluation of meditation and the mental silence experience, and was completed at the School of Community Medicine, UNSW, and the Royal Hospital for Women.

Ramesh is the founder and convenor of Generation Next, a national initiative dealing with youth mental health. He is currently a senior lecturer at the Department of Psychiatry at Sydney University. As part of his long involvement in medical education he chairs a series of seminars for primary health professionals that focus on family medicine and women's and children's health.

Ramesh is regularly sought out by the media for comment on various health and medical issues, complementary medicine and meditation. He is frequently engaged to speak to audiences in the community, educational, public and corporate sectors.

Silence Your Mind is his first book.

www.beyondthemind.com

Silence
Your Mind

Dr Ramesh Manocha

Pseudonyms have been used in this book and other details altered where necessary
to protect the identity and privacy of people mentioned.

If you have a specific health condition we strongly suggest that you continue
with your conventional treatments for that condition. If you have a serious illness
we urge you to notify your supervising health professional that you have
commenced a trial course of evidence-based meditation.

It is the author's opinion that people who are currently suffering from, or have a
history of, serious mental illnesses should not do any kind of meditation without
specific permission and supervision by a suitably qualified mental health professional.

This edition first published in Great Britain in 2014 by
Orion
an imprint of the Orion Publishing Group Ltd
Orion House, 5 Upper St Martin's Lane,
London WC2H 9EA
An Hachette UK Company

1 3 5 7 9 10 8 6 4 2

A CIP catalogue record for this book is available
from the British Library.

Trade Paperback ISBN: 978 1 409 15393 1

Printed and bound in Great Britain by CPI Group (UK) Ltd, Crydon, CR0 4YY

The Orion Publishing Group's policy is to use papers that
are natural, renewable and recyclable products and made
from wood grown in sustainable forests. The logging and
manufacturing processes are expected to conform to the
environmental regulations of the country of origin.

Every effort has been made to fulfil requirements with regard
to reproducing copyright material. The author and publisher will
be

To you, the reader

Contents

In addition to the information given in this book, the website **www.beyondthemind.com** *offers further practical help, online resources, information, and advice about places where Sahaja yoga classes are held should you feel like receiving some face to face instruction. All of these resources are effective and free of charge.*

How to Meditate
A guide to the practical sections

You can use these instructions at your own pace to help you to meditate, whether or not you have read the chapters around them.

You are not your problems.

You are not the things you own.

*You are not your body any more than you are the clothes that
  hang on it.*

You are not your career, your achievements, nor your failures.

You are not even your thoughts, memories or emotions.

You are something beyond all of these things, beyond the mind.

*You are the infinite silence that is hidden in the space between
  each thought.*

When you silence your mind, you will find yourself,

*In the eternal present moment, the pure awareness, reality and
  joy,*

The self itself.

This is true meditation.

Ramesh Manocha

Before we begin

Ask yourself these questions:

- How often have I been unable to sleep because I can't switch off my thoughts?
- How many times have I walked into a room looking for something, only to realise that I have forgotten what I was looking for?
- When I want to think about or do something, do unnecessary thoughts distract me?
- How many times have I noticed that when I am upset, stressed or angry, my thinking activity increases? At these times are my thoughts helpful or distracting? Do they make the situation better or worse?
- There is a constant stream of background mental chatter going through my head. How much of it is useful? Most of it? Half? A quarter? Less?
- What proportion of my thoughts is generally positive and what proportion negative? What proportion contributes to my wellbeing and what proportion doesn't?
- Can I stop that background mental noise, that constant thinking, whenever I want to?

Everything that you will read in this book, especially the practical exercises, is aimed at changing the way you will answer those crucial questions.

Silence Your Mind is different from any other book you may have read about meditation. It sets out to liberate you from the common myths, the misinformation and the many clichés that have arisen around this ancient practice. Meditation is not just about reducing stress but also about realising our potential for optimal wellbeing and our capacity for high performance. *Silence Your Mind* will show how meditation can be used by anyone, at any age; by people with religious or spiritual beliefs, or no beliefs at all. It can be practised anywhere – you don't need to go to a special room or a retreat to do it – and you can feel the benefits of meditation with just 10 to 20 minutes of practice each day.

The meditation technique described here can take you from the limitations of the thinking mind into the experience of non-thought known as 'thoughtless awareness' or 'mental silence', the state beyond the mind. It challenges you to realise your full potential and gives you a set of simple, practical tools to do so.

Meditation is not about modifying, editing or slowing your thoughts; it is about *stopping them altogether.* It is not about mindfulness but *mind-emptiness.* Not quieting the mind so much as silencing it in its tracks if, and whenever, we want to. In true meditation we remain alert, in control and yet free of all thought. It is the experience of complete inner silence that enables us to master the mind and the mental content that it creates, rather than be the mind's servant. Our awareness, no longer cluttered by unnecessary thoughts, becomes capable of experiencing our self and our world more richly and with more joy.

Martial artists call this state *mushin*, the state without mind, elite athletes call it 'the zone' and musicians or artists might call it 'flow'. It is a state of optimal being, something that occurs not just when we sit in meditation but a living experience that should be carried with us throughout the day, enhancing our moment-to-moment experience of life and our ability to engage constructively with it.

The ancient Eastern traditions that come from the *Bhagavad Gita* and the teachings of Lao Tse, Confucius and the Buddha, say that the state beyond the mind is not only achievable but essential. For if we cannot master our own mental content, how can we truly be masters of ourselves and our destinies?

But how is it possible to switch off our mental activity – the background noise that most of us accept as a normal part of our inner environment? For most people the mind is *never* quiet. We have anywhere from dozens to hundreds of thoughts per minute, few of them useful, many of them unconstructive. How many of us can switch off this 'self-talk' at will to give our minds a rest?

In the East this constant mental chatter is known as the 'monkey mind' – the mind jumps from thought to thought and object to object, while we daydream, ruminate over relationships, dwell on the past and worry about the future.

When your mental noise distracts you from the task at hand, makes you forget what it was that you walked into the room for or keeps you awake at night when you really need your sleep, you are a victim of your own monkey mind. When that monkey mind is allowed to do whatever it wants, you lose touch with the simple joys of life, lose your natural balance and start to get stressed.

Fuelled by our 24/7 culture, an all-pervasive media and the relentless pursuit of consumption, for many people the monkey has morphed into a 400 kilogram gorilla with an attitude problem. It is this rampaging primate between our ears that is responsible for the epidemic of stress, mental dysfunction and loss of wellness that is now more prevalent than ever before. This book spells out a solution to this problem and the scientific evidence to support it.

For most people, mental silence seems unachievable. However, the results of more than a dozen years of scientific research tell us that this fundamental reality is not the exclusive realm of secluded monks, Zen masters or 'gurus'. With a small amount of regular practice, using the techniques that appear in this book, anyone can experience it. We have found that in their first meditation session, on average about 10% of people will experience 'complete mental silence', and a further 20–30% experience being 'mostly silent'. With further practice, progressively greater numbers of people attain the mental silence experience and are able to deepen it. So while I can't promise that it will be instantaneous for everyone, I can say with reasonable confidence that the majority will get there with regular practice. Moreover, the experience costs nothing to learn and is as natural and effortless as riding a bicycle.

Here is an interview between myself and an eight-year-old girl about the benefits of meditation.

GIRL: … it's hard to think about not thinking.
RM: Yes?
GIRL: Yeah.
RM: Did you manage to do it?

GIRL: Yes.

RM: Really?

GIRL: Yeah.

RM: And when you got into that sort of state where you weren't thinking, how did it feel? Was it nice or was it yucky?

GIRL: It was nice, it felt good. I felt happy and calm, yeah. And being calm. Happy and calm. For the rest of the day I felt pretty happy.

—

For him who has conquered the mind, the mind is the best of friends; but for one who has failed to do so, his mind will remain the greatest enemy.

Bhagavad Gita

Silence Your Mind presents a combination of explanation and evidence regarding the benefits of a specific and unique understanding of meditation, the central feature of which is an experience known as 'thoughtless awareness' or 'mental silence'. I did not develop the meditation techniques that are the subject of my research. As they are currently taught around the world free of charge I do not have any financial stake in their popularisation either. Nevertheless, I do sincerely believe that there is so much that every person can gain by using them on a daily basis that it is my ethical obligation as a doctor and researcher to communicate this information to the public. Author royalties from this book will be directed to further research and educational activities in this field. It is my fervent hope to contribute to the democratisation of this experience by sharing with you the techniques that have proved so liberating for me and many others.

Important: If you are receiving medical treatment

If you have a specific health condition we strongly suggest that you continue with your conventional treatments for that condition. If you have a serious illness we urge you to notify your supervising health professional that you have commenced a practice of evidence-based meditation.

It is my opinion that people who are currently suffering from, or have a history of, serious mental illnesses should not do any kind of meditation without specific permission and supervision by a suitably qualified mental health professional.

How to use this book

This book starts with my own experience of meditation then expands into a broader journey of scientific discovery, providing not only the evidence but the practical methods by which you can verify it for yourself. The information in this book is based on more than fifteen years of unique research into a phenomenon that I call 'mental silence', or 'thoughtless awareness'.

There are two kinds of evidence given in this book. First, scientific evidence derived from clinical trials and laboratory experiments with varying levels of scientific rigour. Second, remarkable stories and experiences which, although less scientific, provide an important insight into the personal dimension of the 'mental silence' experience. Many of these were provided by regular meditators from around the world in response to my requests for their personal experiences of how the mental silence experience has impacted on their lives. These stories are included here precisely because they are remarkable. They will not necessarily apply to every person who chooses to practise the techniques laid out in the following chapters.

I encourage you to be open-minded but sceptical with regard to this book's claims and assertions. The intention of this book is not to fill your head with facts and figures but to encourage you to engage in a profound personal experiment – the attainment of mental silence, the authentic basis of meditation. Ideally it will inspire you to meditate daily, for it's not the words on these pages so much as your own experience of mental silence that will persuade you of the benefits of regular meditation practice. As such, I have included extensive practical guidance in the 'How to meditate' sections of this book.

Every moment spent in the state of mental silence will enhance your experience of the present and is an investment in your future wellbeing and fulfilment. Isn't it worth committing to some regular practice to master that monkey mind and thereby awaken your potential for greater wellbeing, dynamism and happiness? It's a no-brainer.

Men are not prisoners of fate, but only prisoners of their own minds.

Franklin D. Roosevelt

PART I
MY STORY

1
The ants

This silence, this moment, every moment, if it's genuinely inside you, brings what you need.

Mevlana Rumi

It is 1988. I'm studying medicine and handling the stress that comes with it by drinking and partying hard. I convince myself that it's a legitimate way to let off steam but it's becoming obvious that this approach – which is more or less the established way in which medical students and many medical professionals handle the pressures of a medical career – has its limitations.

I find it difficult to sleep; a constant stream of thoughts keeps me awake into the small hours of every morning. Those thoughts – what psychologists call 'self-talk' – seem to be controlled by a sadist who has taken up residence in the back of my head. A sadist flying high on anabolic steroids and a degree in psychology. At night, as my head sinks into the pillow in anticipation of drifting to sleep, the sadist springs into action. Just as the precious sleep comes tantalisingly close, the sadist switches on a tape recording of the whole day's events. It's a kind of fast forward that usually takes about 30 to 40 minutes for a full review of the day. Just when it seems as if it's over, the sadist rewinds to the worst parts and plays them again. Usually in slow motion.

The sadist is a relentless taskmaster, controlling my mental content, surfing the YouTube of my mind as I lie helpless in bed, staring into the night. The ruminations are an endless circle: *Why did I make that stupid comment in the anatomy tutorial? Did everybody hear it? Does everyone think I'm stupid now? I wish I was smarter. What's it like to be really smart? Exam next week. Need to study, don't want to fail. What would happen if I failed?*

On and on and on it goes. My clock radio emits so much light from the electronic numbers that I cover it with a towel to stop it from reminding me of how long I haven't been asleep. Alcohol becomes a useful option at this point and so there are many days when, having drunk myself to sleep, I oversleep and turn up late and hungover to lectures, or sleep through them altogether.

This mind of mine is finding it increasingly difficult to focus, and my performance in exams is slipping rapidly. I decide that it's time to find a solution that's sustainable, and doesn't involve the consumption of alcohol, marijuana, sleeping tablets or all-night house parties. I start looking for something else, without knowing exactly what it is that I need.

Finding meditation

The traditions of meditation, contemplation, prayer and yoga are deeply intertwined in the culture of India. Even those

Indians who have left their native land carry these ideas imprinted on their collective psyche. Many of these ideas are wrapped up in religious traditions, rituals and observances with their roots in ancient Hinduism. While some of these traditions provide profound insights into the nature of reality and human experience, others have become the basis of superstition, prejudice and fanaticism. This has caused many Indians to develop an unfairly sceptical attitude to much of their own culture, overlooking the many positives that it contains. So, despite the scepticism I felt towards my own cultural roots at that time in my life – my parents are both Indian – I realised that meditation could well help me to escape the negative cycle I seemed to have trapped myself in. There was only one problem: I didn't know how to meditate. Hands-on instruction was going to be necessary.

In 1988 there was no internet or Google, and the closest equivalent was the Yellow Pages phone book. But as I searched the pages, I hit a problem: in the great Eastern tradition, meditation was never marketed as a commodity. It was a way of accessing a higher state of awareness that could not be commercialised. You can't buy inner peace, I reasoned, and anyone who was trying to sell me a version of it – by advertising it – logically couldn't be offering the kind of connection I was looking for. Running down the list of entries under 'Meditation', a small, nondescript ad caught my attention. 'True meditation, absolutely free', it read. The phrase 'true meditation' immediately signalled to me that whoever had written this ad understood that there were lots of people selling fake products to unsuspecting consumers. The technique being advertised was called Sahaja yoga and it seemed like it was worth a try.

In India if you wanted to learn meditation you might go to a local temple or to an ashram where monks would hold sessions for laypeople. Those who were especially keen would climb up a mountain in the Himalayas to reach a remote monastery, or trek through dense forest to find a hermit ensconced in his cave. Yogis in robes or in loincloths might give discourses under trees in parks. I, however, caught a bus to a brick-veneer house located in a middle-class suburb of Canberra.

I rang the doorbell and a very respectable looking Anglo-Saxon lady greeted me and led me into an average looking lounge room. Sitting on the sofa was an Anglo man wearing a flannelette shirt, tracksuit pants and woolly socks. *Decidedly unspiritual*, my mind said, constantly muttering. Nearby was another man with wavy reddish hair, a beard, another flannelette shirt and green corduroy pants. What could these people, so clearly Westerners in their appearance and manner, possibly know about the ancient Indian tradition of meditation? *And what's with the flannelette shirts?*

They explained to me that Sahaja yoga is not 'yoga' as many people in the West understand it – that is, a practice of postures. The word 'yoga' actually means 'to join'. It relates to the idea that the meditator attains 'yoga' when they establish a connection with their deeper self. A major feature of Sahaja yoga is the experience of mental silence or what is known in Sanskrit as *nirvichara samadhi*, meaning 'thoughtless awareness'. Practitioners should experience an inner awakening or awareness that can be felt as a state of being that is not ego, mind, intellect or emotion – something that is beyond all thought and the mind that produces those thoughts.

After experiencing a brief guided meditation and a significantly longer conversation in which life, the universe and everything else was discussed – accompanied by a cup of tea – I left to catch the bus home. Walking down the street I felt nice, but I couldn't say that I'd had any specific experience that I would call 'meditation'. My mind decided that a debate was necessary.

'Feeling good,' said the scientific part of my mind, 'is not proof that it is genuine. In fact, feeling good is a subjective experience that is difficult to measure and which can be triggered by any number of factors. For example, they gave you some chocolate biscuits at the end of the session. You know you like them. This could have clouded your judgement and biased your assessment.'

'True,' said the non-scientific part of my mind, 'but you feel better now than you did before, and basically that's what you were looking to achieve, wasn't it?'

'Feelings are not scientific,' the scientific one insisted, digging in its heels.

'Well,' interjected a third part of my mind that had volunteered to umpire the debate, 'you do feel good. It costs nothing, so it would be stupid to not continue at least for the time being.'

And so it was decided.

Once back in Sydney for lectures, I managed to find a group of meditators who practised the technique I had learnt in Canberra. Each week, with about fifteen regular meditators, I sat on a lounge or the floor, wherever I could find a space, trying to 'do' meditation. They were nice people and they seemed to be really motivated by their meditative experiences – none of which I was sharing. They told me not to 'do' it but, rather, to 'let it happen'.

'The present moment is an experience, not an action,' they told me.

Words are cheap, I thought, *especially fluffy, unscientific ones.*

So there I was, feeling a little guilty because my mind was telling me that I should really be in the medical library studying, or anywhere that didn't require me to face the mental content that floated through my head. Those continuous thoughts – the constant muttering narrative describing what I was doing, replaying things that I'd said, rehearsing things I was going to say – occupied my mind when I was bored, kept me company when I was alone, told me truths and half-truths in random order and clouded my perception when I most wanted clarity. Yes: *clarity.* That's what I was looking for. Clarity and silence.

I leant against a wall and closed my eyes, breathing regularly and gently, trying to focus my attention on the space between the thoughts rather than the crazy thoughts themselves – in the way the more experienced meditators had told me.

This time it was different. Gradually I sensed a change in my inner perception. It felt as if I had grown about a metre taller, yet I knew that my physical dimensions hadn't changed. It was as if I was staring down from a great height, like looking out of an aeroplane window, and I saw a string of objects, dozens or possibly hundreds of shapes moving slowly in a line, like cars on a highway. Somehow my distance above the ground increased and the rows of cars began to resemble a row of ants growing smaller and smaller.

A feeling of peace grew as I watched the ants; a subtle sense of joy was bubbling up from somewhere, and I wondered what those ants were that I could see dwindling away so far beneath me. It was not a thought so much as a desire to know. And then a most unexpected answer emerged in my awareness: that string of ants was my thoughts! Each ant was a single thought and the row of ants was the thought-stream that normally occupied my entire awareness, constantly ticking over in the back of my head. The row of ants became so small that they disappeared completely. The insect-like stream of thoughts on its narrow highway became a cavern of pure, crystalline silent awareness within me. Timeless, profound and innately refreshing.

It felt as if the various pieces of my being had each fallen into their natural place, perhaps for the first time. I felt in control, fully alert and uniquely well. My sense of time seemed to have merged with the stillness of the present moment. The experience was joyful, simple and somehow complete.

I opened my eyes and the experience began to slowly fade, although not entirely. Turning to look at the other meditators in the room, it seemed that this was what they must be experiencing as well. *So this is why they are so motivated*, I thought, and realised that was the first thought that had entered my mind in the past 20 minutes. Somehow I had touched a timeless aspect of my being that left me feeling refreshed, positive and free from stress. It was my first experience of a state of being that I thought must exist in all of us: that is, being beyond the mind.

The experience stayed with me, in a less intense way, during the walk home. My perception of the night air, the sounds in the trees, the way that I walked, the way that my breath moved in my chest and the energy that I drew upon were all somehow clearer, richer and more real than before. There was a subtle shift in the quality of my vision so that colours around me seemed a little richer, shapes and outlines a little sharper, like looking through a window that had just been cleaned. Much of this clarity seemed to be linked to a distinct and tangible quietness inside myself. The constant mental background chatter had subsided, leaving behind a sense of flowing silence within.

I started a regular morning meditation routine and, like a surfer, would try to catch the wave of mental silence and see how long I could ride it. That state of inner quiet began to filter into the rest of my day. Often I would see a connection between the day's productivity, achievements and experiences and how profound a silence I had experienced during the morning's meditation. When I achieved a period of mental silence, my attention span after meditation was unusually long, my ability to retain information was greatly increased and the way in which I related to others was considerably more positive, unpretentious and enjoyable. But on some days the silence was less achievable, and sometimes I didn't experience it at all.

I found that meditation in the early morning was best. Waking at about 6 a.m. to immediately sit down to meditate, I was surprised that I did not fall back to sleep. Instead, the silence would gently wake me up, refresh my mind and prepare me for the day. Even when I'd had less sleep than usual, I would emerge from the meditation alert and refreshed, rather than groggy and tired. At night, getting to sleep was no longer a process of uncertainty. I found that by meditating just before going to bed, my state of mental silence could be extended from when I was sitting in meditation to the time when I climbed into bed and my head hit the pillow. As a result, the sadist's replay of the day's events and the associated in-depth analysis just didn't happen. Falling asleep became effortless, as it had been when I was a child and, in general, it continues to be so to this day. I also found that many of the random and sometimes bizarre dreams that I used to experience almost every night became rare events. The sadist in the back of my head was dead!

Before these experiences of mental silence, I had looked down on what I considered to be the superstitious and spiritual hocus-pocus of my Indian roots. I had considered myself to be a scientific, rational and objective thinker; my personality unswayed by the irrationalities of feeling and subjective emotion. I preferred the hard-edged realities of objective data and logical analysis. Yet, despite my scientific view of the world, I couldn't deny the personal impact of my 'unscientific' meditation experience. It wasn't long before I started to wonder what the textbooks and scientific journals had to say about meditation.

The *Oxford English Dictionary* defines meditation as 'To think deeply and quietly', and the *Cambridge Dictionary of English* states that meditation is 'To think seriously about something for a long time'. This was very different from the complete inner silence that I had experienced. I went to the biomedical library and pored over medical research journals and physiology textbooks that mentioned scientific evaluations of meditation and yoga – but none of them spoke about this experience of inner silence. In fact, while the books defined meditation in many different ways, none contained any mention of the experience of the state of non-thought.

I continued to meditate for the rest of my medical training, always pondering why the Western scientific establishment had failed to identify an experience that seemed to be so easily accessible to an average person like me, in an average lounge room on a daily basis. In many of the lectures I attended in

medical school, especially those on mental health, I felt that
there was a great need for a technique that could elicit an
experience like the one meditation gave me, and yet none of
the textbooks or research journals had come even close to
identifying it, let alone studying its potential benefits. I began
to realise that this knowledge gap had important ramifications
at many different levels: cultural, social and scientific as well as
in physical and mental health. I had enrolled in medical school
because I wanted to do something with my life that would help
society. It seemed ironic that my fascination with medicine and
my desire to help others was leading me back to the ancient
origins of meditation and human experience, rather than
taking me to the further reaches of modern science.

While still a student I spent six months in India, travelling
around, trying to understand the culture of my forefathers
and how it related to the meditative experience I was having.
Staying in a yoga centre, I observed how meditation was used
by people who wished to maintain their peace of mind, and
also by those who were unwell and wanted to improve their
mental and physical wellbeing. Many of my days were spent at
a Jesuit seminary in New Delhi where a vast library of religious
texts had been established. Every day I would read through
translations of Eastern and Western spiritual commentaries,
looking for references and explanations of meditation and
mental silence. To my surprise, I found many. (The most
significant of these have been included in Chapter 6 and there
are many more at www.beyondthemind.com.)

A chance meeting led me to Professor Umesh Rai, who
headed the Department of Physiology at the prestigious Lady
Hardinge Medical College and the All India Institute of
Medical Sciences in New Delhi. Professor Rai had done the

first clinical trials on Sahaja yoga, looking at the impact of
this meditative approach on sufferers of chronic disease such
as asthma, hypertension and even epilepsy. The studies that
he conducted were, by the standards of the day, small but well
designed and well executed. They yielded some fascinating
outcomes indicating that the meditation technique appeared
to have some practical, unique and specific effects on the body
and the mind.[1]

   Despite the promising findings, Western scientific journals
had not picked up on Professor Rai's work. It became clear
to me that it would be important to evaluate his approach in
Western institutions using methodologies and terminology
that were taken seriously by Western scientific journals, with
direct application to Western populations. Professor Rai was
very encouraging and he and I would go on to correspond for
many years about research projects and ideas.

2
The path to research

Silence is the element in which great things fashion themselves together.

Thomas Carlyle[1]

It's my first day as a real doctor. Standing in a room with about thirty other eager young interns, I'm going through orientation at the hospital I have been assigned to for my internship. Tomorrow we hit the wards for the first time. After years of study and exams we will finally be practising medicine, albeit under the supervision of a hierarchy of experienced doctors.

As part of the orientation process we meet the heads of the various departments, who are keen to inspect the new recruits, earmarking the ones who look promising. During an informal lunch, the head of the Department of Medicine is working the room, speaking to each intern, asking them what their interests are and whether or not they want to go into a specialty of some kind.

One of my colleagues explains his interest in immunology, another in emergency medicine, a third wants to do orthopaedics. The professor's gaze turns to me.

'Do you have a particular interest that you'd like to pursue?' he asks.

'Yes,' I reply. 'I'm actually interested in research.'

His eyes light up. He has a reputation as a prolific researcher, so perhaps I might be worthy of a little more of his precious attention.

'Oh really?' he replies. 'What area did you have in mind?'

Sensing his interest, while at the same time completely misreading his mindset, I reply, 'I'm very interested in meditation.'

The professor smiles at me. I smile back, waiting for an invitation to his office for a longer chat on the subject or, possibly, an offer of help to get a project going. Instead, he continues to smile. After a few moments the silence becomes uncomfortable. My intern colleagues seem to have quietly sidled away so as not to be classified as known associates. The professor's smile, I realise, is actually a smirk and his body language has changed from that of someone with a genuine interest in me to that of a person looking at a strange insect under a magnifying glass. He seems to be musing on whether to squash the insect now or let it wander about and get squashed by somebody else in the hospital system. He chooses the latter option and, without saying anything more, turns to the next intern and asks her about her career intentions.

An invisible cloud of disapproval hangs around me for the rest of the orientation session. It slowly dawns on me that I have been earmarked as an intern with potentially lunatic tendencies.

A path less trodden

The reaction of the professor typified the response of most mainstream medical researchers in the nineties. Back then it was frustrating and, sometimes, downright hazardous to disclose my interest in the topic of meditation. To me, science was about having a completely open – although critical – mind, so I was perplexed to find that when it came to meditation, the minds of many researchers were completely closed. Their perceptions were negatively influenced by the many fake gurus and other people of dubious character who were clearly taking advantage of people they thought were naive and stupid. To them, meditation was mumbo jumbo that disguised only a placebo effect.

Meditation enthusiasts, I discovered, were at the other extreme. They perceived the practice of meditation to be a unique method for developing holistic harmony, higher consciousness, peace, love and good will to all. They often talked about it as a magical universal panacea that somehow harnessed the power of the mind over the body. They felt that scepticism blocked these scientists from seeing the obvious benefits of meditation and, conveniently, that the scientific evaluation of meditation's benefits was irrelevant. 'What do a bunch of stuffy old scientists know, anyway?' was a common line tossed at me when I tried to convince the enthusiasts to engage with the scientific community.

The answer had to be somewhere in the middle. The meeting point between these two extremes had to be scientific evidence developed from open-minded but rigorous inquiry. Because both the stubborn sceptic and the indiscriminate enthusiast were suffering from the same thing: lack of reliable scientific knowledge about meditation.

Despite that fateful meeting with the head of department, I completed my internship and started some general practice work, all the while thinking about how to begin research into meditation.

As a first step, and without any specific experience in how to provide meditation within a health centre context, a small handful of my colleagues and I decided that the best way to start the research was by observing the response of patients in and around my own general practice.

This is how the Mind–Body Meditation Clinic was established. It was a not-for-profit service set up in a large group general practice in suburban Sydney. It gave us the opportunity to develop practical experience in how to teach meditation to 'health consumers', learn which kinds of medical conditions responded to meditation, and find out how the mainstream medical community might view this rather unusual concept.

Surprisingly, many patients were sent to us by referral from other doctors in the area. Others came by word of mouth and some just appeared. Most of the patients suffered from chronic conditions for which mainstream medicine had afforded little relief. We found that the majority reported improvements in their mood and general sense of wellbeing within a few meditation sessions. Quite a few reported improvements in their specific disease symptoms as well, although this seemed to take longer than the changes in their general sense of wellness and did not occur in every case.

Remarkably, some of the toughest cases went into complete remission with diligent practice of the technique. I recall the local butcher who had inflammatory bowel disease – a lifelong condition characterised by recurrent gastroenteritis-like attacks caused by inflammation of the lining of the large intestine. He found symptomatic relief with regular meditation.

'I have medications that give me relief from the attacks,' he explained, 'but the meditation is just as effective.'

An elderly lady who had suffered regular migraines for many years and took morphine for pain relief, reported that not only had the frequency of her headaches reduced dramatically but she no longer needed the morphine.

A man in his twenties who had been diagnosed with depression in his early teens, and medicated with anti-depressants for many years in an ongoing struggle to manage his illness, continues to be one of the most memorable examples of the efficacy of meditation. He presented to the clinic with the characteristic facial expression of the chronically depressed: a frown deeply engraved on his face, and dark circles under his eyes, which made him look much older than he really was. Yet, after a few weeks of daily meditation the frown started to disappear and soon a younger, brighter face emerged. One day he came to the evening meditation session smiling, which was something he said he had not been able to do for many years. It was cases like this that inspired us to more thoroughly explore this phenomenon that was unfolding before us.

My first lucky break happened when one of the specialists I interned for, Professor Guy Marks, indicated that he had some interest in yoga and meditation in relation to asthma, his area of research. Professor Rai's work on asthma intrigued him, so Professor Marks and I designed a thorough study using meditation to help treat asthma.

In the course of planning the study, Professor Marks, who knew that I practised meditation, raised a concern that my personal views should not be allowed to bias the outcomes.

The vast majority of research into meditation continues to be undertaken by those who are themselves meditators, so I agreed that this was an important issue to address and we put into place a number of rules to ensure that the study would generate reliable evidence. First, we agreed that neither he nor I would know which participants were learning meditation and which were not. Second, we agreed that I would not deliver any meditation instruction to the participants – all instruction had to be delivered by instructors who were independent of the research project. Third, the meditation had to be compared to a legitimate and active treatment, so we chose a stress-management programme that was being used for asthma sufferers and was in fact supported by the state's Department of Health. Fourth, I would not analyse the data nor be involved in its interpretation.

These strategies gave us the confidence that the outcomes of the study would be reliable. We also used these rules wherever possible in subsequent studies. Data from projects was always analysed by independent expert statisticians; we involved non-meditators in the development and execution of our projects and as co-authors in report writing; and we conducted all of our projects in conjunction with respected, independent research institutions. The Royal Australian College of General Practitioners (RACGP) awarded us a $26,000 grant to kickstart the project. I enrolled as a masters student, and the study commenced. It was completed more than a year later.

The results of the asthma study were promising, indicating that there was an effect specific to meditation that had both physical and mental health implications, and further investigation was clearly warranted.[2] However, we found that there were few people or organisations that wanted to support research into meditation. The crystals, incense and philosophies of the New Age industry that had wrapped itself around the practice inflamed the scepticism of those who came from more mainstream medical backgrounds; many respected researchers regarded our research as amusing, and few were prepared to take it as seriously as we did.

Despite this prevailing attitude, we did find a small segment of the medical and health community that was interested in meditation. For the most part these doctors and other practitioners were sympathetic to complementary and alternative medicine. Yet even these people didn't seem to comprehend the potential significance of mental silence. This community of meditation enthusiasts seemed fixated on every idea about meditation *other* than mental silence. They perceived meditation in many different ways: as a form of profound relaxation, a way of focusing attention or a way of observing the activity of the mind without reacting to it (mindfulness). When we approached them to share our insights, rather than welcoming the idea of meditation as mental silence, many felt challenged by the proposition that mental silence might be an authentic definition of meditation worthy of scientific attention – because this was not the idea *they* had about meditation. Our discovery about the effects of mental silence challenged the status quo even among those who themselves had been marginalised by the larger status quo of mainstream medicine. We were the underdogs of the underdogs – the alternative to the alternative perspective.

We spoke with major stakeholders in the New Age industry hoping that they might fund some research only to learn that some of this industry actually profited from the lack of scientific clarity about what meditation is. A vague definition meant that any kind of practice could be labelled as 'meditation' and then marketed to the public. These stakeholders had a vested interest in not assisting us in solving the problem of definition since the development of a specific and scientifically verified definition would necessarily make it much harder to sell the many meditation courses, CDs, books and other products that relied on keeping ideas about meditation vague. A meditation technique that was potentially effective and yet not amenable to commercialisation was challenging to those who had spent many years cultivating our potential audience into a lucrative niche market.

One day, while watching the evening news, I saw a segment about a professor who had established a research unit focused on the evaluation of natural therapies at the Royal Hospital for Women in Sydney. Associate Professor John Eden was one of a few medical practitioners who was prepared to take a genuinely unbiased and scientific look at complementary and alternative medicine. When I contacted John he explained that his area of interest was in therapies used by women, especially menopausal women. He was interested in my meditation work but said that, unfortunately, there were no positions available for such research at his unit. *So near yet so far*, I thought.

Despondent, I began to resign myself to the fact that I would be unable to continue my research. I was close to being broke, as I had not worked very much while running the asthma project. I had married only a year previously and my wife, who shared my passion for the topic, was nevertheless understandably keen to live off more than a credit card. She had also developed a habit of starting conversations about babies whenever I entered the room.

So I applied for regular medical jobs, not knowing how I would juggle these responsibilities while at the same time completing the asthma project. As I had an interest in paediatrics I applied for several positions in that field. Soon after a screening interview for one position I was advised that I had made the shortlist and that I should fax through the basic information they needed to progress my application.

It sounded like I would get the job, and although I wasn't really sure that I wanted it, I put together the requested documents and took them to the fax machine.

Well, here we go! I thought as I arranged the papers in the machine. I moved my hand to the big green 'Send Fax' button. Once that button was pressed, I was signalling the end of any serious research. But there was no point doing research if I couldn't even pay my bills.

My index finger hovered above the button and, as if on cue, the fax machine – which was also a telephone – rang. I picked up the receiver, expecting a wrong number or a telemarketer, as only a handful of people knew the number of this machine.

'Ramesh, do you want a job?' asked the voice on the other end of the line. It was John Eden.

I took a few seconds to register what he had said. He explained that one of his researchers had left suddenly and he desperately needed another medically qualified person to fill the role. In addition, he said, it would be possible for me to continue doing my own research. The offer was for an immediate start in a full-time capacity.

I hung up the phone, took my finger away from the green button and marvelled at the coincidence. To this day I still don't know how John got that phone number.

Within three months of commencing the position, John

offered me my next big break: a PhD scholarship that would allow me to continue my meditation research. The scholarship was very modest – less than half of what I would earn as a junior medical officer and about one-third of what I could earn in general practice – but it would enable me to get some serious research work done. I supplemented the scholarship income with locum work on the weekends. It was exhausting.

There was still the question of how we were to pay for the costs of the research itself. Again, John Eden came up with a potential solution. He ran an annual conference that should have been successful in theory, but was not attracting enough delegates even to cover its costs. The conference was directed at GPs but for some reason they weren't registering. If I could use my experience as a GP and seminar organiser to revitalise the event, the profits could be used to fund the research programme, John proposed.

I took the conference materials home with me and contemplated how I might be able to turn the event around. The answer came while I was sitting in meditation one day – when my mind was still the solutions had more opportunity to emerge in my awareness. The original conference was a three-day event, which was a format GPs were traditionally supposed to prefer for their professional education, but it occurred to me that with the changing economic climate and shifts in the culture of the medical profession this was no longer a correct assumption. I wondered if the duration of each lecture, scheduled to be an hour long, might not be what GPs really wanted.

It occurred to me that the best way to answer these questions was to conduct a survey of GPs, which would also be a useful way to find out what topics the doctors wanted in the conference. How could this survey be done without spending a great deal of money? Once more, I followed my intuition and contacted Russell Norden, the editor of Australia's biggest GP publication, *Australian Doctor*. To my surprise, Russell immediately agreed to carry the survey and also to sponsor the seminar that would happen as a result of it, thereby giving us free advertising for the event.

Literally hundreds of GPs responded to the survey. No one had ever thought to ask them what they wanted in their education and they were more than keen to tell us.

Instead of the forty or fifty GPs from the previous year, the event attracted more than seven hundred. It made a healthy profit and soon became established as the largest GP meeting in the country. The event continues to this day and for its first five years generated sufficient profits to support all our research needs.

This experience demonstrated to me that the mind-emptiness of meditation seemed to facilitate 'lightbulb moments' of intuitive insight and inspiration that were profoundly helpful. Meditation made it easier for me to think outside the square because it directly neutralised the entrenched and habitual thinking habits that otherwise stifled my creative problem-solving skills.

Later, taking another intuitive leap, we experimented with the same format in other cities, with equally impressive results. Within a few years we had established the biggest seminar series of its kind in Australia, attracting several thousand delegates each year.

The multinational medical education companies were as stunned as we were with the success of the approach and they couldn't understand how an unknown local GP was able to do something that they hadn't, despite their best efforts, vast experience and massive resources. In fact, more than once I was called to meet my competitors, who wanted to find out how we managed to get our formula so right. What they didn't realise was that almost every one of the strategic decisions that guided the establishment of this event series had been developed intuitively through the clarity of perception and judgement that mental silence allowed. I was tapping into an intuitive way of working that was made easier by the inner silence. It was the first of many examples that taught me about the potential of meditation not only for health and wellbeing but also for performance, cognition and creative problem-solving.

These days, in my research, clinical and business activities, I know that the most important part of my preparation is to ensure that my mind is clear and my attention focused, and that the silence is flowing within. From that point I can access all the necessary mental faculties while also maintaining the flexibility that allows me to innovate, strategise and succeed.

Instead of headbutting a problem until the solution falls out, it is now more like extending my meditative antennae and waiting for the solution to be transmitted to them. And the more silent my mind, the more sensitive the antennae and the clearer the reception. As psychologist Guy Claxton said in his book *Hare Brain, Tortoise Mind*: 'Intelligence increases when you think less.'[3]

Mental silence – the new frontier

The contribution that the mental silence experience made to my ability to work dynamically was another revelation for me. Considering meditation as a therapeutic and preventative health strategy alone, which is what scientists and clinicians have done for the past forty years, is in fact failing to recognise meditation's potential to enhance performance. I was struck by the fact that the very modern, Western ideas of 'flow' and 'peak experience'[4] – often referred to by those involved in sport, creativity and other high-performance fields – closely parallel the ancient Eastern ideas of meditation and mental silence, and yet very little scientific work has been done to study this relationship. Our understanding of meditation as a means of reducing stress and improving health, although it is clearly effective at doing both, is only the beginning. Perhaps meditation – especially mental silence – could be better understood as a method that facilitates the attainment of an 'optimal performance state' or 'optimal state of being' in which physical and mental health are only part of a larger array of benefits and features.

Since 1996, when I started on this journey of scientific discovery, much has changed. While there is still scepticism about the efficacy of meditation, the social mood and attitude towards it have shifted; a groundswell of interest even within the previously conservative ranks of the medical profession and scientific community is happening. Much of this is because of the research carried out by groups such as ours, carried out in spite of the resistance of the professions that are now starting to show genuine interest. As a result, the new challenge that faces meditation research is no longer about whether or not it is worthy of scientific attention but how we should conduct good quality research to more fully understand its potential. What are the most important questions that we need to answer about meditation so that the hardened sceptics are satisfied, the indiscriminate enthusiasts are more informed and the public is provided with reliable information that it can use practically and easily?

Despite the spectacle and power of the new technologies available to scientists, the two fundamental, interrelated questions about meditation have not really changed over the past several decades. First, what is the definition of meditation? Second, does meditation have a real effect above and beyond that of placebo? Chapter 3 explains why these questions are important and how we developed a unique strategy to tackle them that ultimately resulted in outcomes so different from the rest. These results create a clear picture of what meditation actually is. They also show how it can be used to improve our health and wellbeing and also our ability to fulfil our potential as human beings.

Words from meditators

I used to keep all kinds of health books by my bedside — a comfort, I guess, in case I found something that stood out and had meaning. Once I learnt how to meditate, the answers were there at my fingertips, everything made sense and I felt at peace. I've often said to my kids 'go with your heart not your head', so I did too. I've learnt never to let negativity take over and my attention and memory have improved. I feel confident — no longer frightened or insecure. The connection is such a wonderful, refreshing experience, bringing me energy, love and peace.

Jill, Australia

When I achieve the state of thoughtless awareness, I can feel a complete change physically and mentally. It's as if my walking posture becomes straight, my attitude becomes positive, my confidence builds up and I start enjoying the tiny things happening around me. In my thoughtless awareness I can think pleasantly and decide what is right for me – the decisions that I make when in thoughtless awareness seem to be the most optimal. Before learning to meditate, my mind would be consumed by irrelevant thoughts. But with deep meditation, an inner silence prevails and I start observing the subject at hand with fresh concentration.

Rama, India

PART II
WHAT IS MEDITATION?

3
Defining meditation

The greatest obstacle to discovery
is not ignorance – it is the illusion of
knowledge.

Daniel J. Boorstin[1]

tanding on the stage behind the lectern, I open my eyes. In front of me an audience of 330 middle managers sits in pin-drop silence. We are at a major corporate event in Sydney's Darling Harbour, this industry's annual conference, and I have been invited to speak on meditation for about 45 minutes and then go through a brief guided meditation session. I'm amazed that within just 10 to 15 minutes such a large group of executives, from a company that is among *Forbes* magazine's global top fifty, could be now sitting in meditation.

They all look calm and quiet, I think, but how many are actually tapping the specific state of silence that my lecture was about? Is it possible for a roomful of complete novices to tap into the experience within a single session?

My questions are soon answered by the chairwoman who introduced me to the audience; she is also a vice-president from one of the company's many divisions. Turning to the audience immediately after the meditation session, she announces, 'I've been meditating for ten years but this is the first time that I've been able to successfully stop my thoughts!'

If that was the first time she'd been able to stop her thoughts, I think, what has she been doing for the past ten years that she regarded as meditation? This executive is clearly highly educated and capable, yet somehow she has been convinced to do something that wasn't delivering the authentic experience.

This quandary neatly sums up the two key challenges that science must address regarding meditation – what is meditation and does it have more of an effect than simple placebo? In fact, it is impossible for our scientific understanding of meditation to make any significant progress without taking on these questions.

What is meditation?

How is meditation defined? What are the fundamental features that distinguish it from, say, relaxation or prayer or imagination or dreams or sleep or coma or psychosis? The earliest scientific studies of meditation began appearing in Western scientific journals in the late 1960s and have continued ever since. Despite more than forty years of scientific research, though, there is still no simple, commonly accepted definition of meditation. This has led to tremendous confusion in both the public and scientific domains – a confusion often exploited by the unscrupulous.

In my own research, I combed through the scientific literature to see how scientists define meditation, and I was surprised to find that there were twenty to thirty definitions floating around, of which three have achieved particular prominence. The most common is that meditation is a method for achieving relaxation. The idea that meditation is a sophisticated method for achieving the 'relaxation response'[2] was pioneered by Herbert Benson in the 1970s and gained traction with the public and within the scientific community. Another popular idea is that meditation is a method of focusing the attention. More recently it has come to be understood as a means of changing the way we think about, and how we react to, our own thinking, that is, it is mindfulness. The paradox is that all of these major definitions have been subject to evaluation by what is currently the gold standard of medical scientific evaluation – the randomised controlled trial (this will be covered in more detail later) – and none has yet shown any convincing evidence of an effect beyond that of placebo,[3] indicating that these definitions don't really capture the true meaning of meditation.

Without a definition that we can all agree on, we can't be sure that what is being scientifically tested is consistent, let alone whether it is actually meditation. If different researchers use different definitions then the results of research using one definition can't be fairly compared to studies using a different definition. You aren't comparing apples with apples. This important issue has not been properly addressed despite more than forty years of research. Some self-proclaimed experts have tried to convince us that the issue of definition is irrelevant since, they claim, all forms of meditation achieve the same goal. However, modern brain studies do seem to show that different types of meditation can bring about different patterns of brain activity, further highlighting the importance of determining which definition, and hence which kind of brain activation, if any, is correct, desirable or effective.

In general, scientific research generates two kinds of findings: high-quality and reliable or low-quality and unreliable. Unfortunately, in applying this to meditation we found that more than 95% of research findings fall into the 'low-quality' category.[4] It has been this body of low-quality research that has made many extraordinary, often highly commercialised claims about the supposedly unique effects of meditation. It is also this type of research that has been frequently reported on by the media, which is always on the lookout for something to talk about, but at the same time needs to simplify complex information down into a two- or three-minute story.

On the other hand, the very small amount of high-quality research made the rather unglamorous finding that, using the most popular definitions, meditation is no more effective than placebo; what many researchers in psychology call the 'non-specific' effect.

In contemplating these facts, my own experience of mental silence resonated within me. It made me aware of the specific and unique nature of the meditative experience and this allowed me to search through the traditional literature on this subject with a different perspective from those before me. Could mental silence be the missing piece of the puzzle? I was able to identify a long and unbroken tradition describing the central importance of mental silence in meditation. For example, in the *Mahabharata*, an epic Sanskrit text from ancient India, we find what is probably the most ancient definition of meditation, when the sage-storyteller describes a meditator:

He does not hear; he does not smell. Neither does he taste or see, or experience touch. Likewise his mind ceases to imagine. He desires nothing, and like a log he does not think.[5]

Also, in the *Tao Te Ching*:

Empty your mind of all thoughts.
Let your heart be at peace.[6]

Even though mental silence was described as being of central importance in the traditional Eastern meditation texts, I could not find any substantive discussion or even acknowledgement of this experience in the Western scientific literature. Could we have had a cultural 'blind spot' that stopped us from appreciating the importance of mental silence as a definition of meditation? This might explain why scholars have focused on so many conceptualisations of meditation that haven't included it.

Yet it was precisely this definition of meditation as mental silence – mentioned throughout many of the ancient Eastern texts from different places in time, culture and location – that, we believed, could claim to be authentic.

Thus, having selected the definition of meditation we would use for our scientific research, we turned our attention to how the research should be conducted. Our examination of the existing research revealed the second main challenge to furthering our scientific understanding of meditation: the placebo effect.

The placebo effect

Recently my four-year-old niece fell over and scratched her knee; it was so minor that it didn't even break the skin. It was probably painful, but surely not enough to warrant the tears that followed. Remarkably, as many adults learn, the application of a brightly coloured bandaid along with some TLC reduced not only the amount of noise produced by the patient, but also the amount of pain that she perceived. A bandaid has no obvious medical effect and yet the patient immediately feels better – this is a simple example of how the mind can strongly influence our sense of wellbeing. It is one example of the placebo effect. The placebo effect's influence occurs regardless of whether or not the treatment is real. That's why it is the main source of misleading results (what scientists call 'bias') in studies of any kind of treatment, including meditation, hence the challenge it created for us.

The placebo effect is probably one of the most profound demonstrations of the mind–body connection. As shown in my niece's experience with a bandaid, placebo effects aren't confined to pharmaceuticals: they can be observed in association with almost any activity that has an expectation of improved wellbeing attached to it. That's why activities as ancient as tribal dance or as modern as a surgical procedure can be associated with a beneficial effect even though they might not act directly on the disease or condition concerned. Sometimes the beneficial effects occur no matter what the therapist administers to the patient, whether it's a sugar tablet, a sympathetic bedside manner, an injection of a small amount of saline, or a brief session of guided relaxation. These can all generate a positive impact on wellbeing that is not specific to the treatment itself.[7]

When researchers have compared different types of behavioural therapy they have found that, despite their overt differences, the therapies often cause similar benefits.[8] It appears that the participants' involvement and interaction with the therapist, not to mention their conviction that they are involved in a therapeutic process, has its own effect regardless of the specific features of the therapy. This phenomenon has been labelled the 'equivalence paradox'. In the context of stress, for example, the equivalence paradox is such that any form of stress-management or counselling may reduce stress or anxiety, but not necessarily because of its specific properties. That's why in meditation research the 'placebo effect' is often called the 'non-specific effect'.

It was important for us to determine whether or not meditation has a specific effect rather than just a non-specific effect if we were to give it the special status that its many enthusiasts – and the ancient tradition – think it deserves.

There are very few behavioural therapies that have been shown to have more than a non-specific effect. Cognitive behavioural therapy, when done properly, is one.[9] This book presents evidence that meditation based on the experience of mental silence is another.

4
Specific effects – understanding the evidence

Perplexity is the beginning of knowledge.
Kahlil Gibran[1]

In the course of our research we read and analysed what had already been discovered about meditation by other researchers. Using databases, hand searches and a predetermined set of criteria in a process called a 'Systematic Review and Meta-analysis', we waded through forty years of scientific databases covering every English-language health, medical, nursing, psychological or allied health journal in the world. We were one of the only teams in the world to have conducted such an exhaustive search and analysis of all the scientific evidence. Despite there being more than 3000 articles on meditation, many of them describing scientific trials of one form or another, to our surprise there was no conclusive proof of anything.[2] All we found out was how much the scientific establishment *didn't* know about meditation.

Another research group at the University of Alberta, headed by Maria Ospina, conducted a very similar project and came to the same conclusion: there has been no consistent proof of a meaningful effect beyond placebo, regardless of whether the information was analysed according to specific disease states, physiological parameters, or techniques of meditation.[3] That is not to say that the existing research has not been useful – it has provided a foundation for more thorough evaluations. However, it was now clear that the mainstream media's representation of these poor-quality studies as proof of meditation's effectiveness, which occurred frequently in the 1970s and 1980s, was misleading. Poorly researched ideas were fed to the media which then encouraged a trusting but ill-informed public to patronise the meditation industry. This led to a self-perpetuating cycle that was both financially lucrative and successful in preventing the public from developing a clear understanding of meditation.

Randomised controlled trials and meditation

Any drug that a doctor prescribes has been evaluated using a randomised controlled trial (RCT). In essence, an RCT works to prevent the kind of factors such as the placebo effect from skewing the results of scientific evaluation.

At its simplest, conducting an RCT involves randomly dividing a group of research participants into two. One group receives the real treatment and the other receives a placebo. The participants are assessed before the treatment commences and again at the end of the treatment period, then the outcomes of both groups are compared. If all other influencing factors have been kept as unchanged as possible during the treatment period, the scientists can say that whatever differences exist between the two groups at the end of the treatment period are due to the real treatment rather than the placebo. This approach provides a method by which we can determine if a treatment really works. RCTs are now considered essential for the objective evaluation of any kind of health strategy. For our research, it was the only way that we could determine if meditation has a specific effect.

Often, meditation enthusiasts argue that using scientific methodology to evaluate meditation is unnecessarily intellectual and applied at the expense of the real meaning of meditation, or that the scientific approach is not subtle enough to detect the effects of meditation. Yet the RCT is intellectually straightforward since it is really no more than the application of common sense. Also, these days it is easy to find measurement strategies that are designed to pick up nuances, whether they are nuances in heart rate, chemicals or emotions. So if we are unable to detect effects in a sensitively designed RCT, there probably isn't an effect.

The conventional RCT to test drugs uses an inert tablet, traditionally made of sugar, that has exactly the same appearance as the 'real' tablet. The participant has no idea whether they are taking the real or placebo treatment. This allows the researcher to control for the patient's expectations that inevitably arise from knowing whether or not they are receiving a treatment (or a fake).

A meditation equivalent of the sugar tablet is much harder to devise because the patient has to actively, consciously and enthusiastically participate in a specifically defined meditative task, rather than just swallow something. The difficulty is that the 'fake' meditation must be real enough to motivate the subjects to participate with enthusiasm and conviction while at the same time be sufficiently different from real meditation to *not* have any actual effect. This 'placebo meditation' can itself be a very resource-intensive challenge.

Our review showed that when faced with this challenge the majority of researchers gave up. Instead, they typically designed their studies so that half the participants in an RCT were receiving instruction in meditation while the other half received no treatment at all but were instead put on a 'waiting list', with a promise that once the trial was finished they too would receive instruction in meditation. This strategy is fundamentally unable to screen out the placebo effect that might occur in the treated group and hence it is extremely likely to produce skewed and misleading results.

Our research has shown that the majority of RCTs that did not make serious attempts to exclude the placebo effect reported that meditation was highly effective. In contrast, of the RCTs that did make serious efforts to exclude the placebo effect, the majority found that the meditation techniques tested were mostly *not* any more effective than the sugar-tablet strategy that they compared them to. In fact, in a substantial number of studies the sugar-tablet strategy was *more* effective than the meditation. The only conclusion that can be drawn from this is that the meditation techniques studied so far – and, hence, the definitions of meditation that they used – are no more effective than placebo.

When I have presented this information to audiences – especially audiences of meditation enthusiasts – it is remarkable how many times otherwise peace-loving meditators have reacted with hostility. The suggestion that the technique they've been practising is, according to the scientific evidence, not as special as they'd thought is sometimes too confronting for them.

How do you make a sugar tablet for meditation RCTs?

For our meditation RCT to be effective, we needed to come up with a sugar-tablet strategy, and there were two ways to do this. One was to use a 'sham' version of the real treatment, which is a common strategy used in psychological research. The other was to compare meditation to an existing treatment method that was accepted by the research community – for example, progressive muscle relaxation or a stress-management programme that could seem very similar to meditation but was hopefully different in crucial ways.

To create a good-quality sham meditation, a researcher must include every aspect that makes the sham seem like meditation but at the same time exclude that part of meditation that is the 'active ingredient'. The conundrum for researchers is that if we don't know what the active ingredient of meditation is then how can we design a sham version that we can be confident doesn't include the active ingredient? In fact, if we don't know what the active ingredient is how can we tell what the real thing is? And what if, instead of using a sham meditation, we used an existing treatment method such as relaxation – how would we know if relaxation is sufficiently different from meditation to warrant comparing it to meditation?

To resolve this conundrum, we chose a unique and ambitious strategy. We would use a completely new definition of meditation – that it is the experience of mental silence – and we would conduct a multifaceted research effort to evaluate whether or not it had an effect that was greater than the more widely accepted, but relatively ineffective, Western definitions, none of which were focused on the mental silence experience.

An overview of the research

Could the reason for the disappointing outcomes reported in the scientific literature, despite the enthusiasm of the public and the health and scientific community, be because they had been assessing the wrong definition? With its emphasis on the experience of 'thoughtless awareness', the Sahaja yoga technique seemed like the ideal meditation practice to research because it focused on the traditional idea of mental silence as its defining feature. However, it was the only practice the scientific establishment hadn't looked at.

The opportunity to do the first Western investigations into this phenomenon was a uniquely attractive opportunity that we grabbed with both hands. We conducted the world's first health and quality-of-life survey of long-term meditators, assessing the health of Sahaja yoga meditators in Australia.

Shanti Gosh, my intrepid research assistant at the time, and Dr Gabby Mane and her husband, Sandeep, worked hard to find meditators from every major city. We recruited more than 350 meditators who used this technique, and they provided detailed answers about their meditation practices, experiences and health.[4] We found that not only did these meditators have better mental and physical health compared to the general population, but that this advantage, especially in mental health, was closely related to how often the meditators experienced mental silence rather than how often they 'sat down to meditate'. This indicated that it was not the quantity of meditation so much as the quality of the experience that was associated with the benefit. This finding provided us with an important reassurance that we were on the right track with regard to our decision to use the mental silence definition.

We then set up a series of increasingly rigorous clinical studies in various areas of health treatment. For example, at the time, many women around the world started looking for non-hormonal options to treat menopausal symptoms. We already had anecdotal evidence from our mind–body clinic about the effectiveness of meditation for menopausal hot flushes, so we invited women in this age group to participate in a clinical trial. Although only a small study, we observed an improvement in menopausal hot flushes that was similar to that which might be expected from hormone therapy (HT). There were also substantial positive effects on psychological and other quality-of-life-related symptoms.[5]

In another case, we were approached by parents who had found meditation effective for controlling attention deficit hyperactivity disorder (ADHD) symptoms in children, and by teachers who were tearing their hair out looking for a simple way to calm ADHD kids in their classes. We combined these two stakeholder groups and conducted a controlled study looking at the treatment of ADHD using meditation. We compared the improvements in the treated group with a second group that was receiving standard treatment for ADHD while waiting for admission into the meditation programme. Over the course of the six-week treatment programme we observed substantial improvements in measures of the severity of ADHD symptoms. A number of remarkable stories emerged from that project (these are described in chapters 11 and 12).[6]

The effects of meditation on the symptoms of menopause and ADHD were very encouraging; however, we needed to gain a more reliable understanding of whether what we were seeing was a real effect or just that of placebo. Conducting RCTs to compare the impact of the mental silence experience with active treatments such as relaxation and stress management was the only way to do this. This kind of RCT should be sufficiently thorough to enable us to confidently exclude the placebo effect and show whether or not mental silence had a real and specific effect.

The right RCT

Asthma is one of the most common chronic diseases to affect Australians. We designed a rigorous RCT to compare the effects of Sahaja yoga meditation on the management of asthma with the results of a standardised stress-management programme.[7] The RCT was designed to focus on the crucial difference between the two strategies, which was the experience of mental silence. We adopted this ambitious design so that we could genuinely control for placebo effects.

The study had two remarkable outcomes. First, it showed that meditation had significantly better impacts on mood and aspects of quality of life compared to the conventional stress-management programme. Second, the meditation group showed significantly greater improvements in a relatively objective measure of the severity of the physical disease, whereas the stress-management group showed none. So not only did we see that meditation improved the psychological aspects of illness but, potentially, the *physical* basis of certain illnesses as well.

We then designed and executed the world's largest RCT of meditation for work stress.[8] Again, we compared meditation to a relaxation method that was developed specifically to allow us to compare mental silence to relaxation-oriented meditation. The results of this RCT showed that the mental-silence approach was substantially more effective in reducing stress and improving depressive symptoms than the other techniques. The outcomes of these studies provided strong evidence that mental silence was associated with a specific, therapeutic effect.

Our explorations of the psychological and physical impacts of this approach to meditation began to resonate with the ancient ideas of meditation as a method of attaining 'optimal consciousness'. In modern times, the notion of optimal consciousness is often described as the phenomenon called 'flow'.[9] Western researchers seeking to understand the nature of peak performance identified a state where a person becomes so intensely engaged in an activity that they lose track of time, access higher-than-usual ability and occasionally transcend mundane self-awareness to attain a peak experience that is self-renewing and innately rewarding, with salutary effects on wellbeing. People from many different vocational backgrounds have claimed to experience this state, but it is most commonly associated with elite-level sports, performance arts and computer programming. Remarkably, the descriptions of high-quality flow states closely resembled descriptions of meditation – especially mental silence.

We compared standardised measures of flow experience, developed by Susan Jackson, an Australian sports psychologist and researcher at the University of Queensland,[10] to ratings of mental silence and found that there was a relationship between the two. Moreover, the flow experience appeared to increase with meditative practice. This raised an intriguing prospect: that meditation, especially mental silence, provided a way for people to tap into the flow state at will. Thus, the ancient practice of meditation might be best understood not as a method of relaxation but as a strategy for attaining an optimal state of being. (Our exploratory research into this is described in Chapter 13.)

How this applies to you

The aim of this book is to provide you with both the scientific and personal evidence to show why meditation as mental silence has so much to offer. The ancient authentic experience is a very specific, very natural state of inner silence that is at once simple and yet immensely self-empowering.

The idea that our full potential is reached not when our mind is thinking but, rather, when it is in the state of non-thought – when the mind is silent – is intriguing to say the least. That this state can be practically achieved more or less by anyone using the simple techniques described in this book, makes mental silence of profound individual and social significance to us all.

PART III
MEDITATION IS MENTAL SILENCE

5
Mental silence – a unique discovery

I know the secret of silence . . . If we agitated souls were to understand the importance of silence, then half the troubles of the world will be solved . . .

Mohandas K. Gandhi[1]

In 1947, India achieved its independence from Great Britain's 300-year occupation without firing a single bullet. Despite Britain's overwhelming military and economic superiority, Indian independence was achieved using an unprecedented strategy called non-violent non-cooperation. One visionary man pioneered this approach to political revolution, and he became known worldwide as Mahatma Gandhi.

Speaking about the source of his unique inspiration and moral force, Gandhi said:

For a seeker of truth like me, silence is of great help. The soul can see its path clearly during silence and everything starts looking crystal clear, which otherwise would have been difficult to grasp or possibly misunderstood.

Gandhi encouraged others to seek out silence, as he had:

Listen to the voice of the great silence within us. If we are ready to listen, the divine radio is always singing within us, but without silence it is impossible to hear it.

Gandhi demonstrated to the world what one person can achieve when energised by the ancient and authentic understanding of meditation, which is what he was describing – the experience of mental silence is the way that meditation has been understood and described in India for thousands of years.

Compare Gandhi's comments to those of a group of children at a school in Queensland who had just gone through a school-based meditation training programme. They and their parents gave me permission to record their descriptions of the meditative experience, some of which follow:

RM: What did you experience happening inside?
14-YEAR-OLD BOY: Well, I went quiet and didn't think of anything.
RM: How did it make you feel inside?
14-YEAR-OLD BOY: Relaxed.

One thirteen-year-old boy said, 'I experience complete silence. A lot of my thoughts go away and, yeah, I focus much better.'

A fifteen-year-old boy said, 'I sort of go calm, like you say, stop the thoughts, stop the thoughts going through my head and sort of just blank and sort of relax my body.'

The interview with the eight-year-old girl in the introduction is another eloquent description of how to 'think about not thinking'.

Both Gandhi and these Australian children are describing the same phenomenon: the cessation of mundane thought and the experience of mental silence. From texts going back 5000 years, right through to the modern day, descriptions of the mental silence experience can be found if we know what to look for.

Origins of the concept

Mental silence is a phenomenon that has been described in various ways and contexts across histories and cultures.

We are not our thoughts, nor are we the mind that generates them but, in fact, something much more profound that is entirely discoverable in the state of mental silence. Mental silence becomes a window through which we can develop a clearer understanding of ourselves and our world.

The ancient Taoist meditation text *The Secret of the Golden Flower* states this simply as 'all methods end in quietness'.[2] Indeed, Eastern cultures, particularly that of India, have recognised the importance of mental silence and have systematically explored ways to cultivate it, developing the yoga/meditation system as a result.

The architecture of our thinking

One way to understand the relationship between thinking, not thinking and meditation is by using the diagrammatic representation of thought activity represented below. We have developed a simple self-assessment survey based on this. You can download it from www.beyondthemind.com to help you monitor your own progress.

Usual mental activity

Each wave in this drawing represents a thought, and the series of waves represents a stream of thoughts – the constant mental chatter that bubbles away in the back, or front, of our head all day, every day. As one thought-wave passes through, another follows right behind it. Often the waves are so close together that we don't perceive a gap between them at all, just a continuous stream of thoughts. The speed at which these thought-waves appear varies depending on one's mental and emotional state at the time.

As an exercise, close your eyes and notice your own mental activity, paying attention to the speed and intensity of the thoughts rather than the meaning of the thoughts themselves. When we are at our 'usual' level of thinking activity, most of us experience what might best be called the 'constant background mental chatter'. This is the stream of thoughts that accompanies everything we do, often distracting us from the task at hand and sometimes keeping us awake at night.

This thought-wave represents the 'idling speed' of our internal monologue. Psychologists call it 'self-talk' and it is estimated by some experts to be anywhere from 300 to 1000 thoughts per minute as we process events and perceptions as they occur around us. Many of us are quite attached to this background noise because it entertains us when we are bored, giving us something to think about when we have nothing else to do. This monologue has been around for so long that we might feel lost without it.

When we are busy doing several things at once, the mind becomes busier and produces more thoughts than usual, as shown in the diagram below. These busy thoughts might help us build a list of mundane daily tasks that we have to do, but many of them can also be unnecessary and distracting.

More thinking than usual

When we are feeling very stressed or unhappy most of us will find that the number and speed of these thought-waves increase dramatically. These ruminations not only keep us awake at night or distract us from important tasks, but can colour our entire perception with a distorted, often pessimistic, view of everything in our lives.

Sometimes, in extreme situations, they create a sense that our mind is racing (as shown in the diagram below).

More thinking than ever before

Many people experiencing the onset of mental illness will describe incessant, negative, anxious or even bizarre thoughts. In the extremes of mental illness that occur in psychosis and mania the thought processes can become so intense that they are completely uncontrollable and overwhelming.

Slowing down the thought-stream

When we start to relax, our stream of thoughts slows down. This might happen when we practise a relaxation exercise or distract ourselves with music, food or a holiday. The physical act of relaxation reduces the electrical and chemical stimulation of the brain, thus allowing the rate of thinking to slow. By taking a holiday, for example, the things that commonly trigger increased thinking are avoided. This allows our mind to relax and our thinking activity to slow down even further. The consumption of alcohol, sedatives or substances such as cannabis, which reduce the activity of brain cells or brain circuits, can act to chemically slow the brain's thought-producing activity even further. Unfortunately, the by-product of chemically induced slowing of the thoughts is temporary and can cause permanent damage to those cells and circuits.

When the thought-waves slow down (represented in the image below) we feel more relaxed, which produces a sense of wellbeing. In fact, our research has repeatedly demonstrated a very strong link between slower thought-waves and improved mood.

Less thinking than usual

You will probably find that your thought-wave pattern doesn't seem to have many gaps in it. However, as the speed of thoughts slows down you might be able to perceive a space between each of them. Just as we understand each wave to be a thought, the ancient tradition of meditation explains that the trough between each wave – the potential space between the thoughts – is in fact a brief moment of complete silence. When we are thinking furiously due to stress or general busy-ness, it's not possible to perceive the space between the thoughts. But as our mind slows down during moments of relaxation, we become better able to perceive one thought rising and then subsiding, and the next thought rising and subsiding.

As each thought subsides we might perceive a small gap. It is precisely this gap that the ancient meditative tradition aims at widening, because it is in this gap that the meditative state exists. The meditative state is *not*, however, a loss of thinking activity, ability or control. This gap between each thought is actually where the state of mental silence can be found, and it is the gap that is cultivated in order to expand and develop the experience of meditation.

Thus the first step in meditation is to reduce the speed of thinking so that we can start to identify the gaps between the thoughts. The commonality between this stage of meditation and relaxation is probably why many Western researchers have assumed that the two phenomena are the same. However, the next step in the meditation process distinguishes it from relaxation.

After slowing down the thought-stream, the meditator aims to expand the spaces between the thoughts until they are larger than the thoughts themselves. As the space widens we might perceive only a few thoughts followed by a noticeable space of non-thought, and then a few more thoughts, and so on (as shown below).

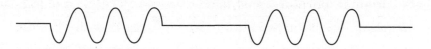

A few thoughts separated by brief spaces of non-thought –
partially silent

With more practice we will experience only a single thought or two, followed by a long space of silence, as shown in the next diagram. Eventually those spaces between the thoughts become so large that there are no thoughts at all.

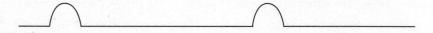

One or two thoughts separated by longer spaces
of non-thought – mostly silent

When the thoughts slow down and become so minor that they disappear, like the ants in my first experience of meditation, we are left with just the infinite silence between the thoughts, and yet we remain fully alert and in control of our faculties. This flatlining of mental activity gives rise to the mental silence experience, the true definition of meditation. The traditional Sanskrit term for it is *nirvichara samadhi* or 'thoughtless awareness'.

No thinking activity – completely silent

Contemplation, relaxation, mindfulness and mind-emptiness – what's the difference?

The thought-waves diagrams can also help us to understand the original purpose of strategies such as contemplation, relaxation, mindfulness and mind-emptiness, how they might all fit together and why there is so much confusion between them.[3]

Contemplation

Contemplation is a method to direct the attention and mental activity away from the hustle and bustle of life's demands to more profound and meaningful issues. By contemplating these deeper ideas, the meditator can more clearly understand the value of connecting with higher ideals and awareness, and thus become more motivated to attain those states. The practice of contemplation also assists in bringing the contemplator's attention away from externalities and more towards his or her inner being. As a result, contemplation can assist in slowing down one's thinking activity, especially if one starts in the category of 'more thinking activity than usual'.

Relaxation

Relaxation naturally follows contemplation as the person sits quietly, reducing the physiological arousal of the body which, in turn, reduces the chemical and electrical signals that normally drive high rates of thinking. That's why sitting still and calming the body is often a necessary first step for meditation, since slowing the thought-stream brings the meditator closer to the goal of stopping the thoughts altogether.

Mindfulness

To further reduce the frequency of thoughts, mindfulness strategies can be helpful because mindfulness practice not only involves the process of physical stillness and some relaxation but also a deeper insight into the workings of the mind. Mindfulness is based on the recognition that many of our thoughts are provoked by other thoughts. The mind's natural tendency to think and react to its own thoughts and reactions has a snowballing effect that results in one's awareness being rapidly filled with often unnecessary mental content and activity.

Mindfulness is a skill aimed at observing the activity of the mind without reaction. It reduces the degree to which the mind gets involved in thinking about the various stimuli that usually provoke more thinking, of which the mind's own thoughts and feelings are the common source. By preventing this mental snowballing it can help to slow mental activity but, since it can rarely stop the thoughts themselves, it is distinctly different from the zero-thought state of true meditation. Mindfulness is best understood as a method designed to facilitate progress towards the state of mind-emptiness, but it is mind-emptiness that is the meditation itself.

There is no doubt that mindfulness has its uses though, as is becoming increasingly apparent in the field of psychology. As an introspective tool it enables the individual to develop a more profound understanding of the workings of their own mind, thus providing them with useful insights into how the mind can negatively influence their mood, behaviour and mental health. As many mental health professionals will tell you, 'Insight is cure'.

Since mindfulness is designed to prevent the snowballing of thoughts and reactions, it can also reduce (but not eliminate) mental activity, especially in conjunction with relaxation-like methods. It can be beneficial for people who are suffering from excessive thinking, especially repetitive negative thinking or what psychologists call 'rumination' or 'negative self-talk'.

As mindfulness practice can assist in the management of common psychological problems, there has been an explosion of mindfulness-based psychotherapies and mental health programmes. While positive in itself, its growing popularity has helped to perpetuate the public's confused understanding of meditation.

Mind-emptiness

As one learns to slow down the thoughts, by using the methods outlined in this book, for example, the meditator will start to perceive a small gap between each thought. Ultimately the thoughts stop completely while the meditator remains fully alert and aware, but experiences no thinking activity. This is 'mind-emptiness' or mental silence.

Having worked with thousands of people over a number of years, we have found that many participants described being able to skip directly from quiet relaxation to mind-emptiness after just a few weeks of practice; the children in our research programmes were particularly good at this. Once the experience of mental silence was established, mindfulness methods actually became less necessary.

A Buddhist perspective on the mind, mindfulness and mind-emptiness

The revolutionary idea that the Buddha introduced into mainstream society was based on an explanation of the stress-producing effects of the mind. Rather than being enticed or repulsed by the activity of the mind, we should accept it with equanimity and, by understanding its nature, learn to master it.

The mind, the Buddha explained, is responsible for interpreting events as either an 'up' or a 'down'; it is also responsible for us having these ups and downs, since it is the nature of the mind that relentlessly seeks out ups without realising that each up inevitably comes prepackaged with a down. In its relentless search for ups the mind becomes impossible to satisfy. Once it has obtained one thing – which leads to an up – it becomes bored or dissatisfied with that thing – which leads to a down. It then tries to convince us to find another thing so that it can have another up.

When that monkey mind is allowed to do whatever it wants, it makes us run around getting and doing things that it thinks are important, and filling our heads with the increasing din of its demands. That's when we start to get stressed.

The system the Buddha developed to facilitate mastering the monkey mind had two important stages. The first was comprised of intense self-observation; what might best be called introspection. It reached its most sophisticated level as the practice of mindfulness – observing the movements of the mind without being seduced by its charms.

The Buddha's innovative teachings were not, however, intended to stop at the point of mindfulness. Instead, they progressed to the second stage where we learn to observe the fluctuations of the mind and also to master and ultimately transcend the mind. The goal was not just to observe the mind and be aware of its dual up-and-down way of being, but to go beyond it and into the experience of mind-emptiness. This state is traditionally known as 'non-duality', and is sometimes also referred to as 'the void'. In this book we call it mental silence.

Mindfulness enables us to observe the antics of the monkey mind, and by not provoking it, that naughty monkey can often settle down. But with mindfulness alone the monkey is still not fully tamed: it continues to pace the room, it still does some silly things when we are not really alert, and can at any time decide to make a ruckus. With mind-emptiness, however, we are able to assert complete control over that monkey. Then, when we wish, it is allowed to come out and play, but the moment it starts misbehaving, doing destructive things or just making too much noise and distracting us, we can put it back in its cage where it won't make a sound. It's an important distinction.

Can beginners experience mental silence easily?

A number of yoga and meditation 'experts' believe that while mental silence may be the ultimate goal of meditation and yoga, it is an experience that is only achievable after a lifetime of practice, if at all. Our research contradicts this: it appears to be achievable for most people with just a little diligent practice using the methods in this book.

We have found that most people can obtain the experience of meditation quite easily, although children do seem to be able to achieve it a little faster than adults. We conducted a session with a group of 343 beginners in a senior high school. They were taught a simple guided meditation based on the Sahaja yoga technique. We assessed their mental activity before and after the session using a survey based on the thought-waves diagrams.

As expected, the majority of participants indicated that the 'usual mental activity' thought-wave best represented their mental state just prior to the meditation session. After the meditation session, 12% of participants indicated that they had experienced the 'completely silent' state, while 26% indicated that they were experiencing 'an occasional one or two thoughts separated by longer moments of silence', that is, 'mostly silent'. And 32% were experiencing 'a few thoughts separated by brief periods of silence', that is, 'partially silent'. The remainder experienced 'usual' levels of mental activity. Given that this was the first session of meditation they had ever done, it was an impressive result, and yet this pattern of response has been consistently observed in many separate instances. This indicates that people are able to achieve the experience even with only a brief introduction to this meditation skill.

For another example, in a completely different setting we assessed 250 participants from a major corporate office, with no prior exposure to meditation, who had a similar single session of meditation during their lunch hour after which they rated their mental silence levels. About 10% reached the state of complete mental silence while about another 20% described being mostly silent. With repeated practice over a further six or so sessions, a substantially larger proportion of those who continued with the practice at subsequent lunchtime sessions reported the experience of complete silence during the meditation sessions.

This evidence shows that the experience is achievable with a relatively small amount of practice even by beginners.

What about long-term meditators?

We assessed long-term meditators in two ways. First, we asked a group of 143 regular Sahaja yoga meditators in

Sydney to meditate as a group for a single session of about 10 to 15 minutes and then indicate their 'thought activity' using the same survey the beginners used. In this group of regular meditators, 35% experienced 'complete mental silence' while 42% were 'mostly silent' and 16% were 'partially silent'. The remainder experienced 'usual' levels of mental activity. This indicates that regular practitioners are also obtaining this experience and are more able to do so than novices.

Our survey of more than 350 adult long-term practitioners of Sahaja yoga meditation included a simple question: *How often do you experience thoughtless awareness for a few minutes or more?* The results were revealing, with just under half saying that they tapped into the experience 'several times per day or more'.[4]

Long-term meditators survey

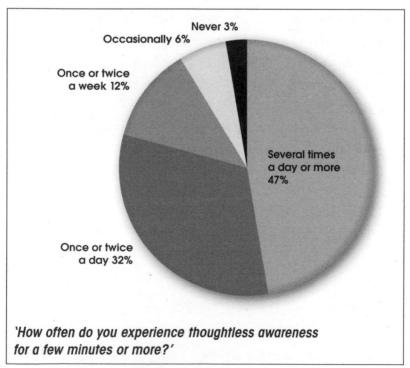

Never 3%
Occasionally 6%
Once or twice a week 12%
Several times a day or more 47%
Once or twice a day 32%

'How often do you experience thoughtless awareness for a few minutes or more?'

These results meant that the vast majority of Sahaja yoga practitioners were tapping into the experience on at least a daily basis. In many instances these meditators were reporting that they were also experiencing mental silence outside of the formal meditation sessions. This reflected my own experience of 'catching the wave' of silence during morning meditation and then trying to maintain that state throughout the day.

As you will see in chapters 10 and 14, this study also found that the health and wellbeing profile of the long-term meditators was significantly higher than that of the general Australian population. We discovered that the more often meditators experienced mental silence, the better their health and wellbeing levels. The survey even found that those meditators who experienced mental silence for just a few minutes once or twice a week had better mental health than the general population. The health advantage correlated with the experience of mental silence more than any other factor that we measured. The relationship with mental health was particularly strong, as is discussed in more detail in Chapter 9. (To download a copy of the original research publication go to www.beyondthemind.com.)

6
The ancient paradigm

When a man knows the solitude of
silence, and feels the joy of quietness, he
is then free.

Buddha

Despite the evidence that shows the effectiveness of mental
silence, the idea of it is still foreign to Western culture.
Why have our modern researchers, despite their obvious
intelligence, failed to appreciate the potential significance
of this phenomenon? We need to look at the historical and
philosophical roots of both Eastern and Western thought to
understand how one culture 'got it' while the other seems to
have missed it almost completely.

Thinking and being

The *Oxford Dictionary* defines meditation as 'To think deeply
and quietly', and the *Cambridge Dictionary* states that meditation
is 'To think seriously about something for a long time'. Neither

of these definitions mentions anything about *silence*. How did Western contemporary popular notions of meditation become almost diametrically opposed to the original ancient Eastern ideas? One reason is that most translators and scholars in the West seem to have a cultural 'blind spot' about meditation that can be traced back to the historical roots of modern Western thinking.

The Cartesian mind trap

When René Descartes (1596–1650), the Catholic mathematician, philosopher and scientist, made the philosophical statement *cogito ergo sum* ('I think, therefore I am') in his text *Principles of Philosophy*, he laid down a foundation element of the Western world view: 'I exist *because* I am thinking.'[1] This statement found enormous popularity and influence because of its emphasis on the celebration of humanity's growing individualism and intellectual power at that time.

The metaphysical implications of Descartes' phrase over the centuries were that thinking activity became equated with the essence of self-existence. Its influence on Western thought is widely acknowledged and cannot be overstated. It also explains why the idea of mental silence is missing from the Western scientific literature: Western scholars, having been educated under the influence of Western philosophy and *cogito ergo sum*, have difficulty understanding the possibility that a state of full consciousness that is also devoid of thought might be possible, let alone useful, desirable or possibly even superior.

Yet the concept of mental silence is thousands of years old – and thousands of years older than Descartes' statement.

The history of mental silence

Following are some key descriptions of mental silence taken from the most ancient sources to those from the modern day. You don't need to read all of them, however I have provided a fairly comprehensive selection here for you to muse over. (There are many more at www.beyondthemind.com.)

The Mahabharata: *'Like a log he does not think',* about 3000 BCE

The idea of meditation as a state of mental silence can be traced as far back as India's most ancient text, the *Mahabharata* ('The Great Story of India'). This text is dated by Western scholars as being 2000 to 3000 years old, by archaeo-astronomers as possibly 7000 years old, and by traditional Indian legend as vastly more ancient still.

Ten times longer than Homer's *Iliad* and *Odyssey* combined, the *Mahabharata* is a dramatised education about the nature of humanity, consciousness and our place in the larger cosmos. It is the most influential story in Indian culture and it is here that we find the most ancient definition of meditation known to man. The sage-storyteller describes a meditator thus:

> *He does not hear; he does not smell. Neither does he taste or see, or experience touch. Likewise his mind ceases to imagine. He desires nothing, and like a log he does not think. Then the sages call him 'yoked', 'one who has reached Nature'.* [2]

These simple lines lay out the key Eastern ideas about meditation. The first is that meditation is specifically characterised as the state of non-thought. Second, the term 'yoked' (as in an animal yoked to a cart, or Sanskrit *yukta*) is the origin of the word 'yoga', and in this context it means a kind of profound connection that involves the state of inner silence. Third, the idea that in the state of silence the meditator has reached 'nature' and has become at one with the fundamental reality of themselves and the cosmos. This optimal state of being has also been called *sahaja*. Thus 'yoga' came to mean the connection with higher consciousness; a perfect harmony between psyche, soul, body and cosmos in which the state of inner silence is the main feature.

On one level the *Mahabharata* is an allegory for the struggle in society for moral behaviour. More deeply, it is about the yogic struggle for self-mastery that each individual must engage in to bring his or her own mind under control and how, through meditative practices, the individual can achieve the state of inner silence that is the ideal way of being. Life, according to the *Mahabharata*, is a journey of personal evolution toward the optimal state of being. Central to that journey is the ability to master the impulses of the mind. In the *Bhagavad Gita*, the spiritual climax of the *Mahabharata* legend, that struggle is simply put:

> *For him who has conquered the mind, the mind is the best of friends; but for one who has failed to do so, his mind will remain the greatest enemy.*[3]

The Upanishads: 'When reason itself rests in silence', 1500 BCE

A thousand or so years after the *Mahabharata*, ideas about mental silence emerged in the *Upanishads*. These ancient metaphysical treatises form another cornerstone of Eastern culture. They are less concerned with heroic stories and more focused on the direct metaphysical questions of life and the nature of consciousness. Juan Mascaro, an eminent translator of Indian spiritual texts, was a Western scholar who successfully grasped the importance of mental silence. In his authoritative translations he eloquently summarised the Upanishadic ideas on meditation and consciousness:

> In the infinite struggle of man to know this world and the universe around him, and also to know the mind that allows him to think, he comes before the simple fact that life is above thought.[1]

In his translation of the Katha Upanishad:

> When the five senses and the mind are still, and reason itself rests in silence, then begins the path supreme. This calm steadiness of the senses is called yoga. Then one should become watchful, because yoga comes and goes.[5]

In the Kaushitaki Upanishad it is stated, 'It is not thought which we should know: we should know the thinker.'

Later, teachings arose that not only spoke about mental silence and the meditative experiences that lie beyond it, but also the methods by which the state could be achieved and maintained.

Patanjali's Yoga Sutras: 'The emptiness between thoughts', 500 BCE

A thousand years or so after the *Upanishads*, Patanjali, a physician and sage, compiled what are known as the 'yoga aphorisms' or *Yoga Sutras*. His work brought together many of the traditional texts that describe various practices for the cultivation of consciousness, and synthesised the information into one of the most well-known yogic treatises on meditation. Patanjali's *Yoga Sutras* was the first 'how to' guide for those aspiring to experience higher consciousness or self-realisation. It described an eight-fold discipline – comprised of ethics, cleanliness, postures, breath control exercises, discipline of the senses, training of the attention, meditation and yogic experience – in which all eight limbs (as they are known) work to support attainment of higher awareness.

Patanjali describes the practice and experience of meditation as the *emptiness* between the thoughts:

> *By being aware of the silent void moments pervading the emptiness between thoughts, one can glimpse and expand the skill of thought subjugation which leads to transformation.*[6]

This is an experience that culminates in a state of perfectly integrated consciousness that Patanjali called *sahaja samadhi*.

Lao Tse and the Tao Te Ching: 'Sitting in oblivion', 500 BCE

At about the same time as Patanjali was writing, Lao Tse ('Old Master'), the founder of Taoism, lived in China. Legend has it that he worked as the Keeper of the Archives for the Royal Court of Zhou. During his life he attracted a great number of students and disciples, eventually becoming so popular that even the emperors of the Tang Dynasty claimed to be his descendants. Towards the end of his life, apparently at about 160 years of age, he dictated the poetic *Tao Te Ching* or 'The Way' to one of his disciples. It describes in beautiful poetry, and sometimes enigmatic riddles, the nature of the universe and the way to enlightenment.

The human mind, according to Lao Tse, is the chief obstacle to higher awareness. By overcoming the mind one attains the state of mental silence and, as a result, inner peace and profound wisdom follow. The *Tao Te Ching* warns against the intellectualisation of spiritual wisdom and spiritual pretentiousness, instead advising people to seek out their real self by being spontaneous and free of social and mental artifice. It says that in living life by flowing with the moment, one becomes in harmony with the cosmic consciousness or *Tao*.

Lao Tse described meditation as the state of 'sitting in oblivion' in which the mind is emptied of all thoughts and physical distractions:

> *Empty your mind of all thoughts.*
> *Let your heart be at peace.*[7]

Confucius: 'Fasting of the mind', 500 BCE

An important contemporary to Lao Tse was Confucius. Legend has it that they even met to compare notes. While Lao Tse focused on how the inner state of the individual should be attuned to the cosmos, Confucius focused on the outer world and how individuals and institutions should behave to create a society that was fair, just and benevolent, and therefore also in tune with the cosmos.

Confucius' teachings focused on personal and governmental morality, correctness of social relationships, filial loyalty, justice and sincerity, which eventually gave rise to a system of philosophy called Confucianism, which was spelled out in the *Analects of Confucius*. Confucius' Golden Rule was essentially, 'Do unto others as you would have them do unto you.' It would, however, be a mistake to say that Confucius was simply a social conservative. To achieve such a standard of behaviour requires tremendous self-discipline, and so Confucius also spoke about the importance of controlling the mind in order to achieve his ideal, writing: 'Emptiness is the fasting of the mind.'[8]

The Buddha: 'The multiplicity of things disappears', 500 BCE

The most well-known contemporary to both Lao Tse and Confucius was the Buddha, who lived in northern India around 500 BCE. This prince who renounced his power, family and wealth to become a pauper–saint travelled across India explaining his insights to whomever would listen. Like Patanjali, the Buddha did not just talk about morality or metaphysics; he also mapped out, in unprecedented and practical detail, the way in which our mind obscures our perception of reality. He developed a methodology and lifestyle that would allow the practitioner to master her or his own mind, and in doing so take the first fundamental step towards attaining the state of *nirvana*.

In the Buddhist text, *The Awakening of Faith*, several stages in the practice of development are described, the final one being 'the stage of preventing vain thoughts'. In meditative posture the aspirant is instructed that 'all kinds of ideas, as soon as thought of, must be put away, even the idea of banishing them must also be put away'.[9]

In the words of the Buddha, 'when the mind is quieted, the multiplicity of things disappears'.[10] This is a direct reference to the experience of mental silence, and yet much of the Buddhism taught in modern times seems to overlook its importance. The experience of mental silence can provide us with a much more profound perspective on Buddhist teachings. The Buddhist idea of 'suffering', for example, can be understood as a description of the effects of the untamed mind. Rather than being the experience of non-existence, the idea of 'void' can be understood as the profound state that arises when one's awareness is emptied of thought and the individual mind disappears and a higher consciousness emerges.

The Secret of the Golden Flower: 'All methods end in quietness', 800 CE

For centuries after Lao Tse, Taoist aspirants sought out methods and practices to bring about the experience of mental silence. Inevitably they came to know about the yoga systems of India, particularly that described in Patanjali's *Yoga Sutras*. By combining Taoism and Patanjali's practices, 'Taoist yoga' emerged in China.

The Secret of the Golden Flower is probably the most famous Taoist yoga text. Richard Wilhelm, a highly accomplished scholar of Chinese culture who was responsible for the most authoritative translation, dated it to approximately 800 CE. Like Patanjali's *Sutras* and Lao Tse's *Tao Te Ching*, *The Secret of the Golden Flower* describes the methods and mechanics of higher consciousness. Again, the experience of mental silence is given central importance in this process of awakening:

> *If the thoughts are absolutely tranquil the heavenly heart can be seen ... It demands the deepest silence ... When the desire for silence comes, not a single thought arises.*[11]

Gyaneshwara: 'The functions of the mind and body stand still', 1200 CE

As the name *The Secret of the Golden Flower* implies, the knowledge contained in this text was a jealously guarded secret. So too in India were the ancient scriptures and texts dealing with meditation, yoga and consciousness kept out of the public eye for thousands of years.

Born in Maharashtra, central India, Gyaneshwara (1275–1296) made it his mission to communicate to the common people the previously secret knowledge about the ancient methods for the cultivation of higher awareness. He did this by writing his famous commentary on the *Bhagavad Gita* called the *Gyaneshwari*, wherein he explained and demystified the process of self-realisation and higher consciousness. Gyaneshwara's contribution was unprecedented both in its detail and, more importantly, because it was written in the local language (Marathi) rather than the exclusive Sanskrit.

For the first time, Gyaneshwara revealed to the general population that the process of consciousness development necessarily involved the cleansing and strengthening of *chakras* (the 'wheels' of energy within the body) and *nadis* (the channels of energy in the body), followed by the awakening of a dormant energy called *Kundalini*. *Kundalini* awakening – which describes the energy rising from the base of the spine, where it is believed to lie coiled in the sacrum bone – was itself the energy of meditation. Its awakening, he said, was necessary for self-realisation and was associated with a variety of experiential phenomena, including mental silence: 'the imagination subsides, activity becomes calm, and the functions of the body and mind become still ...'[12]

Thus ideas derived from the yoga and meditation esoteric systems eventually became the stuff of everyday culture in India. This is why your average Indian understands that daily meditation is good for you, even though they may have never done it themselves, and it's why the Eastern outlook on life is suffused with the unspoken understanding that we are something other than body, mind or thoughts.

Christianity: 'Silent music', 1 CE onwards

Although it is more systematically described in Eastern culture than any other, the experience of thoughtless awareness and its connection to higher states of consciousness is not exclusive to it – descriptions can also be found in the religious and cultural history of the West. However, as these references are not always within mainstream texts, their significance seems to have been overlooked.

For example, in the anonymous book of Christian mystical text *The Cloud of Unknowing*, the writer encourages the development of a profound, introspective understanding of God that is accessible in the non-thinking state: 'strike down every kind of thought under the cloud of forgetting'.[13] St John of the Cross described the state as 'silent music' and 'the sound of solitude'.[14] There are also some references to the silent state in the Bible:

> *For God alone, O my soul, wait in silence, for my hope is from Him ...[15] For God alone my soul waits in silence; from him comes my salvation ...[16] And when he had opened the seventh seal, there was silence in heaven about the space of half an hour.[17]*

Zen: 'The sound of one hand clapping', 1330 CE

Zen is an offshoot of Buddhism. The word is derived from the Sanskrit *dhyana*, which means 'meditation'. The ancient Japanese *Rinzai* Zen tradition elegantly captures the meaning of non-thought with the famous question: 'What is the sound of one hand clapping?'. The answer is, of course, that there is no sound and, similarly, the state of meditation involves no mental noise. The aim of this kind of riddle is to challenge the mind into realising the futility of rational thought, thus triggering a sudden leap of consciousness toward the trans-mind state, described in the Zen tradition as *satori*.[18]

The Book of Consciousness and Life: *'Absence of thoughts is bodhi', 1800* CE

About 200 years ago a Taoist text called *The Book of Consciousness and Life* clearly described the mechanism of higher consciousness. It elaborated on the idea of *bodhi*, originally a Buddhist term meaning 'enlightened intellect'. In the West we would expect a more highly developed intellect to necessarily involve more highly developed active thinking processes, but *The Book of Consciousness and Life* explains to us that the intellect enlightened by higher consciousness is characterised not by more complex and active thought but, in fact, by mental silence – 'absence of thoughts is *bodhi*.'[19]

Ramana Maharshi: 'Self-realisation is cessation of thoughts', 20th century

The lineage continues more or less from ancient times into the twentieth century. In the mid-1900s a sage called Ramana Maharshi became known to a small group of Western seekers, which included the famous English author W. Somerset Maugham, the New Age author Paul Brunton and the father of modern photography Henri Cartier-Bresson.

In his late teens, Ramana was seized by an urge to go into retreat in the south Indian countryside. There, in the forest on a hill called Arunachala, he spontaneously entered into a profound meditative state. Those who discovered him were impressed by the fact that, by sitting in his presence for some time, their minds became silent and yet they were fully alert and aware. As one commentator stated:

> *A short time in his silent presence stilled the raging mind and gently thrust the aspiring devotee into the bliss of the highest state …*[20]

Followers built a small ashram around Ramana, and over time he gained renown for his remarkable ability to not only confer mental silence on those who sat in his presence but for his ability to explain – in extremely simple or extremely complex terms, depending on who the listener was – the nature of self-realisation and spiritual consciousness. His message was simple: forget complex intellectual approaches to inner discovery and instead focus on attaining the state of mental silence. His many comments on this state include:

> *Keep the mind one-pointed or free from thought, the thoughtless state.*

> *There is consciousness along with quietness in the mind; this is exactly the state to be aimed at.*

> *Self-realisation is cessation of thoughts and of all mental activity. Thoughts are like bubbles upon the surface of the sea.*

> *Stillness means 'being free from thoughts' and yet aware.*[21]

Ramana died in 1950, having never left the hill upon which he arrived as a teenager. Henri Cartier-Bresson described that

at the exact time of his death he witnessed a shooting star in
the sky above Ramana's ashram:

> *It is a most astonishing experience. I was in the open space in*
> *front of my house, when my friends drew my attention to the sky,*
> *where I saw a vividly luminous shooting star with a luminous*
> *tail, unlike any shooting star I had before seen, coming from*
> *the South, moving slowly across the sky and, reaching the top of*
> *Arunachala, disappeared behind it. Because of its singularity we*
> *all guessed its import and immediately looked at our watches – it*
> *was 8:47 – and then raced to the Ashram only to find that our*
> *premonition had been only too sadly true: the Master had passed*
> *into mahanirvana at that very minute.[22]*

Such is the nature of one who has attained union with the
cosmos, the ancient Eastern tradition tells us.

The state of union with the cosmos, what might be called
optimal consciousness, has also been called *sahaja*.[23] Ramana
Maharshi himself described the connection between the
sahaja state and mental silence, a condition that is theoretically
achievable by each and every one of us:

> *When we have tendencies that we are trying to give up, that is*
> *to say when we are still imperfect and have to make conscious*
> *efforts to keep the mind one-pointed or free from thought, the*
> *thoughtless state which we thus attain is* nirvikalpa samadhi.
> *When, through practice, we are always in that state, not going*
> *into samadhi and coming out again, that is the sahaja state. In*
> *the sahaja state one sees only the Self and one sees the world as a*
> *form assumed by the Self.[24]*

On another occasion he described the sahaja state:

> *In this state you remain calm and composed during activity.*
> *You realise that you are moved by the deeper self within and are*
> *unaffected by what you do or say or think. You have no worries,*
> *anxieties or cares, for you realise that there is nothing that belongs*
> *to you as ego and that everything is being done by something with*
> *which you are in conscious union.*[25]

Shri Mataji: Sahaja yoga, 21st century

In contemporary times the tradition of the mental silence experience has been maintained by Shri Mataji Nirmala Devi (1923–2011). While Ramana Maharshi spoke openly of the experience, and conferred the experience to those around him, his influence was limited to those who came into his physical presence. For the experience to extend beyond this limitation, a method was needed that could be used anywhere. In 1970 Shri Mataji, an Indian woman, developed a technique of meditation that specifically focused on the experience of mental silence.[26] Similar to Gyaneshwara's descriptions, it claims to utilise an understanding of the subtle energetic system of *chakras, nadis* and *Kundalini* energy to bring about the experience of the meditative state. Uniquely, it could be taught and learnt easily and thus made accessible to the wider population.[27]

The word *sahaja* is derived from the Sanskrit *saha*, meaning 'together', and *ja*, meaning 'born', and can be translated to mean 'innate'. A version of this state can be seen in young children, for example, who are free of the complex adult mind. As a result, children have the ability to enjoy life, behave spontaneously and perceive their world and themselves with fresh eyes, unburdened by pretences and neuroses.

Shri Mataji's method aims to give the average person an intellectual understanding of the importance of meditation and, more importantly, the ability to experience it. Sahaja yoga represents a logical step in the millennia-old progression.

Significantly, like all teachers before her, Shri Mataji did not charge any fees. She propagated the skills by giving public lectures and instructional sessions around the world. As a result, Sahaja yoga is now practised in over a hundred countries taught by a grassroots network of volunteer instructor–practitioners.

Shri Mataji died in February 2011 at the age of eighty-seven; the method she taught continues to be made available at no charge throughout the world.

—

Looking at the full historical panorama of knowledge about meditation in the course of our research, a larger pattern emerged. The knowledge of and methods to achieve the state of authentic meditation began in prehistory as a closely guarded secret. With the progression of time and the coming and going of different adepts, progressively deeper understandings were developed about how to attain the state of mental silence. Along the continuum of spiritual history, this knowledge was slowly released to an ever-widening audience until now we see the knowledge being communicated to the general population in a process that might be called 'democratisation of the meditative experience'.

The historical and cultural provenance of the mental silence experience alone warrants specific scientific attention. The subjective reports from both novices and long-term practitioners collected in our studies appeared to closely correspond to the traditional descriptions of the experience, and consequently urged serious scientific attention. For a meditation researcher, the emergence of a method such as Sahaja yoga represents an ideal opportunity to study the ancient and authentic definition of meditation within a modern scientific context.

Present day

What do William Wordsworth, the eighteenth-century English poet, A. A. Milne, creator of Winnie the Pooh, and George Lucas, director of the *Star Wars* movies, have in common? One feature they share is that they each achieved the pinnacle of their cultural genre; the other is that each has reflected many Eastern ideas of meditation and mental silence in their work. While the experience of mental silence does not seem to have received the same amount of attention in mainstream Western religion as in the East, it's remarkable that references to it appear haphazardly throughout popular culture. Here are just three examples of the many I have found.

Wordsworth refers to it in *Intimations of Immortality*, his poetic exploration of the possibilities and limitations of consciousness: 'Our noisy years seem moments in the being of the eternal silence.'[28] A. A. Milne's Winnie the Pooh has charmed children and adults alike with his Zen-like simplicity. Pooh's adventures and dialogue are now widely understood to contain many references to Taoist ideas, meditation and the state of inner silence. 'Sometimes I sits and thinks, and sometimes I just sits,' says Pooh.[29] One of the central characters in George Lucas's *Star Wars* movies is the guru-like, Jedi master Yoda. Much of Yoda's instruction to

Luke Skywalker is derived directly from Eastern philosophy, including the idea of the Force. Yoda's name closely resembles the word 'yoga', the state of connection with the cosmos, which is what the guru is supposed to give to his disciples – a clear reference to the Eastern concept of meditation. Yoda alluded to the state of mental silence when he spoke of the importance of a clear mind.[30]

The mental silence experience is an important dimension of our potential as human beings. Given orthodox Western culture's difficulty in appreciating it, it's perhaps not surprising that we have turned to popular culture for a more satisfying explanation of the nature of human experience.

Recently, I came across this rather scathing comment in a scientific journal from a Western scientist regarding the authentic ideas that underlie meditation:

> *When we close our eyes to meditate our mind does not go completely blank, void of thoughts at one with the universe, because just as hearts are meant to beat and lungs to breathe, brains are meant to think and will never be completely devoid of thought, perhaps until they are dead.*[31]

Now we can understand why his emphatic rejection of mental silence perfectly illustrates the cultural and personal difficulties that many researchers have had in trying to understand the ancient Eastern paradigm. It is not that mental silence doesn't exist, but rather that the Cartesian blind spot has prevented Western scholars from understanding the authentic ideas of meditation and the concept of mental silence. It's always been there, but until now few of us have been able to see it.

Words from meditators

Sometimes one can retain that meditative mood while walking, driving or even working. Alert but peaceful. I would love to maintain that state all day. It is remarkably silent. The first times I felt thoughtless awareness, I found it a comfort, and a relief. I am naturally chatty and always thinking, planning and reminiscing. The silence is wonderful, and truly relaxing. My experience was usually stronger when we meditated together in one of the programmes. My restlessness and wiggles would just fall away, and I enjoyed a sense of contentment in those long minutes of quiet. Sometimes in the meditation, I still just feel …
as if gentle waves of ocean water are rolling over me, in soothing quiet. Nothing to worry about, for a few seconds. You just can't bear to break that spell. I just wait, very still, hoping the seconds will stretch into minutes. Sometimes it feels as if time itself bends around this moment. Afterwards the whole day seems to go smoother, my steps are lighter, and it's easier to smile … I would recommend this method to anyone who would like to truly enjoy this precious life.

Elizabeth, USA

When you achieve thoughtless meditation you tap into the silence of your being. You connect yourself with a deeper truth, with the essence of your inner joy, with a state of inner balance and total reconciliation with what you are, thus providing a state of inner unity and integration. This state is unique and achieved only when the thoughtless awareness is reached, connecting us with a realm of inner beauty and peace, a realm of understanding oneself and being in tune with oneself, a realm where sincere and pure love for oneself and for others flows, a realm where forgiveness and understanding take on their real meaning. You have the same life but live it with an entirely new awareness, intensity, peace and sense of fulfilment. The feeling after every morning meditation is just awesome; often you don't want to quit the meditation and desire to stay longer and go deeper in this blissful state. You are just sitting and an intense bubbling life of fulfilment and peace is awakened in you, bringing a pure state of joy for no specific reason, just a state. You are then in perfect shape to start your day!

Christophe, France

I think I was searching for some kind of solution. At least at that time I was quite aware of all the confusion there was in my mind, but I didn't know where it came from. Then, one day I saw a poster about Sahaja yoga-meditation in a nearby library. I didn't have a clue what it was, but somehow I wanted to go. It wasn't that tremendous. Just sitting, saying some sentences in my mind and moving with attention on different spots of the body … But somehow it started growing in me. When I first started really going into thoughtless awareness, it was amazing. Just being, no need to think, just being there in absolute oneness with myself. Even when I went home, there was a kind of happy, very balanced and satisfied feeling. Later I also learned how to do it at home. I really don't know when it all happened, but the change is very obvious now. I feel just fine! Little by little it has all worked out so beautifully …

Janne, Finland

Before learning to meditate, I was a habitual thinker. My pastime was to think and think. When my husband was late, I started worrying endlessly and became restless. Practising

*meditation was like training myself to close my eyes and be silent.
I began to notice the calmness in me, then I started to become
aware of nature around me. This feeling of being alive and joyful
is something extraordinary for me. In my daily meditation I feel
so connected with the all-pervading energy above and around and
within. My attention is much clearer and I want more people to
experience this knowledge and joy.*

Celia, Bangkok

7
A thought experiment that ends in silence

You must live in the present, launch
yourself on every wave, find your
eternity in each moment.

Henry David Thoreau [1]

William James, the American philosopher widely considered the founder of modern psychology, was fascinated by the nature of the mind. Exploring both Western and Eastern philosophy, as well as his own experience, James came to a fascinating realisation:

Let anyone try, I will not say to arrest, but to notice or to attend to, the present moment of time. One of the most baffling experiences occurs. Where is it, this present? It has melted in our grasp, fled ere we could touch it, gone in the instant of becoming. [2]

James' discovery is something that has been known and taught throughout the ancient East – that the human mind, while capable of dealing with the dimensions of past and future, is for some reason unable to grasp the absolute present moment. Learning how to focus on the present moment, therefore, is one way to silence the mind.

Following is a thought experiment that you can use. We have found that this exercise, when combined with the other skills and methods described in this book, can be a useful way to maintain and enhance the silent state throughout the day.

While reading, see if you can look inside at your own thinking patterns and apply the following exercise to yourself. For some people, this can be enough to trigger the experience of mental silence. For many, once familiarised with the experience after learning the other techniques outlined in this book, this exercise can be useful to retain or strengthen the experience while going about your daily routine.

If we examine the nature of the thoughts that each of us experience from moment to moment, we will find that they all relate to one of two broad categories:

1. Events that have occurred in the past.
2. Events that we anticipate will occur in the future.

Whether the event was an argument with a friend yesterday (past), an unpaid bill (future), or what we had for breakfast this morning (past), we will find that all of our thoughts have arisen from only the past or future.

The past is comprised of events that have already occurred, but right now those events no longer exist – although we may be living with their consequences. Whether it is something that happened 10 years ago, 10 minutes ago or 10 seconds ago, that event is in the past. If it no longer exists, then it's not real. It may have been real when it was happening but it is not real anymore. Hence, the past itself no longer exists. So, for the purpose of this exercise, let's agree that if the past does not exist, then the past is not real.

The future is comprised of events that have yet to occur. These events are undetermined; they may or may not happen. Certainly, as those future events approach the present it becomes much more likely that they will occur, but until they have actually happened we cannot say with certainty that they will eventuate. So these events that have not happened, that may or may not happen, don't exist. Since they are not real either, then the future itself is also not yet real.

If we accept that the past is not real and the future is not real, then what dimension of our experience can we say is truly real? The answer is that only the present moment is actually real. What is happening right *now* is real.

Once we have accepted that it is only the present moment, the *now* that is real, try this: think about the present moment. Don't think about what's generally happening, just try to think about the absolute present moment. Put the book down and try it with your eyes closed for a minute …

The majority of people who try thinking about the absolute present moment find that it is actually very hard to do. In fact, it is impossible. We find that by the time our mind 'reaches out' to grasp the present moment, that very moment moves into the past. We try again, and yet the next moment that our mind tries to grasp, again, slips into the past. Our mind might try instead to grab something that is *about* to happen, only to find that now it has strayed into the future! Our mind – our thinking processes – are fundamentally unable to grasp the present moment. It's a bit like trying to catch a fish with our bare hands.

While we can easily think about events in the past (even a few moments ago), or events that we anticipate will occur in the future (even seconds into the future), it is impossible to actually think about the instantaneous and ever-changing present moment. Our mind is demonstrably unable to grasp the present moment. Yet, as we've already established, the present moment is the only thing that's real.

Meditation is when we grasp the present moment and stay there. By connecting our attention with the present moment, our thinking – our mind – falls away, leaving us in the thought-free, present-moment experience of reality. By cultivating the ability to focus on the present moment, the mind becomes silent. Its stress-producing thoughts evaporate, leaving us in a state of silent calm and equanimity.

For many of us this is an experience that we may have connected with in childhood, but as our mind became increasingly complex we lost touch with it. The techniques described in this book are aimed at helping you to regain that experience.

This explanation encapsulates thousands of years of Eastern meditative tradition into one simple but profound exercise. Mental silence is in the space between the thoughts, in the dimension of the present moment. It has and always will be. All legitimate meditative methods are designed to give us the ability to make a sustained and repeatable connection with the reality of the present moment.

By now you are probably wondering when you'll get to the 'good stuff'. Here is a guide to using the basic technique of meditation that we employed in our various research projects.

It is a genuinely evidence-based meditation technique that should only take you about 10 to 15 minutes to do, once you are reasonably familiar with it.

Further instructions and resources are available free of charge at www.beyondthemind.com.

> *When he sees a fruit he can think about the fruit, but in the end*
> *he must eat it if he wants to know its taste.*
>
> **Juan Mascaro**[3]

What am I aiming to experience?

As a result of discussions with hundreds of experienced meditators, training thousands of beginners in our own research projects and related initiatives, and my own experience, we can say that the authentic meditative experience boils down to five essential features:

1. The meditator has a heightened awareness of the present moment.
2. The experience of silence is 'located' in the space between any two thoughts. In meditation that space gradually widens until the meditator becomes completely silent within. You can think when you want to or need to, but when thinking is not needed it can be stopped. This leaves us with more mental energy, better focus and an improved ability to think clearly when it is needed.

3. The focus of attention tends to move naturally towards the top of the head or just above the top of the head, where it rests without much effort as the mind becomes progressively more silent.

4. One's mood is pleasant and positive, and there is a sense of equanimity or balance. It's important to distinguish between the quietly joyful state of meditation and the extreme of manic happiness, for example.

5. Importantly, the meditator is fully alert and aware and hence in control of both themselves and the experience. Although meditation necessarily involves, at first, the reduction of mental activity and then ultimately the elimination of it to enter into the state of mental silence, the meditator does not experience a loss of personality, emotion, perception or 'sense of self'. In fact, many meditators report that the mental peace and emotional equilibrium of meditation allows them to feel and experience their own personality, and themselves, more fully than ever before.

These features converge into a single experience that is best described as occurring when one focuses on the cool, silent space that exists just above the head. Feeling 'cool, calm, collected and silent' is a great way to summarise it.

You can't do meditation, you can only be in meditation

Here are some useful points that will assist in developing the experience of mental silence:

1. You cannot *do* meditation, you can only *experience* it. Rather than trying to push yourself into the experience,

you should just allow it to happen in its own time.
Instead of 'trying to make it happen' it is better that you 'desire the experience' and make efforts to create an internal and external environment that is conducive to that experience.

2. It is useful to understand that it is not that you do meditation; rather, there is an energy of meditation within you, a mechanism or ability that needs to be awakened in order for you to experience it. So many of the strategies described here are better understood as ways of **facilitating the effect** of that meditative energy rather than as ways of **making us** meditate.

3. During meditation your general attitude should be directed at enjoying the experience and not getting too worked up if it doesn't happen the first few times. Allow the process to work out in its own time - go with the flow!

General advice about posture

Many people think that to meditate they have to sit in certain postures such as the lotus position. In reality, it is just as effective, or possibly more effective, to sit on a chair or on the floor cross-legged, as you wish.

It may take a few attempts, or a bit of moving around, to work out the best position for you. Some people find that sitting with their back to a wall can provide them with good support. You may also choose to sit on a cushion or folded blankets, but try to avoid sitting on a couch or sofa, as these do not provide good support for the spine. Lying down is generally not the best position for meditation, mainly because there is a temptation to drift off to sleep. Meditation is not napping.

Once you have found a comfortable seated position, rest your hands flat on your lap, palms up, with your fingers gently outstretched. There is no need for any complicated finger positions.

Guided meditation with standard affirmations

- Find somewhere you can sit quietly for 15 minutes.
- Use the guided meditation instructions on the following pages, or download the free instruction card from the website: www.beyondthemind.com.
- It might be easier to do this with a friend who can read out the instructions while you follow. Alternatively, you can go to the website and follow it on audio or video.
- If using it, set up the card where you can see it - stick it to a wall, or frame it so that it doesn't bend (this is important if you are using a candle near it).
- If you wish, light a candle in front of the card, and use some incense. Experiment to see what works best for you. The candle and/or incense are not essential but many meditators do feel that it helps.
- If possible, remove shoes and glasses, and loosen tight clothes such as ties or belts.
- Sit comfortably either on a chair or on the floor (with a cushion if the floor is too hard), resting your left hand flat on your lap, palm up.
- Each affirmation is directed to the energy of meditation, which exists in all of us.
- Place your right hand in the position indicated in the instructions while repeating the corresponding affirmation.

Use the hand positions as shown below.

Repeat the affirmations silently a few times.

Utilise the helpful tips, then gently move to next position.

 Place your right hand on the left side of your lower stomach, just above the left hip.

Affirmation: 'I am the pure knowledge' or 'Give me the true knowledge about myself'

Tip: Take a few breaths to help bring your attention inside.

 Place your right hand on the left side of your upper stomach, just below the ribs.

Affirmation: 'I am my own master' or 'Make me my own master'

Tip: Press a little more firmly here.

 Place your right hand on the heart, a little to the left of the breastbone.

Affirmation: 'I am the spirit' or 'I am the self' or 'I am pure awareness'

Tip: Take a few relaxing breaths.

 Place your right hand on the left shoulder, where the shoulder joins the neck (gently turn your head a little to the right).

Affirmation: 'I am not guilty at all'

Tip: Say this as many times as you need, but it's most important to say it sincerely. Do this without thinking about any specific reasons as to why you should feel guilty. It's important to permit ourselves to recover and grow from our mistakes.

Place your right hand flat on the forehead, gently grasping the temples, leaning your head forward a little into your hand.

Affirmation: 'I forgive. I forgive everyone and I forgive myself'

Tip: Say this from your heart, without thinking of any particular incident or person – feel the release of forgiveness.

Place your right hand on the back of the head, in line with your eyes. Lean the head back a little into your hand.

Affirmation: 'Please forgive me for any mistakes I have made knowingly or unknowingly' or 'For whatever I have done against myself, please forgive me'

Tip: Don't think of any specific issues, just let it go. Relax.

Place your right hand on top of the head, halfway between hairline and crown. Stretch your fingers up a little, lightly pressing your palm onto the head, gently rub the head in a clockwise direction.

Affirmation: 'Please give me the experience of mental silence / self-realisation / true meditation'

Tip: Slowly raise your right hand about 10 centimetres above the head and allow your attention to follow it. With your hand there, you may feel a cool or possibly warm sensation on the palm. It can be useful to focus on this sensation, if you wish.

Return your hand to your lap so that both hands are resting there with palms facing upwards, fingers a little outstretched. Gently maintain your attention above the top of your head.

Tip: Sit quietly with eyes closed and enjoy the peace. If thoughts fail to settle or become intrusive, use the thought-stopping sequence over the page.

At the beginning and at the end of your meditation you can try the 'Tying up your attention' and 'Protecting your experience' exercises that are described on page 171.

Do this meditation at any time, but once or twice a day is best. Make it part of your daily routine and see how it helps you feel better, reduces stress and improves your life in general. Treat it as an experiment for the next few weeks and if you feel that it's working keep it up! If you need to do more to quieten your thoughts, try using some of the tools and clearing techniques described throughout this book and see the tips in the FAQs section on page 264.

This affirmation sequence can be especially helpful to settle the thoughts for people new to meditation. You can continue to use this meditation or try the shorter format on page 170.

Thought-stopping sequence

The monkey mind, especially in the beginning, will struggle against the experience by throwing up all sorts of distracting thoughts, ideas and possibly even images to prevent you from getting or staying in mental silence. Or, after subsiding for some time, it may try to reassert itself. It does this by producing thoughts that enter into our awareness and attempt to distract us from the state of silence. Rather than fighting the mind, we should ask the energy of meditation within us, which is the power of non-mind, to assist in quieting the mind again.

It's simple but it can be very effective, particularly in helping to sustain the silent state once you have gone through the basic affirmations or even combined with other meditations in this book.

When the monkey mind tries to disrupt your meditation experience, try the following strategies:

1. If thoughts or images bubble up into your awareness, just allow those thoughts to come and go, to move in and out of your awareness. Don't allow yourself to be distracted by them, don't give in to the temptation to get involved in them, don't build on them. Just let them move in and then out of your attention. Usually they will subside as the monkey mind gives up trying to distract you. Once the mind settles again, refocus your attention at the top of the head.

2. If the thoughts persist, say silently inside, 'I forgive these thoughts' or 'I am not these thoughts' or 'Please take away these thoughts'.

3. If the mind persists in its attempts to distract and spoil the experience, place the right hand on the forehead and with the eyes closed and the attention gently directed to the top of the head, request that the meditative energy within helps to quieten the mind using those same thought-stopping affirmations.

4. Then place the right hand on the top of the head, so that the centre of the palm is pressing firmly on the scalp. Allow your attention to move to that point. Then raise the right hand about 10 centimetres above the head and allow your attention to move up with it, into the space between the hand and the top of the head. Hold your attention there, as if you were balancing (not visualising) a bubble at the point. Place the right hand back on the lap, palm up, but keep your attention in that space above the head.

5. See how long you can sit and stay silent inside. Whenever the thoughts start to appear, repeat steps 3 and 4.

Did you experience mental silence? A slowing or, ideally, an elimination of thinking, a sense of peacefulness, positive mood and focused attention? Did you notice how being in the present moment has a timeless quality? Remember, our research shows that about 10% of novices experience complete mental silence the first time they try it. A further 20-30% experience being 'mostly' silent. That is, just one or two occasional thoughts separated by longer periods of silence. About 20-30% experience being 'partially' silent, where the thoughts slow down and are separated by briefer periods of non-thought. The remainder experience a slowing of the thoughts. Regardless of how much thinking activity slowed down or stopped, meditators also report improved mood, decreased stress and tension, and an increased sense of calm and peacefulness.

Don't worry if you didn't get there the first time, the main criterion by which you should judge your initial attempts is whether or not it felt good. I encourage you to keep trying. Our research shows that with every further attempt progressively more people get it. The majority of people get it with a week or two of diligent daily practice, and it seems to happen even faster when combined with 'footsoaking' (see page 178).

My advice, whether or not you experience mental silence the first time you try, is to understand that it is a personal journey. Treat it as if it were a personal experiment: do it for 10 minutes twice a day for three weeks and then at the end of this time assess how you feel. If this routine is having a positive impact on any aspect of your life then continue on the journey.

With practice, mental silence can be sustained even in the midst of intense activity, such as in sport, during creative pursuits such as music and art, or while enjoying the company of friends. Of course, it has traditionally been experienced by those who sit quietly, focus their attention inwards and strive towards that transcendent, silent experience that awaits us beyond the mind.

The founder of Sahaja yoga meditation, Shri Mataji, developed a simple series of affirmations and associated hand positions to help people achieve the experience of mental silence or 'thoughtless awareness', as she called it. In one respect it is difficult to explain how such a simple series of steps can trigger the experience. Yet our work in the various research projects described throughout this book has showed that these relatively simple techniques are highly effective in assisting people to achieve the target experience.

One way of explaining the process is that the affirmations are 'psychotherapeutic statements' that, along with the hand positions, allow the attention to focus in on the present moment and hence attain cessation of thought.

Another explanation - the one preferred by Shri Mataji - is based on the idea that the affirmations and hand positions facilitate harmonisation of the yogic energy centres (*chakras*) and their interconnecting energy channels (*nadis*), thus allowing the awakening of the *Kundalini* energy, which then gives rise to the experience of inner silence.

The affirmations are meant to assist in bringing about the experience of mental silence, so try using them at the beginning of each meditation session and experiment a little. The hand positions, just like the process of closing the eyes, assist in bringing the focus away from the external environment, toward a more internalised and subtle awareness. We have found that it is most effective for the affirmations to be 'said' silently. It is best to say them each a few times; it doesn't matter how many times each one is repeated. You may find that there are one or two that work well in facilitating the experience.

People often ask why they are useful, so here are some basic explanations.

Give me true knowledge

In many ways any culture, including our own, tends to convince us to identify with a number of ideas, philosophies and world views that are not necessarily true or good for our wellbeing. These might be simple concepts, such as the notion that we are only a worthwhile person if we have an impressive job, expensive car and a large house. It's easy to see how this idea about ourselves, if taken too far, can lead us to strive so hard for possessions that our whole lives can go out of balance, only to find that when we get these things they may not give us the happiness and satisfaction we were looking for.

There are more subtle ideas that also influence us in harmful ways: for example, the famous saying of René Descartes, *Cogito ergo sum* – 'I think, therefore I am' – has become misconstrued, changed from being a simple philosophical statement to a way of defining ourselves according to the content of our mental activity. Throughout this book we explore the ways in which this very idea has prevented us from developing a more balanced understanding of ourselves.

Sometimes advertisements and the media communicate to us that if we are not rich, famous and beautiful then we are not valuable to society, thereby damaging our self-esteem. And there are many other false ideas that might prevent us from realising our simple, natural state of being. This can lead us to experience feelings of stress and angst. By learning to silence the mind we can effectively neutralise the effects of such false ideas about ourselves. Conversely, by becoming aware of how these false ideas can negatively influence our mental activity we can improve our ability to experience mental silence.

I am my own master

In the closing moments of the Buddha's life, he uttered one of his most profound teachings: 'Be a light unto yourself.' This simple statement sums up one of the most important dimensions of personal growth – that we each must ultimately come to understand the nature and tendencies of our own personality and, by being aware of our strengths and weaknesses, manage our own behaviour so that we can continue to maintain our balance and grow. In past ages we may have surrendered our self-mastery to religious dogma, the local priest or some other 'higher authority'. In the East, particularly in India, every family would have its own local guru who advised on all aspects of life. That guru told us how to live, what was good or bad, and what we should or shouldn't do. However, as we grow we must become responsible for our own values and behaviour. This is not to say that we should reject good advice or the opinions of others so much as we should take full responsibility for our own perceptions, opinions and actions, and ultimately direct our own lives and personal growth. We must, in effect, become our own gurus, in charge of our own destinies. This requires us to have a higher level of self-awareness and self-responsibility, which is possible when we learn to control the activity and content of our own mind. This is self-mastery, or being our own guru.

I am the spirit

This notion has been dealt with at length in Chapter 6, when we discussed the Cartesian mind trap. The affirmation relates to the idea that we must acknowledge that we are not our physical bodies, not our careers, the clothes we wear or the things we own. Even more importantly, we are not even the problems we have; nor are we the responsibilities that we possess; nor are we the thoughts that go through our mind or the mind itself. We are, in fact, something more real, permanent, indestructible and constant than any of these things. In the East this was called the *atma*; Carl Jung called it the 'self'. We can also call it the spirit or just pure awareness.

I am not guilty

This is a very important affirmation, since many of us feel guilty for things that we have done in the past. In many ways, Western society seems particularly focused on the cultivation of guilt. We harbour feelings of guilt for all manner of mistakes that we have made, as a kind of self-punishment. This guilt can become so oppressive that it makes us feel that we are unworthy to enjoy our own lives. In some circumstances, guilt can become a kind of escape mechanism by which we mentally punish ourselves rather than reflect on and change the behaviours that led to the guilt in the first place. It is far better to face our mistakes, whatever they may be, admit that we have done the wrong thing and resolve to learn from those mistakes and strive not to make them again. This is more conducive to personal growth than punishing ourselves, or escaping from reality, using guilt. Guilt can also become a handle by which others can coerce us into doing things we would not otherwise do. By freeing ourselves of guilt we become less vulnerable to unfair pressure from others.

> *If you have behaved badly, repent, make what amends you can and address yourself to the task of behaving better next time. On no account brood over your wrongdoing. Rolling in the muck is not the best way of getting clean.*
>
> **Aldous Huxley, *Brave New World*[4]**

I forgive

This is an important part of the process. A friend of mine sent me this explanation of how she found the affirmation useful, and frankly she has explained it better than I can:

I was really slow. It took me nearly four decades to finally understand forgiveness.

As a fair-minded kid, I first wrestled with the concept after hearing the prodigal son story. Did forgiving mean condoning baddies, saying their wrongs were okay? There was no justice in that. Later, when combined with 'don't take it personally', it became a logic-defying code. Something done to me, was done to me personally. How else could it be taken?

Fast forward to learning Sahaja yoga meditation. As an adult with a bagful of things to forgive, I embraced and applauded the theory, actively forgiving. But more awaited. I still didn't fully grasp forgiveness; unaware I harboured an undetected remnant speck of indignation at possible injustice, that forgiving lets someone get away with something. Until one day, the stars aligned and two perfectly timed things happened.

I saw an article with a photo of two victims of crime. Years after the event, one was obviously still deeply distressed, her face wracked with anger and anguish, adamant she would never forgive. The other suffered an even more vile crime, yet projected serenity. She told of her great relief in forgiving. Click! I got it. It freed her, not the criminal. By not forgiving, we let wrongdoers get away with perpetually tormenting us.

Then someone I knew sat down, unexpectedly saying something scathing to me. It was immediately transparent. She was an 'equal opportunity' insulter and would've scorched anyone next to her. Click! It was clearly about her, and impossible to take personally. The code was cracked.

Claiming no expertise, here's what worked for me. Wrong things that happened were not okay, and it certainly doesn't mean continuing to accept bad treatment. But holding onto anger or hurt is exhausting, painful and futile, as it only harms us. The offender is happily unaware, not giving a second thought. It isn't about wrongs committed, it's about cutting toxic ties that bind us to them, so they don't own us. The past can't change but we can stop being defined by it. General forgiveness is powerful as we get the benefit without putting attention to specific incidents, avoiding dredging up nasty confrontations between our past and present.

How forgiving helped: letting go of a sack of sadness was a plus. It's quicker to find silence. If my head gets crowded, forgiveness empties it by severing emotional baggage. Forgiveness gets stronger with use, short circuiting murky stuff and defusing my reactivity. Sometimes when saying the affirmations, my head and forehead physically relax inside, like it's breathing a big sigh of relief in there. That's got to be good. I tell friends: don't think of specifics, forgive with no strings attached. Do yourself a favour, just forgive.

I forgive anyone who has done anything to harm me. I forgive myself for all my mistakes.

PART IV
HEALTH, WELLBEING AND THE NON-MIND

8

Stress - the noise in the mind

The twentieth century is, among other things, the Age of Noise. Physical noise, mental noise and noise of desire . . .

Aldous Huxley[1]

The majority of Americans – probably the wealthiest people on the planet – are living with moderate to high levels of stress, according to a 2010 survey conducted by the American Psychological Association.[2] Finances and work were identified as the main causes. This may explain why the 2012 Gallup World Poll has found that happiness levels in the wealthy and highly developed USA are basically no different from those in the much poorer and less-developed Costa Rica, despite income levels in the United States being four times greater.[3] It may come as a surprise that the Japanese and the Singaporeans – both living in economic powerhouses with first-world standards of development, wealth and incomes – are actually less happy than the Costa Ricans.[4]

Stress is not just an unpleasant feeling; rather, the modern scientific evidence tells us that it is a toxic state of mind. Many of the common illnesses of our time – including heart disease, hypertension, obesity, diabetes, depression and cancer – are now widely acknowledged by experts as influenced by, worsened by, or possibly even the consequence of, stress.[5] A landmark twenty-year study conducted by the University of London recently concluded that unmanaged stress was a more dangerous risk factor for cancer and heart disease than smoking or high-cholesterol foods.[6]

The stress epidemic

Given the rising tide of stress in developed countries we need to ask how this situation came about and what we can do about it. Many experts believe part of the cause is the pace of modern life, the fact that many of us are locked into a hamster wheel of pressure and overwork to pay for increasingly expensive and demanding lifestyles. The machinery of commerce and consumerism – previously a successful cure for the stresses of material hardship and poverty in poorly developed countries – has become a health hazard in affluent countries. As a result, despite significant material progress, the overall change in quality of life for highly developed countries is not that much better than lesser developed countries.

What the World Health Organization (WHO) has called the 'epidemic of stress'[7] is in many ways the perfect example of what an out-of-control collective mind – fed and encouraged by consumerism and other side effects of modern aspirational culture – can do to its owner and society. Some commentators have come to call this historically unprecedented combination of collective affluence and dysfunction 'affluenza'.[8]

In Australia, 40% of people who have seen their GP have reported experiencing a period of anxiety or stress lasting two weeks or more in the previous twelve months.[9] In the United States it has been estimated that 50–70% of visits made by patients to their doctors involve stress-related issues.[10] The contribution made by stress to the various social problems that characterise our society – from road rage to the rising rates of depression and suicide, not to mention the elevated risk of physical diseases – makes the tackling of stress a major priority for individuals, as well as organisations and governments.[11]

Signs of stress

Brief periods of stress can cause physical and psychological signs that many of us might be familiar with:

- Tiredness, fatigue, lethargy, headaches, stomach upsets and indigestion, muscle aches and tension, change in appetite, teeth grinding, loss of sex drive, chest discomfort, feeling faint or dizzy, change in menstrual cycle.
- Less common signs are: heart palpitations, racing pulse, rapid breathing, shakiness, tremors, tics, twitches, stomach problems such as heartburn, diarrhoea, constipation, dry mouth and throat, sweating, clammy hands, cold hands/feet, rashes, hives, itching, nail-biting, fidgeting, frequent urination, difficulty sleeping, and an increased tendency to use alcohol, drugs and other medications.

- Common psychological signs include: irritability, anger, hostility, loss of motivation, anxiety, nervousness, negative mood, sadness, feeling upset, wanting to cry, intrusive and/or racing thoughts.
- Less common psychological signs include: frequent absenteeism, presenteeism (see page 123), cognitive impairment such as memory lapses, poor concentration, indecision, feeling overwhelmed, changes in personality, depression.

What is stress?

While experts acknowledge the growing significance of stress, and indeed each of us can usually recognise when we are stressed, few of us can easily come up with a good definition of stress.

Strictly speaking, the concept of stress was first proposed by Hans Selye, the 'father' of stress research, to describe the experience of an individual who is faced with demands and circumstances that challenge their ability to deal with them.[12] However, many researchers feel that this definition is too limited.[13] A more popular definition, at least among psychologists, is based on the idea that stress arises as a result of a mismatch between the way we perceive various events and things in our environment (called stressors) and our perceived ability to deal with them. In other words, it is not actually an event or thing that is responsible for our stress so much as the way that our mind perceives and then reacts to that event or thing. The way that our mind reacts to stressors is the thing that determines how stressed we get. While the consequences of those mental reactions are quite physical, the root cause of the reaction is buried somewhere in our psyche – the mind is the key. So, if the poorly controlled mind is a central player in the stress epidemic, does controlling the mind with mental silence lead to less stress? The next few sections describe the outcomes of a number of interesting scientific studies indicating that it does. More information on the psychology of stress can be found at www.beyondthemind.com.

Can meditation modify the way that our mind reacts?

Simon Golosheykin, a psychophysiologist currently at the University of Bocconi in Italy, wanted to test whether or not meditators actually have less reactive minds – that is, minds that are less likely to react to stress.[14] He set up a study involving twenty-five long-term Sahaja yoga meditators and exposed them to a video clip containing stressful images standardised for use in stress research. Usually when a person views these images their mind reacts to whatever negative connotations they elicit, which in turn triggers stress responses in the brain and body that are detected by electroencephalography (EEG), blood pressure and related physiological measurement devices.

In Golosheykin's study the physiological activity of the brain and body was monitored throughout the process and compared to a group of non-meditators who also watched the video clip under the same conditions.

When the non-meditators viewed the clip they typically responded with pronounced stress reactions which were obvious on EEG as well as on the bodily measures of stress. When the meditators watched the same video clip their stress response in the EEG and the body was markedly lower. Since the study was designed to control for any major differences between the two groups, Golosheykin concluded that the reduced level of reaction in the brain and the body was due to Sahaja yoga meditation and, therefore, mental silence.

So it does appear that meditators, especially long-term meditators, experience fewer mental reactions to stressors than non-meditators. The study seems to show that a lower reaction rate is not a case of suppressing the outwards signs of reaction but actually relates to reduced reactivity at the level of the brain. The implications of these findings are that by reducing negative reactions, the meditator is more able to maintain equilibrium, which in turn facilitates greater resilience to stressful events.

Work stress

Work stress can have an impact on anyone, including people who have no other health conditions. Research evidence consistently shows that for most people their job, career and finances are the primary sources of stress. A United Nations report on work stress labelled it the 'twentieth century disease'[15] and a few years later the World Health Organization (WHO) stated that it had become a worldwide epidemic.[16] Recent research has found that this is more so now, post the global financial crisis, than ever before. Factors such as insecurity, working hours, commuting, the behaviour of bosses, colleagues, workplace politics, time pressure, mergers and lay-offs all contribute to the experience of stress at work.

In Australia, it's estimated that stress-related illness is worth $14.81 billion a year to the national economy, mainly due to absenteeism or, where people show up to work but are not productive, 'presenteeism'. On average, each worker loses about three days per year due to stress. As employers well know, when stress levels climb there is a risk of workplace injury, which currently comprises about 10% of workers' compensation claims in Australia. The cost to employers is $10.11 billion.[17] The United Kingdom's Health and Safety Executive (the official body in the United Kingdom that is responsible for policy related to occupational health and safety) estimates 50% of absenteeism in the United Kingdom to be work-stress related.[18] A recent US survey of more than 46,000 employees indicated that medical care costs were 70% higher for those who reported being depressed and 46% higher for those who reported being stressed.[19]

The American Psychological Association's 2010 survey gives us a fascinating insight into what people are doing to help them manage their stress.[20] The good news is that 8% of people in the United States are using meditation to reduce stress, although it's not clear what kind of meditation they practise or whether or not it involves mental silence. Others alleviate stress in a variety of ways: about 52% listen to music, 47% exercise or walk, 42% spend time with family or friends, about 36% use prayer, 32% take a nap, and 30% spend time on a hobby. Now the disturbing news: about 34% manage their stress by eating, about 18% by drinking alcohol, about 16% by smoking, about 4% gamble, and about 16% don't want to or can't do anything about it. So while many people are doing healthy things to reduce their stress there is a large number of people who are taking options that are detrimental to their health. As a result, stress and its indirect consequences are essentially killing them.

Reducing work stress

Generally speaking there are three ways to tackle stress at work.[21] First, change the things that *can* be changed. The most common-sense approach is to tackle those things in your environment that are causing the stress. Many experts correctly state that stress is best managed by improving the way that organisations work since a lot of stress seems to arise from conflicting demands and pressures. If you are overloaded with tasks try to work out how they can be done more efficiently, or if some of the workload can be taken on by someone else. Less-experienced workers often benefit from learning time-management skills, improving office systems and streamlining communication. Reducing interpersonal conflict can be extremely effective at reducing stress in the workplace.

While it is entirely logical to deal with the causes of stress at the level at which they are generated by improving the way that workplaces are run, the reality is that this can't always be achieved in practice. It requires the commitment of managers, the cooperation of staff and the coordination of resources. It can take time to implement and sometimes the changes also generate stress. So if you can't change the situation that is triggering the stress, or while you are waiting for the situation to change, what is the next option?

Second, accept that there are some things that you will never be able to change. In this case, if you can't change your external environment then you will need to change the way that your mind deals with that environment. Given that the stress we experience arises as a result of the way that our mind interprets external events, we need to assess the pathways that our mind uses to put a negative interpretation on those events. This approach can often be highly effective. However, many of us have come to realise that there are some situations where either our mind refuses to rewire itself or it is simply not possible to put a positive mental perspective on things. In Chapter 10 we will explore the strengths and limitations of re-educating the mind, positive thinking and other related strategies in more detail. Once we reach the limits of what psychologists call 'cognitive reappraisal', changing the way we think about things, what is the next option?

Third, implement techniques and strategies to reduce the impact of the stressful experience as it emerges. This is where stress-management interventions such as relaxation and calming skills have been traditionally positioned. Yet, even conventional relaxation and calming skills have been shown to have limitations. For example, relaxation enables us to calm both the mind and the body during a relaxation session. As a result, we think less stressful thoughts and reduce the physical manifestations of those stressful thoughts, such as muscle tension or elevated blood pressure, and hence we feel physically and mentally better. However, as soon as the mind is not engaged in the relaxation strategy, it quickly becomes active again, and soon after that it becomes overactive and then the symptoms and signs of stress reappear. Without addressing the root cause it is difficult to make the benefits of relaxation sessions last.

This is why our research indicates that in many situations a more useful way of understanding stress at the individual level is along the lines of what the Buddha proposed; that is, that stress is the inevitable product of an overactive and uncontrolled mind. Understanding stress within the context of the 'uncontrolled mind' helps us understand why the effects of strategies such as relaxation are real but at the same time limited in their benefit; because although they show the practitioner how to calm the mind and body and sometimes to re-educate it, they don't show how to completely control it. This is where the mental silence experience becomes relevant. By developing the ability to stop the mind's negative activity altogether, the individual is given a fundamentally powerful solution to the problem. When we are unable to re-educate or rewire the mind, rather than just turn down the volume of the mental noise the mental silence of Sahaja yoga allows us to stop it in its tracks.

Mental silence and work stress

Since much of the adult population spends at least half of its waking hours at work, and most workplaces have large numbers of individuals in single locations, the workplace is an ideal environment to conduct stress-management interventions. Surprisingly, few of these strategies have been rigorously evaluated. We designed a series of initiatives starting with some field studies conducted in real workplaces followed by a rigorously designed randomised controlled trial (RCT).[22] In these initiatives we explored the impacts of Sahaja yoga, or secular methods based on Sahaja yoga, on stress and wellbeing. Where possible we looked particularly at the role of mental silence within those outcomes. The outcomes of some of the key initiatives and studies are described below.

The top-tier law firm

The corporate environment is well known for its demands on workers, particularly in the legal profession. We were approached by a top-tier law firm in Sydney to deliver a national series of meditation sessions in their major corporate offices to determine if meditation was a useful option for them. Keiran McPhail, Paul Keetley, Greg Turek and Robert Hutcheon developed a strategy that could be easily integrated into the daily routine of a high-powered corporate office. The strategy was secular in style. Although it drew upon Sahaja yoga, it did not focus on the usual Indian cultural and spiritual concepts. Instead it focused only on the mental silence experience.

The process involved delivering a one-hour combined lecture (45 minutes) and hands-on meditation workshop (15 minutes) to familiarise participants with the rationale and benefits of meditation, followed by actual instruction in a 'secularised' version of the Sahaja yoga meditation technique suitable for the corporate environment. This alone was enough to give the participants the skills to practice meditation at home or in the workplace, in conjunction with a resource kit (CD, instruction card, etc.) that we gave them. Designed to accommodate a single lunch hour, the event was advertised internally by the human resources department. It attracted more than 250 legal and administrative staff across its three major offices (Sydney, Melbourne and Brisbane). This was a record turnout and an eye-opener for the company, and it was quickly realised how much the staff were looking for help.

Our assessment of participants before the programme started was that their emotional wellbeing levels were relatively low compared to their contemporaries in the United Kingdom and the United States.

At the end of the first session, participants were asked three questions about how the meditation made them feel.

Approximately one-third of participants experienced a significant degree of 'mental silence' (defined as a greater than 50% reduction in their mental activity), 80% of participants experienced a significant improvement in feelings of 'calm and peacefulness', and 62% of participants experienced a significant improvement in 'stress, anxiety and tension'. There was a strong positive correlation between participants' ratings of the 'mental silence experience' and their 'sense of reduced stress' and increased sense of 'calm and peacefulness'. In other words, the meditation was helping them think less, and as their level of unwanted thinking subsided their sense of stress declined and their sense of calm improved dramatically as well. Less thinking was strongly associated with feeling better.

Following this, for those who were interested, a three-week follow-up programme providing 30-minute in-house lunchtime meditation sessions twice per week at each office was organised, facilitated by experienced instructors. One hundred and twenty staff participated, most attending once a week for the full three weeks. At the end of the three-week programme we reassessed their emotional wellbeing and found that it had improved by between 55% and 65%. They were now the same or better than their UK and US counterparts. Qualitative feedback from the participants was extremely positive, with many requesting that the initative be made a regular event.

Medical practitioners

Health professionals, especially GPs, are among the most highly stressed professional groups. Stress and its consequences can lead to a reduced ability to make important, sometimes life-saving, decisions. In fact, health professionals have some of the highest rates of depression, alcohol and substance abuse, and suicide. Yet, in Australia there is very little support made available to help them cope with the pressures of such an intensely responsible profession.

To assist them, some health professional colleagues of mine, Dr Amy Gordon, Kabir Sattarshetty RN and Minakshi Pearce RN, organised a special health professionals' wellbeing programme, which was endorsed by the Royal Australian College of General Practitioners so that participants could earn professional development points essential for their medical registration.[23]

The programme involved an afternoon of lectures on stress, work–life balance and meditation. These were followed by three consecutive 15-minute meditation sessions designed to teach participants basic, intermediate and advanced skills in a kind of 'crash course' for these very time-poor professionals. The technique used was again a modified version of Sahaja yoga. Three hundred and twenty GPs participated. At the end of the day, 40% experienced a greater than 50% reduction of mental activity and 18% experienced a greater than 70% reduction in mental activity; more than 90% of subjects experienced an increase in their sense of 'calm and peacefulness' and a reduction in their sense of 'tension and anxiety'. Again, the improvements correlated strongly with the degree to which participants experienced mental silence.

For those doctors who wanted more than just the crash course, a self-directed two-week home practice programme was developed for which they could get additional professional development points. Approximately 120 GPs did the home practice. Using a standardised instrument designed to assess emotional wellbeing, called the Kessler 10,[24] we were able to develop a reliable profile of this group's mental state. At the beginning of the programme, 54% of the GPs were in the elevated risk category. The Australian population by comparison has only 36% in this category. At the end of the two-week home-based programme however, half of the participants in the elevated risk category had improved sufficiently to shift back into the normal range. Importantly, we asked participants to rate their experience of mental silence and found that the higher their mental silence rating, the better their emotional wellbeing was and the lower their risk for developing anxiety and depression.

Managers

Recognising the potential of meditation to not only reduce stress but to also change perceptions and behaviour, Professor Maurizio Zollo, at Bocconi University, has begun to explore the impact of meditative strategies on the decision-making behaviour of managers.[25] He coordinated one of the largest research projects to date in Europe, focusing on the study and integration of Corporate Social Responsibility in multinational corporations. In his study, the same mental silence approach to meditation was shown to have significant impacts on the psychological factors that influence socially responsible behaviour in managers. During the course of a six-week coaching programme, managers showed significant shifts in their attitudes: more weight was given to considerations about the impacts of their decisions on the wider community, there was a shift in their personal values in favour of nature rather than public image, higher levels of positive emotions and lower levels of negative emotions were reported, as were more frequent experiences of calm, inspiration and determination, and more consensus-oriented decision-making and cooperative conflict resolution. Although further research needs to be done to tease out the specific effects of mental silence, this is a very promising area for further research.

Is meditation uniquely effective in reducing stress?

Professor Umesh Rai's work assessed the impact of meditation on conditions such as epilepsy, asthma and hypertension by measuring changes in the parameters specific to the disease including seizure rates, lung function and blood pressure. He also measured the stress that these patients were experiencing by assessing electrodermal activity, skin temperature and stress hormones in each of his major studies. He observed that as the participants' medical conditions improved so too did their stress indicators. These studies are described in more detail at www.beyondthemind.com.

The field studies at the top-tier law firm, the workshop with medical practitioners and Professor Rai's research in India show that the mental-silence-based meditation techniques are effective at reducing stress and improving mental wellbeing. But we needed more rigorous evidence to tell us if mental silence is specifically effective for work stress.

To do so we designed and implemented the Meditation for Work Stress project.[26] Involving 178 participants, it was the largest RCT of meditation for occupational stress ever done. It was specifically designed to determine how effective Sahaja yoga was at reducing stress and whether or not this approach to meditation was more than just a relaxation response or placebo effect.

The Meditation for Work Stress treatment programme was eight weeks in duration and involved hour-long evening sessions twice weekly, delivered at Sydney Hospital in the Sydney CBD. Participants travelled directly from work to the sessions. They were divided into three groups. Group One was asked to practise mental silence meditation using the Sahaja yoga method twice daily for approximately 10 to 15 minutes each time, with the aid of written and audio materials. Between classes, instructors made themselves available to take queries or give specific advice to participants.

Group Two learnt a meditative strategy that focused on the conventional Western idea of meditation (relaxation and contemplation) rather than mental silence. Group Three comprised a no-treatment waiting list to show us what happened to the group that received no treatment at all across the same period of time.

Classes for both the meditation groups were conducted at the same location, in similar rooms, at the same time of day, and were of equal duration. Both groups had experienced health professionals as principal instructors. Thus, the two interventions were structured identically, with the core experience of mental silence being the only major difference.

At the beginning and end of the eight-week programme, participants in all three groups were assessed using scientifically validated measures of work stress, depressive symptoms and anxiety. At the end of the eight-week period, the mental-silence group demonstrated significantly greater improvements, especially in levels of work-related stress and depressive feelings. Improvements occurred in anxiety levels but not as much as the other two measures. The reduction in work-related stress in the mental-silence group was 27%, compared to 15% in the non mental-silence group and 7% in the untreated group. Depressive symptoms improved by 66% in the mental-silence group, 39% in the non mental-silence group and 10% in the untreated group. Anxiety levels improved by 24% in the mental-silence group and 12% in the non mental-silence group, and worsened by 5% in the untreated group.

The diagram on the following page illustrates the improvement in stress, depression and anxiety scores in the three groups. The untreated group actually worsened across the same period, which is an indication of how quickly untreated stress can grow into a bigger problem.

It has been generally assumed that meditation reduces stress by reducing its physiological impacts. So we decided to include some additional measures that assessed the way the participants perceived their own ability to cope and the availability of resources in their workplace to help them cope with stress, as an indicator of the way that their 'cognitive appraisal' of the stress at work might change over the duration of the study.

At the end of the study, the mental-silence group showed significant changes in this dimension, indicating that mental silence not only mitigates the impact of stress but also improves the way that the meditators think and, thus, their fundamental propensity to be stressed.[27] These changes did not occur in the non mental-silence group. Remarkably, the cognitive reappraisal process occurred despite the fact that the Sahaja yoga training programme focused exclusively on training people to experience mental silence. There was no instructional content aimed at intellectually educating participants about how to change their perceptions and attitudes to stress at work.

Work stress
Mental silence vs contemplation

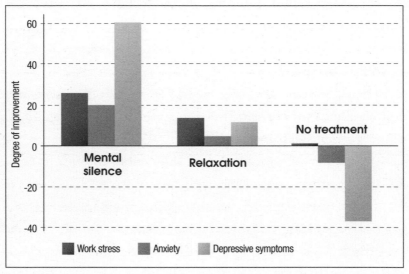

Since the major differentiating feature of Sahaja yoga is mental silence, it is reasonable to conclude that this experience might have somehow modified the way that the participants thought and felt about the various factors in their environment that contributed to stress. At least some of the positive effect of mental silence arises from its ability to directly reduce negative perceptions, thoughts and interpretations.

There may be additional ways in which mental silence works that our research has yet to tease out. It is, however, now clear that Sahaja yoga appears to be more than just a method of relaxation, since it not only calms the mind but also seems to positively change the way it thinks and perceives as well.

A physiological paradox

The traditional way that scientists explain how our mental state can influence our physical health is by pointing to the fact that stress causes changes in the body that increase the likelihood of certain illnesses. Similarly, the traditional way that scientists have tried to explain the benefits of meditation is that it negates the effects of stress and triggers the relaxation response. Yet when our trials have compared Sahaja yoga to relaxation or other forms of stress-management, the mental-silence-oriented technique seems to be more effective than conventional approaches that involve the relaxation response.[28]

Why? Sitting quietly and not thinking is probably much less stressful than having a head full of thoughts, especially negative ones. Could it be that mental silence works by simply triggering a more profound level of relaxation? Or is there more to it than that?

If Sahaja yoga – or, more specifically, mental silence – is basically a form of profound relaxation, then we should be able to see the same physiological effects that occur in the relaxation response also occur during the experience of mental silence. So it was surprising for us to find that some of the physiological effects of mental silence are, in fact, different from those of relaxation in some remarkable ways. To understand this we need to keep in mind that the basic physiological features of the relaxation response are widely understood to involve:

1. Decreased heart rate and blood pressure.
2. Decreased respiratory rate.
3. Increased galvanic skin resistance (also known as electrodermal activity).

4. Diversion of blood flow away from the skeletal muscles towards the organs of digestion and the skin, causing skin temperature increases in the palms of the hands and in the feet.
5. Decreased diameter of the pupils.

Professor Rai's research in India found that something different occurred during a mental-silence experience. In his studies, although the meditator's heart rate and blood pressure decreased as would be expected in the relaxation response, the skin temperature also decreased, which is the opposite to what should occur during relaxation. While there are several studies that describe *increases* in skin temperature in association with meditation (coincidentally, none of these studies used the 'mental silence' definition of meditation) there are no other studies in the scientific literature that describe *decreases* in skin temperature. Rai's studies were the only ones that used the 'mental silence' definition, clearly implying that the reduced temperature effect is probably associated with the key differentiating feature – the mental silence experience.

We wondered if we could replicate these unusual findings in Australia. Using a psychophysiology laboratory in Melbourne's Swinburne University, we took a group of regular meditators who used the Sahaja yoga technique and put them in a temperature-controlled room. We attached delicate temperature-measuring devices to the palm of a hand of each group member as well as a monitor to assess heart rate. We then took a second group of non-meditators and attached the same measurement equipment to them. The non-meditators were asked to relax for 10 minutes and the Sahaja yoga practitioners were asked to go into the state of mental silence for 10 minutes while we monitored their skin temperature and heart rate.[29]

The non-meditators performed exactly in accordance with the principles of the relaxation response – their heart rates reduced and their skin temperature increased. Now, the orthodox understanding of meditation as a form of relaxation predicts that the same thing should happen in the Sahaja yoga practitioners.[30] However, what we found was that heart rates reduced – but skin temperatures, rather than increasing, also reduced. When they were asked to rate their degree of mental silence using a simple scale where ten was 'completely silent inside' and one was 'thinking more than ever', we found that this correlated very closely with the degree of skin temperature reduction.

Although a small study, the results corresponded closely with the findings of Professor Rai and are difficult to explain using our conventional understandings of the physiology of relaxation. One might try to explain the findings by pointing out the possibility that although both the non-meditators and meditators appeared to be sitting quietly, perhaps the meditators were not actually relaxing but, rather, feeling very tense and stressed. As a result, rather than triggering a relaxation response they were actually triggering a fight-or-flight response (see www.beyondthemind.com for an explanation on this) and this would explain why the skin temperature went down instead of up. However, for this to be true the heart rate in the meditation group should also have increased and yet there were no differences in heart rate between the two groups. Alternatively, one might propose that the meditators have trained themselves to reduce their skin temperature in much the same way that some people can train themselves to control their heart rate. Yet when I looked through the scientific literature, I was unable to find even one example of anyone being able to voluntarily reduce their skin temperature. So this is also an unlikely explanation.

In our various research projects, many research participants and Sahaja yoga practitioners reported a subjective sensation of skin-temperature cooling on the hands during meditation, suggesting that the skin-cooling phenomenon was tangible and apparently quite common. The findings of our research provide evidence that these sensations are neither imaginary nor the product of suggestion but, in fact, a reflection of real, although poorly understood, physiological phenomena.

The implications of these preliminary findings are important for several reasons. First, they provide some objective evidence to indicate that mental silence is physiologically different from simple relaxation. Second, since many meditation and related non mental-silence techniques focus on triggering the relaxation response, the findings suggest that mental-silence-oriented meditation is physiologically different from the vast majority of meditation techniques currently available in the New Age marketplace. Third, they provide some potential indications as to why, when we compared mental silence to conventional stress-management or relaxation methods in our research, we observed significantly greater effects in those using mental silence – presumably because they were using a different set of physiological responses that were not triggered during the relaxation response.

The challenge now lies in designing larger, more thorough studies to further understand what the possibly unique physiology of mental silence really involves – we have only scratched the surface.

The mind and body are cooled and soothed, by the touchstone of truth.

Guru Nanak Dev[31]

Who, having abandoned attachment and aversion. Who has become cool, free from conditionings. Above overcoming the entire world. That one I call a brahmana.

Dhammapada[32]

Kundalini ... Cools internally the body ...

Gyaneshwara[33]

Implications

Mental silence appears to act at both the 'cognitive reappraisal' level and the 'stress-management' level. It is more effective at reducing stress and improving mood than simple relaxation because it teaches the practitioner how to switch off the constant mental chatter rather than just slow it down or reduce the volume. It also facilitates positive changes in the way that the mind interprets things, so perceptions and reactions at the level of the brain that normally lead to stress are reduced.

In many ways, the Buddhist aphorism that 'life is suffering' could be more accurately reinterpreted as 'life lived with the stress of an untamed mind is suffering'. However, in the state beyond the mind, stress is naturally eliminated since the root cause of stress, the uncontrolled mind, has finally been tamed. What is perhaps most fascinating is the possibility that when the mind is silenced a unique kind of physiological activity emerges. Could this biological pattern be specific to mental silence? If so, this provides an important clue to help us understand why it is more effective at reducing stress and improving health than simple relaxation.

Mental silence tackles stress at its psychic roots by conquering the mind's stress-producing tendencies, thereby making the meditator more resilient, less reactive and potentially more productive as well. A simple, low-cost, evidence-based technique of meditation may be all that is needed to combat the 'stress epidemic'.

Words from meditators

I began practising Sahaja yoga meditation some seventeen years ago, and felt myself really change from the inside. I was relating to life and to others in a different way.

Before, I came across as a career-minded, rather confrontational sort of person, but now I am much calmer. I am doing a degree that I always wanted to do but never thought I could achieve. I know Sahaja yoga makes a difference to me emotionally and mentally as well as physically. I feel and look younger.

Philippa, USA

I suffered from chronic headaches for about ten years and was continuously on painkillers. The painkillers caused chronic gastritis, so I had to put up with the headache or gastritis. The headaches became worse when I had some personal problems. It was a throbbing pain. I could hardly concentrate on anything when I was in pain. I was practically living with the pain every day. I had trouble sleeping and at times the painkillers didn't help. The doctors could not diagnose the problem even

after a few scans. They concluded that it was related to
stress. I began attending meditation classes. I meditated in the
morning and in the evening. Going into thoughtless awareness
definitely helped to relieve the pain. Within one week, I found
myself becoming a calmer person. After just two weeks of
regular meditation, I stopped taking the painkillers completely.
Since then, I have never experienced headaches to the same
degree. At times, due to work stress and bad weather, I may get
a headache but meditation and a good night's sleep relieves it
immediately.

Manjula, Malaysia

Back in 2000, I was a busy manufacturing manager. The job
involved a lot of stress, anxiety and fear, and at the same time I
had to balance my time with the family. I frequently visited the
doctor for tranquillisers to keep me calm, but one day the doctor
told me: 'You are a Type A (result-oriented) person. You need
to look for an alternative to change your behaviour rather than
relying on these pills.'

Searching for alternatives, I came across meditation and have
been practising it for the last ten years. I've experienced many
positive changes as a result, at physical, mental and emotional
levels. The regular experience of thoughtless awareness brought
a total change in the way I approached my peers, colleagues and
family.

The feedback from my colleagues, including my boss,
is that they see that I have changed: they find me more
calm, approachable and able to control my emotions in any
circumstance. My daughter told me that she used to fear me
as I was very hot tempered, but now she finds me much more
approachable and understanding.

Thoughtless awareness has helped me not to react, but to look into every single challenge as an opportunity to improve myself.

Patmah, Malaysia

I started my career as an engineer at the age of twenty-four. Due to work pressure, I regularly suffered from indigestion, headaches and even vomiting. I tried fasting, diets, yoga, jogging, walking, etc. All this helped me to a small extent but I was still very much affected. Eventually I came upon Sahaja yoga meditation, which I began practising religiously. Slowly my confidence level improved leading me to be more dynamic and confident at work. I also gave up smoking and drinking without much effort. All my indigestion problems and headaches subsided. I also felt less angry and more able to forgive. I am now sixty years of age and have no health problems at all.

Ashok, India

9
Beyond the mind-body connection

There is no better medicine than silence.

Talmud

The connection between the mind and the body has long been recognised. Scientific minds, however, have struggled to define and harness it.[1] Could mental silence, the 'non-mind', be the missing piece of the puzzle? Fascinated by research from India along with our individual experiences of meditation, Peter Kenchington, a mental health nurse, Greg Turek, a dentist, some other meditation instructor colleagues and I established the not-for-profit Mind–Body Meditation Clinic on the top floor of a medical centre in Sydney in the mid-nineties.

There, many people learnt to achieve peace of mind or reduce their stress. What also emerged were some intriguing stories from those who found that what they learnt assisted them in more profound ways. I recall the local butcher who had inflammatory bowel disease finding symptomatic relief with regular meditation; the young man in his twenties diagnosed with depression in his early teens who rediscovered his ability to smile – something he said he hadn't been able to do for many years; a lady whose migraines remitted completely after only a few weeks. All of these people continued with their mainstream treatment but the addition of meditation seemed to make a difference that they had previously been unable to achieve.

The trickle of patients that we hoped would give us an opportunity to explore the potential impact of meditation on their lives soon became a flood. On some evenings more than a hundred people would cram in so there was standing room only. They were eager to learn a skill that might assist in enhancing their health. It was a skill that they wanted, but it had been out of their grasp.

Modern medicine has made tremendous advances in the war against disease and the effects of injury – quite literally, we can't live without it. Yet at the same time its limitations, particularly with regard to chronic disease and mental health, are becoming increasingly obvious to those of us working on the front line of healthcare delivery.[2] As a general practitioner I came across patients every day looking for help to fill the gaps left by mainstream medicines in their disease and symptom control. Many of them would ask me what else they could do to improve their health that didn't involve more drugs.

The cases we saw in this clinic gave us confidence that more serious research into meditation would be worthwhile. After two years of ad-hoc experience in the Mind–Body Meditation Clinic we closed its doors and shifted our attention to full-time, formal research.

Professor Rai

Professor Umesh Rai, the professor of physiology in New Delhi who had conducted the first research into Sahaja yoga, had suffered from serious angina attacks for many years, but found that with regular meditation he experienced an improvement that he had been unable to achieve using mainstream treatment alone. Although impressed by this, Professor Rai recognised that one person's experience was not scientifically reliable, so he decided to design and implement a more thorough investigation under scientific conditions. With the assistance of a number of his postgraduate students, he set up a multifaceted research project to examine the purported effects of Sahaja yoga meditation.

He focused on chronic illnesses that could be improved with conventional medicines but not permanently cured. In a randomised controlled trial (RCT) where Sahaja yoga was used to treat asthma, Professor Rai observed significant improvements in the symptom profile, rate of exacerbations and even lung function of asthma sufferers who were not experiencing sufficient relief with conventional medication alone. When he applied the method to people whose high blood pressure was unresponsive to normal medications, he found that there were impressive improvements in just three months. Among sufferers of epilepsy, the rate and severity of seizures were observed to improve with regular practice over several months.[3]

Before establishing the Mind–Body Meditation Clinic, I had doubts about whether or not we would be able to conduct the sorts of studies that Professor Rai had undertaken with such apparently remarkable success in India. But the results from the clinic demonstrated that the skills and experience easily translated across cultures. It was now clear that we both could and should set up some more systematic studies.

Our research into the mind–body connection led us to study several different conditions, and to observe the impact of mental silence experience on the health of the subjects.

Andrew: Taming the brainstorm

One case that taught us a great deal was that of a young man named Andrew, whose mother brought him to the clinic. Two years earlier, Andrew had contracted encephalitis, a viral infection of the brain tissue, which put him in hospital for several weeks. His condition was so critical at one stage that he spent many weeks in the intensive care unit. Although he survived, the viral attack had left him with chronic epilepsy. Doctors said that this was the result of subtle scarring in his brain that caused it to intermittently 'short-circuit', producing overpowering waves of electrical signals. The ensuing brainstorm caused the uncontrollable muscle contractions that typify epileptic seizures, sometimes several times per day. The condition was permanent.

Medical science has failed to establish a meaningful understanding of a number of diseases, of which epilepsy is one. While we know that the epileptic seizure arises because of massive electrical misfiring of parts of the brain, the reason this misfiring occurs in the first place remains to be answered. As a result, treatment is directed at controlling the misfiring rather than dealing with the fundamental cause. The treatment is usually a drug that reduces the electrical excitability of the brain. Sometimes it may only be partially effective and this is when sufferers look for other ways to solve the problem.

Andrew's seizures were so frequent that he could neither resume his schooling nor keep a job. Dependent on his parents for everything, their lives had also become considerably restricted by their son's illness.

Professor Rai's epilepsy research had shown that patients who practised the meditation technique consistently experienced reductions in the amount and severity of the seizures they suffered. While we could not promise that Andrew would experience similar benefits, the research gave us some confidence that he might find meditation useful. Even if it was simply to help him feel better, rather than make any physical change, we believed that would be a worthwhile outcome.

Andrew learnt quickly and practised diligently. The first changes we noticed were in his face: his eyes lost their usual dullness – they looked clear and bright. When we had first seen this nineteen-year-old boy he looked like an old man: hunched over, his face drawn and dark rings under his eyes. Now he started to look young again and what I could only describe as a dark shadow that had seemed to hang over him had lifted. After a few weeks he would even come to the class with a smile where before there had been only a frown. Andrew's progress was obvious to us and his parents told us that his seizures were reducing in frequency.

One day his mother came to the clinic to invite us to their home for dinner. Andrew, she told me, had not had a major seizure in four weeks, she and her husband were planning to go away for the weekend and, for the first time in years, life was starting to look normal for them. They had re-enrolled Andrew in school and started planning their life after epilepsy. My colleagues and I were surprised by the progress Andrew had made and we were optimistic about his prospects. We had learnt an important lesson about how powerful the impact of meditation can be.

Some weeks later we learnt a second, more sobering lesson. Andrew's mother contacted us, concerned that, although the meditation seemed to be helping, Andrew had lost interest in his daily meditation, preferring to watch TV and play video games. He had had several weeks with no seizures, but she was worried that this would not last if he did not continue with the meditation. We agreed that while we didn't fully understand why he had experienced the improvement, it did seem logical that by stopping the meditation he was likely to lose the benefit.

We explained to Andrew that meditation was probably not a one-shot cure and should instead be considered a long-term lifestyle change. He seemed to listen, yet he still could not summon the motivation to meditate, even though he claimed to enjoy it and understood that he only really needed to do it for about 10 minutes twice a day. We had no option but to wait and watch, and we were disappointed but not surprised when Andrew's seizures returned.

The second important lesson that emerged from our experience with Andrew was that even though regular meditation might be able to bring about remarkable outcomes in some cases, ongoing practice is essential to maintain the benefit. Patients who experience improvements must understand that to maintain those improvements they have to continue to practise diligently, and that meditation is not a 'miracle cure' so much as a regular discipline with positive side effects that include better health and wellbeing.

I had the impression that while part of Andrew wanted to get better – to return to the normal process of growing up into a fully functioning adult and member of society – there seemed to be another side that liked the idea of never having to go back to school, of being a couch potato all day at home and having his mum do everything for him (she was a really great mother, I must say). Attachment to the 'sick role' and the resulting 'learnt dependence' on caregivers is a well-known phenomenon that can prevent people with chronic illness from finding the motivation to improve.

From this experience we also realised that while meditation might have positive impacts on health, not everyone wants to meditate. Meditation may provide an opportunity for better health, but it can't create motivation. Meditation – like any self-help strategy – is unlikely to be of benefit if a person is not genuinely motivated to get better.

Nevertheless, cases such as Andrew's and many of the other patients' offered evidence for the potential impact of this method. The fact that those clinical benefits could be lost as easily as they were gained was an important realisation for us.

Menopause

Hot flushes are a common problem among women in their menopausal years. In fact, most women can expect to experience menopausal symptoms, of which the hot flush is the most common. This is an experience characterised by the flushing of skin on the upper part of the body, sweating, a sensation of heat and associated feelings of being unwell. The hot flush can be worsened or brought on by stress. Many women report that high-pressure situations greatly exacerbate the number and severity of the flushes they experience. Also, women report that their flushes improve somewhat when they are calm and relaxed.

For many decades, probably up until the 1980s, women with menopausal symptoms were misdiagnosed as having everything from infectious diseases to lunacy. Then came hormone therapy (HT). Women using HT not only noticed an improvement in their menopausal symptoms but often improvements in their skin, general mood and libido. For many, HT was an essential treatment to control debilitating symptoms, while for others it was a way of holding on to their sense of youth and femininity.

Uptake of HT throughout the Western world was massive, until the Women's Health Initiative (WHI) study, published in 2001, revealed the treatment's risks.[4] The WHI studied the impact of HT on elderly women and found that the risk of breast cancer increased from a background of about 0.3% up to 0.38% with the addition of long-term use of HT. However, the media chose to report the data in a different way, representing it by asserting that HT led to an increased risk of breast cancer of 26%.[5] It didn't report that the risk related to users of HT in very specific circumstances – the elderly and in the long term – and not to the average menopausal woman in whom the risk is substantially lower. Nevertheless, the perception had been created and millions of women all over the world were flushing their HT pills down the toilet. All of a sudden these women were looking for a non-hormonal treatment.

The Natural Therapies Unit, Royal Hospital for Women – where I worked under Associate Professor John Eden – had a longstanding interest in scientifically evaluating alternative therapies for women's health problems, of which menopausal symptoms were a major focus. Our unit worked in parallel with the Sydney Menopause Centre, which conducted rigorous research into mainstream drugs for menopause. This allowed us to apply pharmaceutical-grade research methods to the field of natural therapies. Our unit had evaluated a wide variety of natural options from soy and wild yam to 'bio-identical' hormones for menopausal symptoms. Sadly, it seemed that none of these strategies could compare to the effects of HT. In fact, under scientific conditions few could be demonstrated to work at all.

So with the tide of women coming through the doors of the Sydney Menopause Centre now looking for non-HT treatment options, especially something that was 'natural' (because, in their perception, 'natural' equated to 'safe'), we thought that meditation was probably the most natural option we could offer. It did not involve the consumption of any substances, relying instead on existing mechanisms within the body, and it was unlikely to generate the kind of side effects that HT was becoming associated with.

Study of menopausal hot flushes

We set up a small trial in which fourteen menopausal women were enrolled in an eight-week programme.[6] The frequency and severity of their hot flushes and other menopausal symptoms were recorded using standard methods before and after the programme was run. The results were impressive, with all women experiencing improvements in their conditions. In fact, nine of the women reported greater than 50% reductions in the frequency of their hot flushes. Six of these women had a 65–70% improvement in their hot flushes, which, after eight weeks of meditation 'treatment', is comparable to that seen in conventional HT, yet presumably the only chemicals these women were using were the ones produced by their own bodies. In addition, standard measures of quality of life and symptom profiles showed similar degrees of improvement.

Eight weeks after the trial ended we reassessed the participants and found that all but one had maintained the benefit. I wondered why that one woman had experienced the complete return of her symptoms.

'That's easy to explain,' she told us. 'I stopped meditating.'

She couldn't explain why she had stopped even though she acknowledged that meditation had seemed to work for her across the weeks that she was practising it. Nevertheless, she was adamant that meditation was not her cup of tea.

Once again, it was clear that regular practice was essential for maintaining the benefits of meditation. It was also clear that not everyone would find the idea of meditation, or mental silence, attractive.

Attracta's story

Attracta worked at the Royal Hospital for Women as a nurse's aide, so she was already familiar with the work of the Natural Therapies Unit. She had seen her mother and two sisters develop breast cancer and, at fifty-four years of age and menopausal, she was faced with a choice of either HT or several years of enduring the bothersome and distracting hot flushes of menopause. Her concerns about her own chances of developing breast cancer were so great that she ultimately decided against HT.[7]

Eventually, Attracta's menopausal symptoms became so severe that she became desperate for some relief. When she heard about our clinical trial she decided to participate. Initially I had the impression that Attracta was sceptical about meditation, or perhaps reluctant to apply herself with full effort to it, but after about three or four weeks she suddenly seemed to 'get the knack' and began not only to experience mental silence, but also to find meditation to be an enjoyable and rewarding experience.

Attracta later told me that her initial scepticism came from the suspicion that the meditation technique might conflict with her Catholic beliefs; however, she came to realise that rather than diminishing her beliefs, the practice seemed to complement them. In concert with her developing ability to still her mind, her menopausal symptoms began to ease and by the end of the eight-week trial her hot flushes had stopped completely. She also felt less stressed about the familial risks of breast cancer.

Some time after the trial Attracta saw me in one of the hospital corridors and said that she was still meditating and still enjoying life without the menopausal symptoms that had driven her to see us in the first place.

—

The results of this small trial with menopausal women added to the growing list of positive experiences that we were seeing. Our confidence that we were on to something of potential significance increased and our enthusiasm to do more rigorous research grew steadily.

An important shortcoming of this trial, however, was the fact that it did not control for the placebo effect. How could we be sure that the improvements we saw were real effects of meditation and not simply the effects of, say, relaxation? Or perhaps the improvements were due to the expectation of a participant that because she was involved in a hospital-based initiative, she would improve? You will recall from Chapter 3 that the only way to differentiate between a real effect and a placebo effect is to use the RCT strategy, and that was clearly the next step in the journey for us.

Asthma

Encouraged by the results that we saw in the menopause study, and aware that we needed to do further work to determine if there was more than just a placebo effect, we knew that an RCT was necessary. Around this time I was approached by a regular meditator who told me that her asthma had been greatly improved by the addition of meditation to her daily routine.

Professor Rai and Dr Deepak Chugh conducted some fascinating studies in India using Sahaja yoga meditation to treat university students with asthma. Their study found that after sixteen weeks of daily practice, the meditators experienced significantly fewer asthma attacks. They also exhibited reductions in stress hormone levels and physiological measures of stress, such as galvanic skin resistance (also known as electrodermal activity), during the course of their treatment.[8] (Electrodermal activity is explained in more detail in relation to stress at www.beyondthemind.com.)

Asthma is a major chronic disease with no permanent cure. Sufferers experience it for years, sometimes for their entire life. Its severity can wax and wane, influenced by a range of factors, including weather, pollens in the air, allergy and stress.

Australia has one of the highest rates of asthma in the world, second only to the United Kingdom. The impact of asthma on sufferers can range from mildly inconvenient to completely debilitating. Any strategy that would reduce the need for medication, reduce symptoms or possibly even provide a cure would be of great importance. Given that mainstream medicine has so far failed to provide a cure, it is only logical that researchers should think 'outside the square' for potential solutions.

Most doctors who treat asthma, and most people with asthma, acknowledge that stress can worsen the symptoms or even trigger an attack. Recognising that asthma may have a psychological dimension, clinicians of various persuasions have developed a range of mind–body strategies for managing it; these include stress-management psychotherapy, acupuncture and breathing exercises such as yoga and Buteyko.

In addition to testing whether or not meditation might help alleviate the symptoms of asthma, we realised that an even more important question needed to be asked: Was there any difference between this meditation technique and other methods of reducing the stress that was thought to contribute to asthma symptoms?

Since we suspected that the uniqueness of the Sahaja yoga meditation technique was the mental silence experience, we needed to find something that was more or less identical to meditation except for that specific feature. After assessing many different options we decided that the course 'Stress Management for Asthma', designed and implemented by the New South Wales Department of Health, was the ideal comparison. The programme taught many things that were also taught in meditation and relaxation programmes – but it did not teach participants how to achieve mental silence. If we compared these two strategies, we could be fairly confident that any differences between the two groups at the end of the treatment programme would be primarily due to the mental silence experience.

Our plan involved selecting a large group of people with severe asthma whose conditions did not properly respond to even maximum levels of medication. These people were randomly divided into two groups. One group received regular instruction in Sahaja yoga meditation while the other group took the standard stress-management programme. The patients were assessed before the trial began and then again after four months of training in either Sahaja yoga or stress management.[9]

The Royal Australian College of General Practitioners funded the project, which ran for eighteen months. The results showed that while both groups improved similarly in a number of measures, there were also clear differences in some of the key outcomes. First, the psychological improvement in the meditation group was 26%, compared to that of the stress-management group, in which there was only a 13% improvement. Second, certain aspects of quality of life also improved more in the meditation group compared to the stress-management group. Third, and most importantly, the meditation group appeared to experience improvements in the way they felt, and they also showed improvements in the severity of the disease process itself.

This was determined by measuring a phenomenon called airway hyperresponsiveness (AHR). AHR is a relatively direct assessment of the level of irritability of the airways of the lungs. In non-asthma sufferers the airways are not very irritable, but in asthma sufferers they are extraordinarily so. This is why inhaling things such as dust particles, smoke or pollens can trigger symptoms in people with the disease but not those who don't have it. The AHR did not improve at all in the stress-management group whereas it improved substantially in the meditation group (see graph below).

Asthma
Meditation vs stress-management

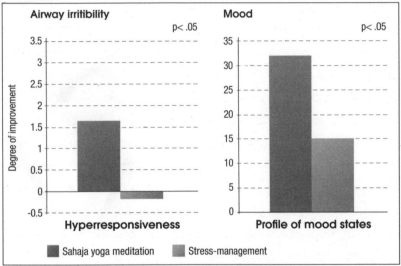

The fact that these results emerged from a rigorously designed RCT in which the strategies used to test and analyse the data were very conservative meant that we could reasonably conclude that Sahaja yoga, and hence mental silence, appeared to have its own specific effect beyond that of standard stress-management. Logically, if meditation was more effective than stress-management it must also be more effective than placebo. It suggested that the results described in our other, smaller studies were also probably real effects.

David's story

David, aged 42, had suffered from asthma since infancy, which had greatly frustrated both his career and sporting ambitions. When we assessed him prior to his entry to the trial, his asthma was in the severest of categories; simply blowing into the spirometer, a machine used to test lung capacity, caused his asthma to worsen.

After sixteen weeks of meditation (which he took to like a duck to water), David returned for reassessment. At the lung function laboratory we saw a changed man. David's lung function had increased, his symptoms had reduced massively and the standard tests that had initially placed him in the severest of asthma categories now indicated that his asthma was in one of the mildest. David told us that his asthma had improved so much that he was sleeping through the night rather than being woken with symptoms, that he was playing sport, and that he had saved more than $1500 in medication expenses since he started the programme. It's important to point out that there were other participants in the study who did not improve to the same degree, although we did observe a handful of remarkable stories like David's in this study.

—

While it was impossible to predict who or by how much an individual would benefit from learning about meditation, we did see time and time again that the highly motivated person was much more likely to reap the benefits. Having said that, it's important not to interpret that statement in reverse, that is, to say that those who do not improve despite meditating have some sort of personal failing. However, I do feel that it is important to explain how the benefits of meditation on health appear to be influenced by the individual's motivation and self-discipline. There are some people who simply don't want to stop thinking. How, then, do we motivate them to pursue the elimination of thinking activity so that they can reap the benefits? I don't yet have the answer to this quandary.

We found the best way to prevent patients from developing excessive expectations – which in themselves would often make it harder to get into the meditation experience – was to explain that meditation is designed to give the experience of mental silence and that any health benefits should be seen as a bonus rather than a guaranteed result.

The long-term effects of meditation on health

Clinical trials reveal the relatively short-term effects of meditation. These trials are important because they can tell us about specific effects by controlling for the influence of placebo, as discussed in Chapter 3.

However, in many ways, using meditation as a treatment when it was actually designed as a preventative strategy is like shutting the gate after the horse has bolted. What potential benefits might meditation have for people who are not sick and wish to remain healthy? Rather than assessing the impact of meditation on people with specific illnesses, what would we find if we assessed the general health of those who regularly practise meditation? After all, meditation was originally developed as a long-term practice, a permanent lifestyle measure, rather than as a treatment for a specific illness.

To answer this we need to turn back to the long-term meditators survey, mentioned in previous sections of this book. To summarise, we conducted the world's first health and quality-of-life survey of long-term meditators. My researchers and I travelled to every major city in Australia and visited meditation centres, retreats and meetings. To ensure consistency of results it was important that we focused on only one form of meditation. Our clinical trials had focused on Sahaja yoga and its central feature of mental silence, so it was logical to centre the question of long-term effects on this technique. We managed to interview and collect information from more than 350 Sahaja yoga meditators, who were diligently practising the technique in Australia.[10]

To assess their health and wellbeing we used the same assessment tools that the Australian Government used in its National Health Survey.[11] These survey tools had been carefully developed over many years of rigorous testing to be able to give a numerical score to each facet of mental and physical health. The fact that they had been selected by the Australian Government gave us added confidence that we were using a validated and respected method of assessment. Most importantly, by using the same survey tools we were able to accurately compare the health profile of our meditating population with the general Australian population in which they were immersed. We also asked the meditators about their lifestyle. This included standard questions about alcohol, tobacco and drug consumption, and also questions about how often they meditated, whether they meditated alone or in a group, and how often they socialised with other meditators. Most importantly, we asked them how often they experienced mental silence. This allowed us to examine the relationship between these important factors and their health scores.

Analysing the data, we found that the health and wellbeing profile of the long-term meditators was significantly higher in the majority of categories when compared to the general Australian population (see graph below).

Health of Australian meditators

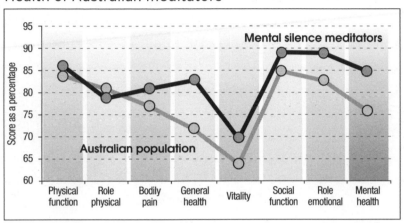

While we had expected that there would be some differences between the meditators and the general population, we hadn't expected the findings to be so pronounced. In six out of the eight standardised categories of health (these categories looked at things such as physical function, bodily pain, the ability to perform basic day-to-day tasks, etc.), the meditators were significantly better off than the general Australian population, and in the remaining two categories they were about the same.

To allay our own doubts we repeated large components of the survey three times, only to see the same pattern emerge. The area of greatest difference was in mental health, where the meditators were more than 10% better off than the general population.

Our analysis showed that there was a robust relationship between the frequency of mental silence experience and health scores, especially mental health. In other words, the more often the meditators experienced mental silence, the higher their levels of health. In the case of mental health, the survey found that even those meditators who experienced mental silence for just a few minutes once or twice a week experienced better mental health than the general population (see graph below).

Relationship between mental silence and mental health

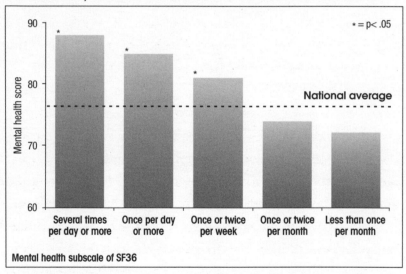

Mental health subscale of SF36

To our surprise, while there was a strong relationship between the frequency of attaining *mental silence* and health scores, the relationship between frequency of *formal meditation* (how often they sat down to meditate) and health scores was minimal. How could we reconcile this seemingly contradictory finding? The question about formal meditation related to how often the meditators physically 'sat down to meditate' rather than how often they experienced mental silence. By comparing formal meditation to 'How often do you experience mental silence?' we were able to differentiate between the benefit associated with the *physical act of meditation* (that is, sitting still and appearing to meditate) and the *actual experience of meditation* (that is, mental silence). It seemed to be telling us that it was the experience of mental silence that was associated with a benefit rather than the mechanical actions of mental silence. This, then, was a case of quality over quantity, mental stillness rather than physical stillness.

A logical question in response to these findings was whether or not other definitions of meditation – or spiritual practices such as prayer – might be associated with similar outcomes. By coincidence, a group of researchers in the United States assessed the health of several thousand Presbyterian ministers, using the same instruments that we used, and compared them to the general population. They found that this population of practising Christians also had better health than the general population, although it was less pronounced than the differences we observed in the meditators.[12] We were fascinated by the fact that the researchers also examined the relationship between frequency of prayer and health advantage. They found that there was a similar, but weaker, relationship between how often the ministers prayed and various aspects of their health. What surprised us, however, was that compared to the relationship between prayer and health in the US study, the relationship between mental silence and health in our study was three times stronger, suggesting that mental silence was associated with a greater health advantage than prayer.

The implications of this survey were significant for several reasons. First, it told us that, for whatever reason, regular practitioners of Sahaja yoga had better health than the general population. Second, this health advantage extended from mental health to physical health, although it was certainly more pronounced in the mental health dimension. Third, the advantage appeared to be connected to the experience of mental silence. This provided powerful evidence in support of the idea that it was the experience of mental silence rather than the outward appearance of meditation that was associated with the benefits.

In India, Dr Anuradha Palta conducted a similar study of Sahaja yoga practitioners and found that long-term practitioners experienced a higher quality of life compared to novices.[13] A group of researchers took this idea one step further under the guidance of Dr Sheng-Chia Chung from the Department of Epidemiology and Public Health, University College, London.[14] With the assistance of Dr Sandeep Rai and Dr Madhur Rai, they brought together a group of meditators who had a variety of pre-exisiting health conditions. Instead of meditating at home, however, they stayed in a residential facility that provided organised meditation-related activities several times a day, in a calm and pleasant environment supervised by experienced practitioners and medical staff – a 'yoga hospital', more or less.

Given that the participants had such a heterogeneous collection of problems, ranging in severity from very mild to severe, the investigators assessed the one thing that is common to all patients: quality of life and anxiety. They observed two groups of participants: the first group was comprised of those who enrolled in the meditation centre and its meditation-based programme, along with whatever mainstream medical treatments that they required, and the other group received only mainstream treatment at a nearby tertiary hospital. Patients stayed in the yoga-retreat facility for between one and two weeks and so patients in the tertiary hospital were assessed over a similar time period. Although the two groups were comparable in demographic and clinical characteristics, the meditation group demonstrated a significant improvement in quality of life, a decrease in anxiety and some other favourable measures, whereas the quality of life of the 'standard care' group deteriorated and anxiety levels increased. This finding provides further support for the idea that regular meditation can be a very useful way of improving the quality of life of people with ongoing health problems.

Non-thought and wellbeing

The discovery that mental silence might have a specific and unique effect on the body and the psyche represents a significant shift in our understanding of the connection between the body and mind. It provides a new and unique perspective that can help us improve our understanding of 'cutting-edge' ideas. Let's look at two examples: positive thinking and mind–body medicine.

Positive thinking

As the field of positive psychology has become more popular, a plethora of books, articles and people have popped up promoting the benefits of 'positive thinking'. Certainly, there is scientific evidence indicating that negative thoughts and feelings can have a negative impact on health and wellbeing.

However, the evidence for the beneficial impact of positive thoughts is considerably less. While positive thinking certainly plays a role in improving certain aspects of health and wellbeing, many health professionals have become concerned that the hype about positive thinking is now extending well beyond its real capabilities.[15] This is to the point now that rather than being of assistance, positive thinking is placing additional pressure on people who have been convinced that their ill health is due to negative thoughts, or the lack of positive thoughts. Some patients strive to edit their thoughts in fear of seeing their health worsen. Others report that the positive-thinking fad makes them feel guilty because they have failed to achieve something that the experts are telling them is their responsibility to achieve.

An advantage of emphasising non-thought over positive thought then, is that many people will find it easier to achieve than positive thought. Non-thought can be taught using specific practical exercises such as those in this book. It does not require people to struggle against their negative thoughts, or force themselves to try to have positive ones. Most importantly, our research indicates that non-thought, rather than positive thought, does in fact have a specific effect on health and wellbeing.

Mind-body medicine

The mind–body connection is something that fascinates scientists, clinicians and laypeople alike. We often hear about researchers trying to unlock the 'healing power of the mind' but finding that while there is clearly a potent connection, the ways to harness that power have proven elusive. Despite this, there are hundreds, if not thousands, of techniques and products claiming to use this connection for better health and wellbeing. Scientific evaluation of these often costly methods usually yields disappointing results, suggesting that most of them work primarily by generating a placebo effect or, at the most, a relaxation response (see Chapter 3 for an explanation of this). Yet we have seen here (and in other chapters) that the evidence for the effect of mental silence on health appears to be real and substantially greater than both placebo and relaxation.

Our research tells us that it is the healing power of the 'non-mind' that may well be a more accurate description of the mechanism. When we eliminate the interference of the thinking mind, the remarkable and significant benefits of meditation emerge. Could mental silence, the state beyond the mind, be the crucial ingredient that facilitates the experience of better health and wellbeing? In our attempts to unravel the mystery of the mind–body connection, it may be that the non-mind is the missing piece of the puzzle that researchers have been looking for.

There is a perceptible drop in blood-pressure when I observe silence. Medical friends have therefore advised me to take as much silence as I can . . . My experience tells me that silence soothes the nerves in a manner no drugs can.

Mahatma Gandhi

The secret of health for both mind and body is not to mourn for the past, worry about the future, or anticipate troubles but to live in the present moment wisely and earnestly.

Buddha

Words from meditators

I had a loud ringing in my right ear called tinnitus, which I had suffered from for some months. During the meditation classes I felt a very distinctive stream of cool air, like a cool breeze, going into my right ear. It was a comfortable sensation. I found that the tinnitus cleared up completely, with perhaps a once-yearly return of the ringing that goes away quite quickly.

Tamara, Ireland

My eldest son was diagnosed as a severe asthmatic at the age of four. He needed to use a nebuliser three times a day, every day, and more often if he was having an attack. After four years of meditating (because he wanted to) he was able to reduce the amount and frequency of medication because his asthma became much less severe. As a young adult he very rarely uses any type of medication. He's found that all he has to do when he starts wheezing is become thoughtless and his body calms down and he can breathe freely again.

Helen, Australia

ENHANCING YOUR EXPERIENCE

Meditating at home daily and, if you wish, attending a weekly Sahaja yoga class for collective meditation will help to strengthen your experience. If you can't make it or prefer not to attend face-to-face classes then www.beyondthemind.com has a wide range of resources that you can use to establish and improve your experience at home in your own time, at a pace that suits you.

Experiment with the different methods given in the following pages and on the website. By trial and error you will find that some give you a more profound experience of mental silence than others, depending on your personal circumstances and whatever may be happening in your life at the time. So be mentally flexible and treat the process as an experiment.

Generally aim to gently direct your attention to the space above your head while you are meditating.

As you experiment with the exercises in this book, you can follow the instructions on the pages, saying the affirmations silently to yourself. However, following a guided meditation by reading from a book can be a challenge for the attention. Instead, you can ask a friend to read them out to you or, if you prefer, use one of the guided meditations provided on www.beyondthemind.com. There are audio and video options on this site that you can play on your computer with or without headphones, or on your phone or portable media device.

The following practices can be used once you are familiar with the basic meditation technique (page 104).

Short affirmation sequence

This meditation uses just the key affirmations. You might use it when you don't have much time, in your lunchbreak for example, or as an adjunct to your regular meditation routine. You just need somewhere relatively quiet for about 5 minutes. Even sitting at your desk when everyone else has gone to lunch can be a good environment.

With your left hand in your lap, palm up, place your right hand ...	Affirmations: repeat silently a few times
on the heart	'I am the spirit' or 'I am pure awareness'
flat on the forehead, gently grasping the temples, leaning your head forward a little into your hand	'I forgive. I forgive everyone and I forgive myself'
on the top of the head, at the halfway point between the hairline and the crown	'Please strengthen my experience of inner silence / self-realisation'
Slowly raise your right hand above your head, allow your attention to follow your hand up into the space just above the head. Then return your hand to your lap so that both your hands are resting on your lap with palms facing upwards, but maintain your attention at, or just above, the top of your head	Sit quietly and enjoy the peace. Use the thought-stopping sequence (on page 106) if you need to. 'I forgive these thoughts'

Tying up your attention and protecting your experience

These are two simple actions that many meditators use to maintain their meditative state beyond the 'formal' meditation session. As our attention becomes more engaged with external tasks and issues, we can become less connected with the meditative experience of mental silence, and the positive feeling that arises in meditation can lessen throughout the day. Ideally, these two strategies should be used together just before meditation as a way of settling the attention and just after as a way of preserving the experience for as long as possible. They may seem a bit simplistic, but they can be quite effective. As usual, I suggest that you take an experimental approach, try it for several meditation sessions and see how it influences your experience of meditation.

Tying up your attention

1. It's preferable (but not essential) to close your eyes.
2. Keep the head, neck and back in a comfortable, straight alignment. Breathe slowly, bring the attention away from external distractions.
3. Rest your hands in your lap with your palms facing up.
4. Put your attention in your hands. It's very important that we always know where our attention is. By the end of this process it should be at the top of your head.
5. Raise the left hand a little so that the palm is facing your belly button or lower stomach area, with the fingers a little outstretched. Move the right hand just in front of the left, also with the fingers outstretched and the palm facing toward your stomach. Now rotate your right hand around your left as if you were winding up some string. While 'winding the

string' move both hands up along the central axis of your body toward the top of the head.

6. When your hands reach the top of the head, tie an imaginary knot at the point just above your head to keep your attention there. Repeat the whole movement twice more to establish your attention. On the last repetition, tie the knot a few times to really establish your attention at the point where the knot is.

7. Now sit quietly with your attention above your head, where the knot was tied.

8. During the day, if you find that your attention becomes distracted or frazzled, take a couple of minutes to sit quietly and then retie your attention slowly. Sit for a few moments with your attention focused in the space above the head where you tied the knot, and then carry on with your various activities while trying to maintain your attention on the inner silence or at the top of the head.

Protecting your experience

1. Put your hands on your knees or lap, with your palms facing up, fingers a little outstretched.

2. Move the right hand toward the left side of the body, near the left hip, and then move your right hand in an arc over your upper body and head towards the right hip and back again, also in an arc. Repeat this movement approximately seven times.

3. Sit quietly and see how this influences the amount of inner silence that you experience.

4. During the day, if you find that the positive feeling associated with meditation is fading, if it's practical, stop for a minute or two, close your eyes and slowly 're-apply' the protection. Sit silently for a minute and then carry on with your various activities while trying to maintain your attention on the inner silence.

Conscious breathing

There was an ancient yogic observation that the thought-stream is influenced by our pattern of breathing. Yogis noticed, for example, that at the peak and trough of each cycle of breath the thoughts actually slowed down. So, to cultivate the experience of mental silence, they developed different breathing methods to utilise this natural slowing down. This is one of the simplest breathing methods and it is highly effective.

1. Find a relatively quiet place to meditate.

2. Sit in a comfortable position with hands in the lap, palms up. Your back should be straight so that the head, neck and back form a natural vertical alignment, but do this in a relaxed way.

3. Close your eyes. Bring your attention away from any external distractions, such as noise or minor discomforts, by paying

attention to establishing a gentle, natural rhythm of regular breathing in and out through the nose.

4. Now pay attention to the breath moving gently in and out of the nose and chest. Observe its gentle rhythm until it reaches its own natural rate.

5. Now breathe in gently.

6. At the peak of the in-breath, pause for a second or two.

7. Breathe out gently.

8. At the bottom of the out-breath, pause for a second or two.

9. Repeat this in a gentle rhythm, ensuring that it feels natural. Don't do it in such a way that makes you feel strained or short of breath.

10. Continue gently for a few minutes: breathe in, pause; breathe out, pause; breathe in, pause; breathe out, pause.

11. You should start to notice that the thoughts progressively slow down and, after a little while, at the peak of the in-breath and the trough of the out-breath they slow down to the point where a discernible space appears between the thoughts. Direct your attention to that space between the thoughts. Allow that space to gently widen.

12. As you become more silent inside, shift your attention to the space just above the top of your head. Or try the thought-stopping sequence (page 106) to further widen the space between the thoughts.

Mindful breathing

This is a simple strategy that enables you to bring your attention inside and focus it on progressively more subtle dimensions of your awareness, and then ultimately on the experience of mental silence in meditation. This is an exercise in observing progressively more subtle aspects of your awareness, resulting in attaining the silence.

1. Find a relatively quiet place to sit.
2. Sit in a comfortable position with your hands in the lap, palms up. Your back should be straight so that the head, neck and back form a natural vertical alignment, but do this in a relaxed way.
3. Close your eyes. Bring your attention away from any external distractions, such as noise or minor discomforts, by paying attention to establishing a gentle, natural rhythm of regular breathing in and out through the nose.
4. First, observe the breath. Pay attention to the breath moving gently in and out of the nose and to its gentle rhythm.
5. Now pay attention to the breath moving in and out of your chest. Observe the breath as it moves into the chest and then out of the chest without mental effort.
6. Second, observe your feelings. Shift your attention from the breath to how you feel within yourself. Don't think about how or what you are feeling, just pay attention to whatever feelings are there without analysing them.
7. Third, observe the slowing of the thoughts. Shift your attention to the space just above the top of the head and observe your thinking activity as it begins to slow and subside. Place the palm of your right hand on the top of the head to help focus your attention, if necessary.
8. Observe the expanding silence between the thoughts.

Bringing back your focus (takes 1 minute)

Sometimes in situations where it is difficult to meditate formally, it is still useful to be able to focus your attention and to put yourself in a meditative mood, even for a brief period. You can do this by taking one minute to refocus your attention at the top of the head and bring your attention to the present moment.

1.   Put your hand at the top of the head (between the crown and hairline).
2.   Press your hand lightly at the top of the head.
3.   Allow your attention to flow up to where the hand is pressing.
4.   Raise the right hand above the head about 10 or 15 centimetres.
5.   Allow the attention to go up above the head and into the silent space that is always there.
6.   Sit silently for a minute.

Attention-based strategies

1.   Once you become familiar with the experience of inner silence, you will find that one way to get into mental silence quite quickly is to use the 'thought experiment' described on page 96. By focusing your attention on the absolute present moment you will find that the thinking activity starts to fall away. Whenever a thought emerges while meditating, bring your attention back to the present moment, away from the thoughts.
2.   Alternatively, you can focus your attention at the top of your head, or on the sensation in the space just above the top of your head. To help, place your hand above your head, facing the palm down. Pay attention just to the physical sensation of the palm of your hand. Once your attention is settled at that point, move your hand back down to the lap but keep your attention at the point above the head where the palm of your hand was held previously. By paying attention to the physical

sensation, your attention is naturally brought into the present-moment experience.

3. Another way to assist your attention to come into the present is to observe your own thought-stream without getting involved in the thoughts themselves. Slowly, the thoughts will slow down and then you should shift your attention to the space between the thoughts. This can be enhanced by using the conscious breathing technique described earlier.

4. A useful way of watching your attention, and therefore preventing it from wandering off, is to simply ask yourself intermittently, 'Where is my attention right now?'

Other centring strategies

As well as the meditations, you might use the following quick techniques at your desk in your lunch or coffee break. These strategies are designed to assist in bringing your attention back to the present moment, the centre between past and future, and from there into the state of inner silence.

1. Look at the sky, the earth or nature. Nature is constantly in the present moment.

2. Close your eyes, bringing the attention inside. By briefly taking your attention away from things that might be disturbing your equilibrium you can re-establish your balance and then re-engage with the tasks.

3. Put your hand and your attention on your heart, or pay attention to your breathing for a minute or two. This again brings the attention back into the present moment.

4. Focus on the absolute present moment, using the 'thought experiment' described on page 96.

Footsoaking and Earthing

The following practices can enhance your experience of meditation and may improve your physical wellbeing. They are of particular benefit if you are feeling tired, stressed or run-down.

Footsoaking

This technique enhances the mental silence experience, relieves the body of stress, and allows for a peaceful and relaxed night's rest.

Sometimes the simple things in life can be the best. In many traditional societies the practice of footsoaking is common. After a long day, or when particularly exhausted, people put their feet in a basin of water with some salt (dissolved) to help deal with stress and tiredness. Many midwives recommend this to women in the late stages of their pregnancy when the mother-to-be seems most prone to becoming hot and bothered. This is probably why so many people find soaking their feet at the seaside, or just swimming in the sea, so relaxing and rejuvenating. The footsoaking strategy is like harnessing that soothing effect of the sea in your own home.

Our experience in the research programmes was that footsoaking was a highly effective adjunctive strategy to enhance the meditative experience, especially mental silence. We recommend it to everyone who wants to enhance their experience. This is helpful at any time of the day, but can be especially beneficial after a busy day's work, especially just before bedtime.

You can buy a plastic bucket or basin for a few dollars, and it is a great investment for your meditation practice. Use the bucket or basin only for footsoaking, not for any other purpose.

Experiment with the water temperature. If you've been very busy or it's a hot day, you might prefer to use cool water straight from the cold tap. I know some participants who found that putting a few handfuls of ice cubes into the water was an even more powerful way of harnessing the de-stressing effects of the footsoaking strategy. If you prefer, use lukewarm water, especially if you are in a cold climate where the water is likely to be chilly (or if your feet are scared of cold water). Sometimes having a full bath with some salt added followed by a short shower might be just the right thing, too. Remember that combining this with the basic meditation techniques explained earlier is essential for you to experience the maximum benefit of this strategy.

Follow this procedure for effective footsoaking:

1. Put a handful of salt into your basin or bucket of cool or lukewarm water (the water should reach your ankles).
2. Sit comfortably in a chair with your hands on your lap.
3. Place your feet in the basin or bucket.
4. Meditate for 10 to 15 minutes using any of the strategies described in this book or at www.beyondthemind.com.
5. You can say some affirmations if you wish.
6. When finished, rinse feet with fresh water, then dry them.
7. Flush the water down the toilet and rinse the bucket. Use the bucket only for footsoaking.

If you are outdoors enjoying nature, it can be very beneficial to take the opportunity to footsoak in a river, lake or the sea. Similarly, try pouring water over your bare feet while standing on the earth, or putting your bare feet on dew-covered grass. See what works best for you; gauge the effectiveness of this and all strategies by how much they impact on your experience of mental silence and general sense of wellbeing.

Earthing

For the same reason that we enjoy spending time in nature or at the park or just sitting in the backyard, we can also use the natural environment to enhance our inner silence.

A simple way to do this is to meditate while sitting outside, preferably on some green grass or natural ground. Use the affirmations given earlier; you may want to listen to them on a media player. Pay particular attention to the effect that physical contact with the earth has on your sense of balance and inner silence.

To further enhance the experience, wear clothes made of natural fabric rather than synthetics. When sitting on the earth, try to orientate your pelvis so that the perineum (the area between the anus and genitals) is relatively flat against the ground. This is actually a Hatha yoga position.

Sit comfortably for some time and observe the impact on the quality of your mental silence.

Some ways to assess your progress

You can use a visual scale as a simple self-assessment tool to help gauge your mental activity levels at any time and your general progress as you practise meditation.

Draw a horizontal line about 10 centimetres long on a piece of paper or, even better, in a word processing programme so you can reprint it.

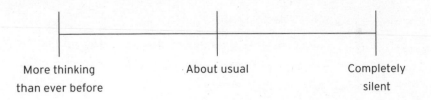

| More thinking than ever before | About usual | Completely silent |

The left end of the line represents 'the most thinking activity I have ever experienced' while the right end of the line represents 'complete mental silence, i.e. no thinking activity at all'. At the midpoint of the line, place a mark that represents your 'usual level of mental activity'.

Now place a mark somewhere on that horizontal line to rate the amount of mental activity you have *right now*. Try this at different times of the day, especially immediately after a meditation session, and then compare it with other times of the day that don't involve meditation. As you continue to practise meditating over the coming weeks, see if there is a pattern of mental peace emerging.

You can also use the thought-waves diagrams described on page 62 or download a simple questionnaire that we developed from www.beyondthemind.com. Complete the questionnaire after each meditation session and compare it to previous sessions to help you understand which methods, strategies and circumstances seemed to give you the best experience of mental silence.

The website, www.beyondthemind.com, has further information, practical help, online courses and advice about places where Sahaja yoga classes are held should you feel like receiving some face-to-face instruction. All of these resources are effective and free of charge.

PART V
HELPING OUR YOUNG PEOPLE

10
Young minds

Learn silence. With the quiet serenity
of a meditative mind, listen, absorb,
transcribe, and transform.

Pythagoras

Despite being surrounded by unprecedented wealth and opportunity, the levels of unhappiness, anxiety, depression and other mental illnesses among young people appear to be greater than ever. A study of nineteen- to twenty-five-year-olds in the United States by Mark Olfson typifies what seems to be happening throughout the Western world.[1] Olfson found that almost half of the participants had at least one psychiatric disorder, albeit some of them fairly mild. Despite this, less than 25% of young adults in the study ended up receiving treatment. Current health figures indicate that in Australia 75% of all mental illness begins before the age of twenty-five.[2] Findings in other countries such as the United Kingdom and Sweden reflect the same pattern. It is compelling evidence that the mental wellbeing of young people has been slowly but steadily declining over the past several decades, moving towards a tipping point that has now pushed the youth mental health crisis to the forefront of national attention. For more information, facts and figures about youth mental health, see www.beyondthemind.com.

Medical science is struggling to understand what causes mental illness and how to treat it, let alone explain why it is an increasing problem among the young. Despite the wealth and development of our society – and the access to better healthcare that goes with that – the situation is getting worse.

Probably the most telling piece of research is that by Professor Jean Twenge at San Diego State University in the United States.[3] Her team has found that up to five times as many US students are facing mental health problems than those who lived during the Great Depression. Twenge and her colleagues analysed data from more than 77,000 students from 1938 to 2007 using the same psychological assessment tool, the Minnesota Multiphasic Personality Inventory (MMPI), to ensure consistency across several decades of observation. They found that five times as many students in 2007 had problem levels in one or more of the mental health categories compared to 1938. In fact, depression, anxiety and 'narcissistic tendencies' were six times greater. This goes some way to explaining why we are seeing so many more young people coming to our clinics, counselling sessions and hospitals seeking assistance for mental health issues or the immediate consequences of them.

Taming the wild things

For some reason our young people are having ever-greater difficulty controlling their mental and emotional content, their inner world. The situation reminds me of the iconic book by Maurice Sendak, *Where the Wild Things Are*.[4] This book was published in 1963 and has since sold 19 million copies, and been turned into two animations, an opera and a feature-length film – such is the strength with which it has resonated in the collective psyche.

It's a story in which a young boy called Max struggles with a bad mood after a day of unruly behaviour and, confined to his room without supper, imagines himself on a journey to an island where he encounters a menagerie of giant monsters. At first they frighten him, but then he tames them with the strength of his glare. Recognising his power over them they make him their king. In their camaraderie they wander the island behaving like self-respecting monsters should. The story climaxes when Max organises yet another session of wild behaviour – the infamous 'wild rumpus'.

The monsters dance and cavort in a wild, escalating frenzy around a fire. There is a vague threat of violence – perhaps even cannibalism – in the air as the monsters plumb the depths of their nature in the wild dance. Max watches them keenly and then, unexpectedly, sends them off to bed. And those big, hairy, scary monsters obediently do as they are told. In the silence while the monsters sleep, Max realises that he actually yearns for a higher feeling – love – and decides to return home. The monsters try to make him stay but Max knows that, having mastered these beasts, his destiny is with his family and loved ones.

In many ways this story illustrates the journey that every young person must go through. In order to mature they must recognise, control and master their thoughts and emotions. The untamed thoughts and feelings – indeed, the untamed mind –

is the wild gang of monsters in each of us that will happily consume us if allowed to go unchecked. For some reason, the 'wild things' in the collective minds of our young people are working themselves into an unprecedented frenzy and the ability to control them, to send them to bed, has vastly diminished.

Developing self-mastery of our mental and emotional content, our inner world, is precisely what meditation aims to do. The experience of mental silence is not unlike the crucial moment in Sendak's book when Max silences the unruly mob of monsters by ordering them to be quiet. He learns to assert utter control over them, to make them be still, even to sleep. In the same way, when we are becoming overwhelmed by a negative feeling or thought – such as anxiety, insecurity, a grudge or a negative feeling or idea that we can't seem to let go of – the initial effect of meditation is to reduce the loudness of those thoughts, to reduce the intensity of the dance of the wild things. Then, with a little practice, we learn to eliminate those thoughts and feelings rather than merely suppress them.

We can use this metaphor to understand the nature of the mind and the difference between mindfulness and mental silence. When Max is intimidated by the monsters and later playing among them, he is neither mindful nor mind-empty. He is like most people: immersed and, for the most part, entertaining himself with his thoughts and feelings, subject to their whim. When he sits and watches those wild things dance and play, but he is trying not to get involved himself, he is exercising mindfulness. When he commands them to be still and sends them to bed, he has achieved the meditative state of mental silence and can thus create a space within his awareness for higher emotions to emerge more freely, such as love of home.

The skill of meditation gives us the ability to still those destructive thoughts and feelings and to send them to bed without any supper. This is the power of mind-emptiness rather than mindfulness. The alternative – to allow them to continue their wild dance, to feed the frenzy of negative thoughts and feelings – will only egg them on towards the inevitable rumpus that undermines our equilibrium and damages our wellbeing, making us think, do and say things that we later regret.

Rebuilding resilience

In our efforts to understand how the rise of mental health problems among young people has come about, we need to take a close look at the environment in which our young people are immersed. Typically they face a range of challenges, from the usual events such as the death of a pet, the loss of a friend or lack of success in some endeavour, to more major but less common things such as the mental illness of a parent, being involved in an accident, the break-up of the family unit or some other traumatic experience.

In addition to these challenges, Jean Twenge and front-line professionals including teachers, counsellors and social workers who work with young people are coming to realise that there are a number of uniquely modern factors affecting young people. These include consumerism and loss of spirituality, a high rate of family breakdown in developed countries, increased drug and alcohol consumption, and a media culture that encourages young people to grow up faster and earlier than ever before. Young people also live in a cyber-saturated world, and the internet and mobile phones place tremendous power in the hands of those who are often not yet mature enough to handle it. As a result we have uniquely modern problems such as cyberbullying and harassment, sexting, internet addiction and 'Facebook depression'.[5]

A common thread connecting the various elements of the cultural storm is that they each chip away at the psyche, creating insecurities, negative thought patterns, self-destructive ideas and dysfunctional behaviours. They erode our young people's resilience – their ability to bounce back from mental and emotional challenges. While young people have always needed coping skills to deal with life's challenges, the evidence from many different sources indicates that today they are less resilient than young people were in previous generations.

Experts have proposed an array of strategies to tackle the problem of youth mental health, ranging from increasing the number of psychiatrists and psychologists to screening and early-detection programmes and internet-based treatment strategies.

It is important to work at a preventative level as well and many researchers are now focusing on identifying how to enhance young people's coping skills and other protective behaviours to help make them more resilient. Generally speaking, resilience strategies aim to make young people more stress-resistant and help them to develop strength, courage and positive mental health.[6]

Meditation seems ideally suited as a resilience-building skill. Also, it is a strategy that can be taught at school and used both at school and at home. The following sections describe some of the outcomes of our scientific explorations in the area of young people's mental health and wellbeing, and the role that meditation can play.

The ADHD clinic

A series of coincidences led to the establishment of a unique clinic set up to help manage attention deficit hyperactivity disorder (ADHD).

A mother who had practised Sahaja yoga for many years approached us and explained that she had successfully used the technique to treat her teenage daughter, who had ADHD. Then two teachers who were also meditators explained that for several years they had been successfully using the approach in their classrooms to deal with children with ADHD. Finally, we were contacted by teachers from a local school who had heard about our programme and wondered if we could do anything for their students with ADHD. We agreed to give it a try.

ADHD is a common problem in Western countries. It is estimated that anywhere from 3% to 9% of children in these countries may suffer from the condition, with some surveys indicating that the prevalence is rising. In the United States it is estimated that almost 9% of children have ADHD, although less than half have been diagnosed and less than a third are receiving appropriate treatment. In Australia, the National Survey of Mental Health and Wellbeing reported that 11% of children and adolescents had behavioural features strongly suggestive of ADHD. The majority of sufferers are boys.[7]

ADHD is poorly understood, with many experts describing it as multifactorial, with social and parental factors being very important. The idea that ADHD might be a by-product of a culture and value system that emphasises fast-paced, unhealthy lifestyles and undermines meaningful relationships, character development and family structure is gaining popularity with the public, but the scientific evidence to confirm this perception is still lacking.

ADHD is characterised by three main behavioural characteristics: impulsivity, hyperactivity and poor control of attention. Meditation is aimed at achieving a state that is the complete opposite, characterised by calmness, focused attention and self-control.

We brought together the two teachers who had been using the meditation approach in their classrooms, the mother of the child with ADHD and a number of Sahaja yoga practitioners who were also qualified health professionals, and devised a strategy for our programme.

The strategy involved 'treating' both the child and at least one parent (preferably the primary caregiver, which in most cases was the mother) using meditation techniques and footsoaking. A six-week programme of twice-weekly sessions began at the hospital campus; forty-eight children were taught meditation skills under the supervision of more than ten instructors. At the beginning of the programme the parents were taught separately from their children, and they were encouraged to practise daily at home.

The programme involved brief guided meditations, often with one instructor supervising a single child at a time. Although the children were often hyperactive at first, they became significantly more settled after the second week to the point where they could participate in group meditation sessions. The children were also taught footsoaking from the first week (footsoaking is described on page 178). It had a remarkably soothing effect on the children's behaviour.

While we knew that the children might not be cooperative, we impressed upon the parents that they could compensate for this with their own meditation. Calm parents contribute to a calm household, which in turn has a calming effect on the children. At about the midway point we began combining the classes so that the parents could supervise the children. At the end of the programme we reassessed the children, and the results were compared to the assessment that was done prior to the children beginning the class.

The results were very encouraging. Of the forty-eight children who finished the programme, more than half were able to reduce the amount of medication they needed. Of that half, a smaller proportion of the children were able to stop taking their medication altogether while maintaining normal behaviour levels with no adverse consequences for their behaviour and no negative alteration of their personality. Overall there was a 35% improvement in behaviour over the six-week treatment period.[8]

Ryan's story

Ryan and his brother were brought to us by their parents. Ryan's condition was characterised by poor control of attention, while his brother had the more stereotypical form of hyperactivity disorder. Like many of the other children in the clinic, Ryan found it difficult to focus, so the idea of meditation was foreign to him. Nevertheless, his parents had experienced significant challenges as a result of having two sons with behavioural disorders and they were prepared to try anything.

Like many people who participated in the programme, the parents were the first to experience the benefits of practising meditation, saying they felt more relaxed and less likely to react to difficult or unwanted situations. Within a couple of weeks, Ryan's mother started to see improvements in his behaviour.

She first noticed that he was less anxious, then observed that he was more able to focus on homework. His brother had also become less restless and was finding it easier to go to sleep at night. These improvements continued until, around the third week, Ryan's mother started to reduce his dose of medication while also intensifying his meditation regime using the techniques she had learnt from the instructors.

By the end of the six-week programme, Ryan was completely off his medication, his behaviour had improved substantially and he was excelling in areas in which he had previously experienced difficulty. For example, Ryan enjoyed school swimming competitions but often experienced anxiety attacks beforehand. The day before his first competition after starting the programme, he developed diarrhoea and stomach pains because of his anxiety. His mother employed the meditation techniques, Ryan's symptoms settled down, and as a result he was able to race. On the day of the competition Ryan used his meditation skills to neutralise any anxiety that might otherwise have affected his performance. He went on to win four ribbons and later told us that he had no doubt that the meditation techniques contributed to this.

When we asked Ryan how he felt about his condition, he explained that before attending the clinic he had felt trapped by his own behaviour but didn't know any way to correct the problem. Now he was able to observe and correct himself in such a way that he was free of medication and the stigma of the condition as well. In Ryan's own words, 'I always knew what I was doing was wrong, but now I can control it.'

His teachers noticed the improvement in Ryan's behaviour, and his paediatrician, who specialised in ADHD, contacted us to express her surprise and delight with his progress. She wanted to send more of her ADHD patients to the clinic. Ryan's brother had also experienced significant improvements, having halved his medication dosage by the end of the six-week period, and his mother felt confident that if his progress continued she would be able to get him off medication completely within a few weeks.

The results

On average there was a 35% improvement in the behaviour of the participants in the programme, despite the reduction in medication. Surprisingly, most of the improvement was seen in the first three weeks of the programme, while the children were still on holidays. The return to school seemed to hamper progress, but when compared to the children on the waiting list (who had also been assessed and were receiving standard treatment, but who had not received any meditation sessions), the relative improvement was even greater, as the untreated children had experienced substantial worsening of their behaviour as they re-entered the school environment.

Feedback from the parents was also very positive, particularly from those who actively participated in the meditation sessions. They all reported feeling generally better, less stressed and more relaxed. Most parents felt that the programme had benefited both them and their children. About half said that their child was less restless and was sleeping better, and that their relationship with their child had improved.

I was surprised by the number of parents who felt deeply conflicted about using stimulant medication to treat their child's ADHD. On the one hand they recognised that the child's behaviour was having an impact on others (not to mention themselves), which led the child to have feelings of alienation and insecurity, as well as compromising their ability to learn and engage at school. The medication did control the hyperactivity and impulsivity which, in turn, allowed the children to function more harmoniously at school and behave less antagonistically towards others. On the other hand, the same medication also suppressed other aspects of the child's personality (a phenomenon called 'blunting of affect'), which made it harder for parents to have an emotionally rich relationship with their child. As one mother put it, 'When I give him the medication his behaviour improves but it's like I lose my child in the process. Now with the meditation programme I feel like I've got my child back.'

Coverage of the positive results on national television has led to a flood of applicants, with a waiting list that is almost two years long. Sadly, we don't have the staff or resources to meet the current demand for the programme, so at the end of the formal study we had no choice but to close down the initiative. And as our experience indicates that meditative techniques that don't specifically deliver mental silence are unlikely to help, we couldn't make a generic recommendation for any form of meditation to those parents who were waiting to place their children in our programme.

Now, when we are approached by parents wanting to use meditation for the treatment of their child with ADHD, we advise them to first learn Sahaja yoga meditation themselves. Once the parents have become established meditators they will be able to teach their children. It's the whole family who needs to learn how to meditate, not just the child with ADHD.

11
Meditation in the classroom

Sometimes I sits and thinks and
sometimes I just sits.

A.A. Milne[1]

In the process of wrapping up the ADHD project and reflecting on what we had learnt, it occurred to us that by focusing on the issue of ADHD we were missing the larger picture: we should be looking at using meditation to *prevent* emotional and behavioural issues rather than treat them. So we decided to take meditation into the classroom.

A number of teachers and parents told us how informal meditation programmes they had initiated in their schools had apparently led to better behaviour in the children, improved mood and more focused and settled students.

At one school, primary school teacher Priya Rapyal had been using meditation in 'Hindu scripture', a replacement for Christian scripture in a school where there was a very large proportion of children from Indian families. Teachers who taught the lessons that came immediately after the meditation sessions remarked on the improved behaviour of the children in their classes. The principal eventually heard about it and became enthused by the idea that something as simple as meditation could have such a potentially significant effect. She encouraged Priya and myself to develop this concept into what came to be known at that school as 'The Reflections Program'.

The principal rightly pointed out to us that it would not be appropriate to use the usual Sahaja yoga approach for this programme since some of its ideas made reference to essentially spiritual concepts and values. Moreover, yogic terminology such as 'chakras', '*Kundalini*', 'self-realisation' and 'spirit' had cultural and spiritual connotations that were not compatible with the state school system's secular ethos. And while many parents – especially those from Asian backgrounds – did not have any difficulty with the terminology, there would inevitably be some who might not be comfortable with it.

The necessity to create a secular version of Sahaja yoga suitable for the state school system was a new challenge. Through a series of workshops and discussions with meditation instructors, schoolteachers and school leaders, we succeeded in stripping out the Eastern terminology and cultural ideas, as well as the spiritual references – boiling the techniques down to truly secular, non-denominational methods that were suitable for use in a secular school system.

Many of the instructors wondered if this secularised version would actually be effective in eliciting the experience of mental silence. Some of the instructors had serious doubts.

We chose several schools in which to test our secularised approach to mental silence: a metropolitan girls high school with a strong reputation for high academic performance; a state co-ed high school in rural Australia with a wide range of socio-economic challenges; an exclusive private boys high school in Sydney's blue-ribbon eastern suburbs; and a high school in suburban Brisbane. To gain a clearer idea of whether or not the students were able to achieve mental silence using this secular approach, we devised a simple survey based on the thought-waves diagrams seen in Chapter 5.

A total of 750 students filled in the survey before and after the meditation session. None of the children had had prior exposure to meditation.

As expected, the majority of students indicated that the 'usual mental activity' thought-wave best represented their mental state just prior to the session. After the meditation session, however, about 10% indicated that they had experienced the mental silence state, and about 20% experienced the state that was characterised by 'one or two thoughts separated by longer moments of silence', that is, a condition where they were 'mostly silent'.

Given that this was the first session of meditation that they had experienced, it was an impressive result and proof that even when the meditation method is stripped of its traditional terminology, or the beliefs that the words might encompass, it can still trigger the crucial experience of mental silence. This was a very important development in our research project's growing understanding of the meditative process. Clearly the process of meditation was entirely independent of the mental framework that surrounded it and must therefore depend on a much more subtle mechanism than even we suspected.

Evaluating meditation in schools

Taking the secularised approach, and confident that it was effective in bringing about the mental silence experience, we now needed to evaluate its impact on practically relevant measures of mental health.

To do this we established an initiative in a state primary school in Sydney with the assistance of Priya Rapyal and Sheetu Aurora, a student teacher. We took a class of Year Three children, aged eight and nine, and added a 10- to 15-minute meditation session, conducted by an experienced meditation instructor, to their usual morning routine. The sessions would take place in the classroom every day before teaching began.

In addition, we asked the classroom teacher to assess each of the children using a scientifically developed measure of mental health called the 'Strengths and Difficulties Questionnaire'. This questionnaire assessed the child's risk of developing mental health problems as well as their social skills. The assessment was done at the beginning of the school year and then at the end of every term. This allowed us to effectively track each child, and the class as a whole, as they progressed with the meditation instruction. These teacher assessments indicated that the class had a mental health risk score of twelve. The average mental health risk score for Australian children of the same age was six, meaning that this class was more at risk of mental health issues than the general population.

Within the first few weeks of practising meditation with her class, the teacher was already remarking on improvements in the children. This was reflected in the mental health measures, which showed a steady reduction in risk across each term and over the full year. By the end of the year the children experienced an 80% reduction in their mental health risk, bringing their score down to two, and a 25% improvement in their social skills (see figure below). This impressive result clearly illustrates the potential of meditation not only to treat problems like ADHD but also to reduce the risk of mental illness in the first place.

Emotional and behavioural wellbeing
Year Three class

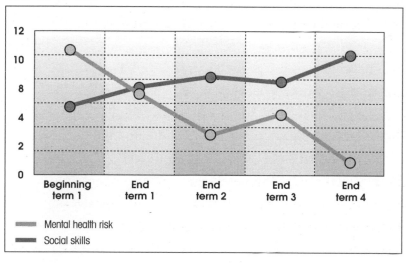

Word got around and we were invited by other schools to work with them in a similar way. At some of these schools we interviewed a number of the children, who each provided candid and spontaneous descriptions of how the meditation skills and experience had worked for them. The teachers also gave their feedback, and they consistently noted improvements in their ability to manage the class and teach effectively. Much of this was the result of the children being more settled, focused and motivated.

Initially, some teachers were sceptical about meditation or concerned about the loss of valuable class time during the sessions. However, they soon realised that while they were losing some teaching time to the meditation classes, they were gaining much more because of the increased ability of the children to work productively. The amount of time that they were spending on teaching, as compared to discipline and behaviour management, had increased.

A principal from a primary school in a particularly low socio-economic area of Queensland gave us his insights into the impact of the strategy after a single term in his school:

> The teachers were probably initially a bit sceptical or unsure about what they were getting into, but the feedback that came back, almost immediately, showed that teachers were really impressed with the changes they saw in the kids. Certainly by the second session they were seeing kids being more relaxed, being more calm. They were noticeably different in terms of the sorts of physical attributes they sometimes display coming in from a lunchbreak or coming in from a transition from a previous class – able to quickly get back to their studies, even the hyperactive kids. So that definitely increases our efficiency for the time we have with students.
>
> We quickly get parents up in arms or concerned if kids go home and say things that are at odds with what the parents and families would like, so the fact I haven't had feedback is actually a good sign. Something like this that helps kids to tap into their inner resources, their inner strength, to deal with life's travails and bounce back and have the confidence to move forward is really, really important. You can't teach kids if they're

not ready to be taught, and the mental stillness and resilience programme was able to put students in that place where they're ready to learn. I think it's shown us the extent to which we can tap into things that support students socially and emotionally and, in turn, the direct and immediate benefits this brings to teaching and learning.

Below are excerpts from interviews that I conducted with children from this school. You'll recall the interview between myself and the eight-year-old girl in the introductory section of this book. Both are elegant illustrations of how children perceived the meditative process assisted them in reducing their stress, improving their mood and, hence, improving their class performance:

8-YEAR-OLD BOY 1: It's helped me in my work and doing maths, trying to make me not to stress when I've got this sum to do and I can't do it.

8-YEAR-OLD BOY 2: When I did my speech, I was only scared for, like, so long. It was only just, like, a few seconds and then it was gone.
RM: And do you usually get scared for longer?
8-YEAR-OLD BOY 2: Oh yeah, I get scared for, like, the whole thing.

9-YEAR-OLD GIRL: When I'm at school, sometimes when I'm doing a test, I get, like, really stressed that I'm going to get it all wrong. But when I do the mental stillness thing I, like, get basically the whole thing right.

The 2011 Mission Australia Youth Survey identified stress as the foremost major concern for young people.[2] Educators are also increasingly aware of how stress can negatively impact on the learning process. We've already seen in Chapter 9 that the mental silence experience is a highly effective way to reduce stress. These simple statements from the children also provide eloquent support for the potential role of meditation to reduce the stress that children and youth are increasingly exposed to.

Engagement

In every lesson that they give, teachers strive to help young people to make an effort in their learning, to understand the material and to internalise the information and the ideas that they are being given. When the student wants to participate and be successful in the learning process, it promotes higher level processing of the information and thus a more enduring level of understanding. Engaged students have a positive feeling associated with learning activities. Below is one teacher's description of how she saw the impact of the meditation initiative that we conducted at her school on student engagement:

> **RM:** Could you give us a general impression of how you found the mental stillness programme and what your overall sort of perceptions and impressions are?
>
> **TEACHER:** Okay, so I've been teaching here for nine years and when the mental stillness programme started I wasn't quite sure what it was and what to expect.
>
> **RM:** Did you find that the stillness programme had any benefits either for the children or for you as a teacher?

TEACHER: I noticed that the students who were targeted, or who also targeted themselves, were kids who were quite outgoing, quite talkative. Once I set it up that they had to come back into the class quietly, I could start seeing the impact it was having on them, particularly a couple of the boys who were in my class. They really quietened down, and would get straight into work once they returned from mental stillness.

RM: Did you notice any behavioural changes in the children who participated?

TEACHER: Definitely. Calmer, they came back to class calm and quiet, quiet of mind, and they were on task. So I could see the benefits of that, particularly after maybe the second or third time that they went, I could really see that they were starting to form a pattern and it was helping them in a positive way.

As our understanding of the process of learning grows, we are coming to realise that what teachers call 'engagement' psychologists call 'flow'. Within an educational context, flow is an optimal learning state that involves three key factors: concentration, enjoyment and interest.[3] Interestingly, meditation also involves concentration (focused attention) and positive mood (enjoyment), and of course these necessarily make the student interested in the experience. This may explain why teachers in our participating schools noticed after the meditation sessions that the children were remarkably more engaged in their classwork and learning.

To further explore the connection between flow and meditation in students, we collected feedback from a group of fifty senior high-school students in rural New South

Wales. We gave them a single session of meditation for about 20 minutes. Before this session they received a lecture on computer safety. We asked them to rate the flow experience after the computer safety lecture and then again after the meditation session. The amount of flow that they experienced as a result of the lecture was moderate, in line with our expectations for something like a lecture which involves a certain amount of focused attention but may or may not be interesting or enjoyable, whereas the amount of flow they experienced immediately after the meditation session was high – more than 50% higher, in fact. Meditation was definitely associated with significantly more flow experience than a standard educational lecture, even though it was only the students' first meditation session. Importantly, when we asked the students to rate how they felt, there was also a strong correlation between their mood and their experience of mental silence. As they became more silent, their mood and their level of enjoyment improved.

Since meditation gives rise to flow experiences it could be a powerful tool to facilitate engagement in the classroom as well.

Teacher stress

Many teachers dream of inspiring and motivating their students but find that the reality of teaching is a heavy workload, difficult student behaviour and immense pressure to produce academic results. Teachers and educators are among the most highly stressed professions.[4] High-school teachers are one of the top ten professionals most likely to make a stress-related work injury claim in Australia. Our other scientific studies – such as the work-stress trial describing reduced stress, depression and anxiety in full-time workers – also demonstrated the potential benefits of meditation for stressed-out teachers. So meditation skills are relevant to teachers and students alike.

In our school programmes, an instructor was provided for the class but the teacher was required to participate and assist. As a result, the teachers also learnt to meditate and susbsequently noted that they too experienced less tension and better moods, which they felt enhanced their ability to connect with their class and teach effectively. Meditation might not only be useful because it can make students more resilient and engaged, but also because the subsequent improvements in behaviour might reduce stress on teachers.

Relationships

Another area of great concern to young people is their relationships with others. Friends, peers, family and teachers are an important source of emotional support for a young person going through the challenges of growing up in a very modern world. Conversely, the conflict that occurs when relationships break down can be profoundly stressful. As young people grow they learn to negotiate the social landscape, and acquire skills to manage relationships and strategies to minimise conflict. An unexpected outcome of the meditation initiative in schools was that the students described how the skills seemed to help them to manage their relationships more effectively outside of the classroom as well as within. Below are some excerpts of interview dialogue from young people describing how the meditation helped them to improve the ways they related to their friends and family.

RESPONDENT 1: Well, you know, fights with friends and family and stuff, you kind of decide not to hold grudges against them and just forgive them for whatever's happened and don't, like, worry about it and just be friends with them again, which is really good.

INTERVIEWER: That's good. And that's in the last few weeks that this …?

RESPONDENT 1: Yeah, I've been fighting with, like, my family a lot and so I decided that I have to be happy around them and just not hold stuff against them anymore.

INTERVIEWER: And what about inside, do you feel better inside as a result of that?

RESPONDENT 1: Yeah, yeah I do. I feel, like, a lot happier and just when you don't fight with people you feel better about yourself. It's good.

RESPONDENT 2: It helped me, like, forgive people a lot. Say they'd say something to me and I'd get angry at first but then I just, it's not … I need to be friends with them and I just be happier towards them and become friends.

RESPONDENT 3: Like at home with brothers and sisters and stuff, I found it easier to sort of not lose my temper and just hold back and sort of restrain, like, have a bit more self-control and be more relaxed. When once I would have sort of been really angry, I was sort of less wound up about it and I sort of just let it go.

RESPONDENT 4: Well, I get blamed for a lot of things, most of them I did, but some of them I didn't do. But I still get blamed. But often it's hard to keep your calm state, but when you do it makes things a whole lot better. Like if I react badly, the situation will just drag on and on with me and my mum arguing constantly. But if I can just accept that she's always right, her mood will start to improve and …

INTERVIEWER: And has mental stillness had any effect on that?

RESPONDENT 4: Yes, yes it has. It's essentially what helps me keep a cool head in those situations.

Preventing depression

Although much of this chapter has focused on young people, the mental health crisis is part of a much larger problem that threatens people of all ages. The World Health Organization has predicted that depression will be the most common illness in the world, regardless of age, by 2030.[5] Can meditation help us stem the tide?

To answer this question, it's worth re-examining the findings of the survey of long-term meditators, described in chapters 5 and 9. Although we have already looked at the relationship between mental silence and general health, there is one more set of findings within this study that relates specifically to depressive illness.

You will recall that more than 350 practitioners of Sahaja yoga meditation took part in this survey. Most meditators were successfully experiencing mental silence on a daily basis. There was a robust relationship between how often meditators were experiencing mental silence and their high level of health, especially mental health.

The important additional information that relates to depression involved another part of the survey. We used a measure called the Kessler 10, which is the same instrument used in the National Survey of Mental Health of the Australian population conducted by the Australian Bureau of Statistics.[6] It is a reliable way of assessing an individual's risk of developing depression or anxiety based on a set of standardised questions about symptoms that are commonly associated with these conditions.

We found that 78% of the meditators were in the lowest risk category compared to 64% of Australians who were in the same category. The low-risk category is the group considered least likely to develop depression. Conversely, only 3.5% of meditators were in the high to very-high risk category compared to 13% of Australians in the same category. This category is thought to represent those people most likely to develop depression in the near future. These pronounced differences indicate that regular meditation or, more accurately, regular experience of mental silence, is associated with reduced risk of developing depression. This finding persisted even after controlling for alcohol and tobacco consumption.[7]

Now, while surveys can provide us with important clues about what benefits meditation might be *associated* with, they can't prove that meditation actually *caused* those benefits. However, there are some clinical studies in which the effects of meditation have been observed from the outset, which suggest that this approach to meditation does in fact cause the improvements. A study by Dr Wolfgang Hackl as part of his doctoral thesis at the University of Vienna compared the effect of Sahaja yoga to the music of Mozart.[8] He took 101 participants and divided them into three groups – one group listened to Mozart, another practised Sahaja yoga and a third received no treatment. Hackl assessed levels of anxiety using the State-Trait Anxiety Inventory – a widely respected assessment tool – before the study and after eight weeks of exposure. At the end of the eight weeks, both the music and meditation groups improved. However, the meditation group experienced significantly greater improvements in 'state' anxiety (that is, the anxiety that they were feeling at that very moment), which was 40% less than when they started, compared to the music group's 20% reduction. A similar pattern, although smaller in magnitude, also occurred with regard to the participants' 'trait' or 'background' level of anxiety.

An exploratory study conducted by Adam Morgan, a psychologist then at the University of Exeter in the United Kingdom, showed that Sahaja yoga meditation had a beneficial therapeutic effect on the symptoms of patients with depression and anxiety.[9] Twenty-four patients with depression and anxiety were divided into three groups, according to the treating health professional's assessment of their suitability: the more 'introspective' patients were referred to a group receiving direction in Sahaja yoga meditation over six weeks, while the more 'outward looking' were allocated to a group receiving the conventional behavioural treatment for depression, that is, CBT. Both groups were compared to a control group that received no treatment. Interestingly, the meditation and CBT groups seemed to show equivalent levels of effectiveness in improving symptoms. In fact, although the study had limitations there was some suggestion that in some areas the meditation was more effective.

You will also recall that we conducted two randomised controlled trials (RCTs) which demonstrated specific positive effects on mood, stress and depressive symptoms. Taking all this evidence together, we could draw a number of important conclusions:

- First, long-term meditators have a lower risk of developing anxiety and depression compared to the general population.
- Second, mental silence has a specific positive effect on mood and was specifically effective at reducing depressive symptoms.
- Third, our work in schools and organisations indicates that it is feasible to introduce meditation-based strategies into the organisational environment, and our initial work is showing that it does have an effect on reducing the risk of mental illness.

Therefore, mental-silence based meditation strategies have great potential as a preventative strategy for depression, and should be seriously considered along with other strategies that health policymakers are exploring to tackle the looming depression epidemic.

Larger-scale research is certainly warranted and we have a number of larger-scale evaluations currently occurring around Australia to help provide further information about this.

Implications

Decades ago, our children and youth were more likely to suffer or die from infectious diseases such as measles, smallpox and polio. Nations worked together to develop effective vaccinations and delivery programmes to tackle these diseases. One of the most inspiring stories from that era was that of Jonas Salk, developer of the Salk polio vaccine. Despite developing the vaccine, he resisted the temptation to patent and commercialise it even though it would have made him incredibly wealthy.

When an interviewer asked, 'Who owns this patent?' Salk replied, 'No one. Could you patent the sun?' Instead, Salk worked to make the vaccine, and the technology used to produce it, as widely available as possible at minimal cost. As a result, polio is now a rare disease. In similar ways, many other childhood infectious diseases have been eliminated.

Today, the greatest health threat to our young people is mental illness. Could mental silence inoculate young people to reduce this risk of developing mental illness? Could meditation be the universal primary prevention strategy that our public health policy makers are looking for as they struggle to find solutions to the growing mental health crisis?

Words from meditators

I was enjoying the deep mental silence, meditating in the midst of a large group, when suddenly I found myself enveloped in what seemed like an immense expansion. It happened just as a thought came in; not so much a thought as a knowing, a sudden recognition of the meaning of compassion within myself. It was like a powerful collective force, but at the same time it was me alone. I was completely inside it and it was completely inside me. It was as if my whole head had opened up at the top and knowledge was pouring in so fast I could not grasp or hold on to any of it. I had a deep feeling that I was being given this immense knowledge, all at once, as a gift. I felt that I could not move; I had to just sit there and receive. And yet I knew I could move if I really wanted to. I didn't want it to ever stop. I felt completely part and parcel of the whole creation. No beginning and no end. The oneness of all things. I knew everything and I knew nothing.

It was pure feeling – powerful, intense, blissful. It must have lasted ten or fifteen minutes before I slowly came back to normal.

The next morning, looking out over a beautiful wooded river valley in the company of others, I put my hands out and was instantly, and totally unexpectedly, in the stillness again. But now it was quite different. My eyes were open; I was not formally 'meditating', just feeling the beauty. What astonished me was that when people spoke to me I heard them and I answered, and it made not the slightest difference to the stillness. It was just there. I could move around and carry on a conversation, all in the state of complete silent stillness. It lasted about ten or fifteen minutes, then faded. The memory of it stays.

There have been times since that quiet, momentous event when everything has gone still and the bliss has poured over me, but not in the same way. I look forward to the time when that depth of stillness becomes a part of everyday living, and not just for me. I know that it can be so. What I do have now is a great measure of peace in everyday living. I used to get tongue-tied, but now words seem to come when I need them. I can mix without feeling self-conscious, I can speak easily to friends or strangers, and I can address a gathering of people with ease. This is a far cry from the old, lonely Katie, who could open her mouth but nothing would come out. Depression and anxiety are long gone now. There's nothing I need that I don't have. I am an independent, free person with many loving friends.

Katie, Australia

Last year someone close to me suffered a debilitating mental illness. As the main support person I attended this person's therapy sessions with a specialised clinical psychologist. The one thing that kept me sane and calm throughout this experience was meditation. At the biggest crisis point in the treatment period, I believe that it was meditation – and the friends who meditated with me and with the person affected by the illness – that helped this person to avoid the much harder and more complex road of hospitalisation.

At the end of the treatment sessions, the psychologist told me that what we had achieved in six months had never statistically been done in less than twelve months in Australia. I fully credit meditation for this better-than-average result.

A mother who wishes to remain anonymous

Children in upper primary and high school, especially senior high school, found the affirmations described on page 104 easy to do. However, children in the younger age groups needed a more simplified approach. Here are some strategies that we have developed and evaluated to help even very young children to meditate. The technique is completely secular, and it works just as well as the original Sahaja yoga practice from which it is derived. The key idea behind this strategy is to get the children's attention focused, in the present moment and then above the head. It works automatically from there.

For the programmes it was important for the instructor to be established in their own experience of mental silence. It seems that unless you are very familiar with this experience it is not possible to help others to achieve it. Adults need to meditate successfully and then teach their children or students.

If you are not yet consistently getting the mental silence experience then we suggest that you use the audio or video resources provided on the website rather than try to take on the role of 'meditation instructor'.

The instructions on the following pages are to be read aloud to children while they are seated comfortably.

What's done to the children is done to society.

Buddha

The magic bubble

1. Close your eyes.
2. Breathe slowly, in through your nose and out through your mouth.
3. Put your hands in your lap, palms up; back straight, legs crossed if you are sitting on the floor.
4. Put your right hand, palm up, just in front of your tummy.
5. Imagine a cool, delicate bubble balancing in your hands.
6. Raise your right hand while very carefully balancing the bubble on your hand so that it doesn't fall off or float away.
7. Very carefully put the bubble on the top of your head.
8. Press gently on the top of your head so that you can feel the bubble balancing there. Move the right hand back to the lap.
9. Let the bubble balance carefully on the top of your head.
10. After some time, feel the bubble float up just above your head, then up to the roof, then through the roof into the sky.
11. Follow it up, feel the bubble floating in the cool clouds.
12. Eventually the bubble disappears. Keep your attention at the top of your head where the bubble was.

The golden string

1. Close your eyes.
2. Breathe slowly, in through your nose and out through your mouth.
3. Put your hands in your lap, palms up; back straight, legs crossed if you are sitting on the floor.
4. Imagine a curled golden string at the bottom of your back.
5. Let that string slowly uncurl and start moving up through your body.
6. The string is moving through your tummy.
7. Now it's moving through your heart and chest.
8. Now it's moving up through your neck.
9. Now through your head.
10. Now it's coming out of the top of your head.
11. It's going up into the sky.
12. Follow it up as it reaches the clouds.
13. Feel all quiet and cool inside, surrounded by fluffy clouds.
14. Raise your hands towards the sky, wiggle your fingers a little bit and see if you can feel the cool clouds moving around your hands and fingers.
15. Put your hands back in your lap and sit quietly.

Tying up your attention

1. Close your eyes.
2. Breathe slowly, in through your nose and out through your mouth.
3. Put your hands in your lap, palms up; back straight, legs crossed if you are sitting on the floor.
4. Hold your hands out, palms up, in front of you.
5. Put your attention in your hands. It's very important that we always know where our attention is. By the end of this process it should be at the top of your head.
6. Now wind up your attention along your body to the top of your head. Do this by moving your right hand around your left as if you were winding up some string. While 'winding the string' move both hands up along the centre of your body toward the top of the head.
7. When your hand reaches the top of your head, tie a knot at the point just above your head to keep your attention there. Repeat all of this a few times to establish your attention.
8. Now sit quietly with your attention above your head.

Rainbow protection

1. Close your eyes.
2. Breathe slowly, in through your nose and out through your mouth.
3. Put your hands in your lap, palms up; back straight, legs crossed.
4. Hold your hands out, palms up, in front of you.
5. Now move your right hand over your body to make the shape of a rainbow. Each movement has a different colour, do it about seven times, once for each colour.
6. Red looks after my legs, yellow looks after my back, green looks after my tummy, blue looks after my heart, orange looks after my neck, white looks after my forehead, all the colours look after the top of my head and the whole of my body.
7. The rainbow protects us from all the bad thoughts and feelings by keeping them out.
8. Put your hands back in your lap and sit quietly.

PART VI
FLOW AND OPTIMAL BEING

12
Meditation and flow

Suddenly, I realised that I was no longer driving consciously and I was kind of driving by instinct only, I was in a different dimension ... I was well beyond my conscious understanding.

Ayrton Senna[1]

A bodysurfer friend of mine, Robert, looks at a particularly beautiful picture of a wave and says, 'It reminds me of a barrel I caught about six months ago, when time stretched right out and everything went quiet – really expansive and quiet.'

A martial artist with a green belt describes a spontaneous state of high performance: 'One night I was sparring with a black belt and everything just happened automatically. Time slowed down. I was blocking every punch and giving plenty back. I knocked this guy to the floor five times in a minute. It was amazing!'

Ayrton Senna, the great Brazilian Formula 1 driver, was well known for his ability to drive a car in a way that other drivers thought was not possible.[2] On many occasions it seemed as though he took his vehicle beyond its physical limits to produce unprecedented lap times and mind-blowing victories. In the qualifying round for the 1988 Monaco Grand Prix, Senna broke all the records for his lap. He was one and a half seconds faster than his team mate, Alain Prost, and two seconds ahead of the next competitor. Prost, himself considered one of the great Formula 1 drivers, found it difficult to believe the extent to which Senna had outclassed him. Senna had somehow pushed himself and his vehicle to a new level of capability. At the same time, Senna described being in a completely different state of awareness, which he explains in the quote at the start of this chapter.

Pelé, the legendary Brazilian soccer star, describes a shift in his consciousness while playing soccer that echoes Senna's experience:

> *A strange calmness ... it was a type of euphoria; I felt I could run all day without tiring, that I could dribble through any of their team or all of them, that I could almost pass through them physically.*[3]

The state 'beyond conscious understanding' is a phenomenon that has come to be known by researchers in the West as 'flow'[4] or sometimes as a 'peak experience'.[5] Over the past several years there has been increasing recognition of the roles that flow and peak experiences play in mental health and in performance. Remarkably, although the concepts of flow and the peak experience have developed independently of Eastern ideas of meditation and mental silence, they correspond almost exactly with them.

Flow, peak experience, meditation and mental silence are not different phenomena, but are just different labels for essentially the same thing – a state that might be best called 'optimal consciousness' or 'the ideal state of being'.

It is fascinating that these ideas have emerged in different parts of the world, in different cultures, at different times, and yet describe the same core features. I was intrigued by how the ideas of flow and peak experience, which have crystallised recently in Western thought, relate so closely to the ancient Eastern understandings of meditation and mental silence. Both of these streams converge on the idea that within each of us there is a capacity to attain a peak performance state connected to an ideal state of being. Perhaps there is an instinctive part of us that is, consciously or unconsciously, seeking ways to access this state.

About flow

Also described as being in 'the zone', 'the pipe' or 'the groove', flow occurs when we become completely immersed in a task. So immersed, in fact, that we are not distracted by external factors – noise, discomfort, the passing of time – or internal factors, such as unnecessary thoughts or emotions.

Mihaly Csikszentmihalyi was the first of the modern researchers in the West to identify this phenomenon, for which he coined the term 'flow'.[6] When he was researching creativity, he wondered what motivated artists to work despite the lack of rewards, financial or otherwise. He noted that many of the artists he studied lost interest in an artwork once it was completed. They seemed to be motivated by something much more profound; the process of creating the artwork was so rewarding that there was no need for any other motivator, not even the completed artwork itself. The process of creation seemed to involve an experience that was more important and more fulfilling than anything else. 'Flow' seemed to best describe this experience.

Csikszentmihalyi, his colleagues, students and many others went on to study athletes, chess masters, rock climbers, dancers, musicians, surgeons and computer programmers, and found that all the participants described a similar feeling of positivity and fulfilment when their attention was completely consumed by their chosen task. The experience of flow was itself a motivator to experience more flow.

Research has shown that many high achievers, regardless of their field of expertise, experience flow more frequently and more profoundly than others. Hence, flow states are associated not only with feeling good but also with increased capability, creativity and performance.

Flow can be experienced in almost any situation that requires total focus, whether knitting a scarf, cooking a meal or engaging in an engrossing conversation. There is a spectrum of flow quality. Low-quality flow happens more frequently and can occur when we are doing simple tasks such as raking leaves or having a conversation with friends. High-quality flow is less common. In addition to being focused and productive, it involves a tangible shift to a state of awareness in which mundane thoughts and feelings are replaced by a sense of timelessness, a loss of ego and a profound sense of positivity. A musician explains: 'I literally imagine the air flowing through my body into the flute and suddenly half my problems take care of themselves ...'[7] This is what Ayrton Senna described as a state 'beyond conscious understanding'. High-quality flow is remarkably similar to meditation and particularly mental silence.

The peak experience

A generation before Csikszentmihalyi, Abraham Maslow (1908–1970), an American professor of psychology, was unusual for his interest in the nature of mental health rather than mental illness, and human potential rather than dysfunction. He felt that great personalities and high achievers, both living and historical, could provide important clues about how to achieve the ideal state of consciousness. He was most interested in what it was within them that allowed them to realise their potential – what he called 'self-actualisation' – when others could not. His research led him to develop an understanding of humans and their potential to achieve an optimal state of being, embodied in the phenomenon that he called 'the peak experience'. Maslow explained that the peak experience involved 'feelings of limitless horizons opening up to the vision, the feeling of being simultaneously more powerful and also more helpless than one ever was before, the feeling of great ecstasy and wonder and awe, and the loss of placing in time and space'. When peak experiences are especially powerful, the sense of self dissolves into an awareness of a greater unity.[8]

Maslow believed that all of us were capable of attaining these experiences. He went so far as to suggest that perhaps all of us have a number of peak experiences in the course of our lives, regardless of whether or not we recognise them as such. He argued that peak experiences provided a pathway to achieve personal growth, sustainable wellbeing and authentic happiness. He strongly advocated for further research into peak experiences, so that strategies could be developed to cultivate them.

Many people who experience intense, high-quality flow are effectively having a peak experience. Csikszentmihalyi and Maslow, as well as other researchers, also found that these experiences, rather than the activity from which the experience comes, were beneficial for one's health, wellbeing and performance. As a result, these phenomena have become interesting to modern psychologists and health researchers because they represent states that are the opposite of mental illness. (Our studies, described in Chapter 9, where we scientifically demonstrate the connection between the mental silence experience and health benefits add further confirmation to this growing understanding.)

In mental illness the workings of the mind and brain have become so disordered that the sufferer experiences mostly negative thoughts and emotions and is unable to function productively. Recognising the existence of flow and peak experience gives us an opportunity to identify the moments when the brain and mind are functioning at the peak of their constructive capacity; when people are at their best rather than their worst. The shift in focus away from mental illness towards those peak states when we feel happy, satisfied and complete, has led to the development of a new field in mental health, called positive psychology.

The obstacle that both Maslow and Csikszentmihalyi, and anyone who works in positive psychology, have come up against is that although these states are important and beneficial, they are difficult to achieve at will. While flow states are often described by high achievers, they also say that it can be difficult to get into flow and to stay there when they want to.

It's interesting that the same idea of optimal being has long been recognised in Eastern culture, where it is known in Sanskrit as *sahaja*. It's another fascinating clue that enables us to draw some important connections between the emerging ideas of flow and peak experience and ancient ideas of meditation.

Sport, mental clarity, flow and meditation

A clear head is essential for good performance in all types of sport. The athlete's awareness must be absolutely clear and free from distractions for the right split-second perception and decision to happen. A mind cluttered by useless thoughts will not allow the necessary focus. Instead, many athletes look for the ideal state, which is a mind completely free of negative and distracting thoughts.[9]

In Japanese martial arts this state of non-mind is called *mushin*, meaning 'without mind'. Derived from the Zen term *mushin no shin* or 'mind without mind', *mushin* is characterised by the absence of thoughts, anger, fear or pride during combat, which gives the martial artist the ability to perform without hesitation, at one with a form of intuition that is superior to mundane thinking awareness.

The role of *mushin* in non-martial sports is well illustrated by one young footballer, who had been taught by one of his parents to meditate. He told me, 'I remember playing a whole game of football in mental silence. It was my best game ever.' Like the martial artists, the footballer's experience shows that the state of mental silence does not only occur when sitting still, but can be carried with the athlete into the intense physical activity of competition, even the frenzy of combat.[10]

Reaching the flow state beyond the mind is an important skill that should enhance an athlete's ability to reduce the negative impact of the mind on their performance. However, my conversations with elite athletes, coaches and sports psychologists have also revealed that while flow is widely acknowledged as being important and useful, it has proven to be such a difficult and unreliable state to trigger at will that many have given up trying to cultivate it. So much so that people claiming to be able to train athletes in developing flow are treated with sceptical derision. Given their difficulties and frustration, I can understand their perspective. Yet I am reminded of my own meditative experience when I was a student. It was both flow and peak experience. Could meditation – particularly Sahaja yoga with its emphasis on the mental silence experience – be a method of accessing this state of high performance more easily by facilitating mastery over our mental content?

In our research programme we focused on evaluating the experience of meditation as a state of mental silence in which the meditator is fully alert and aware, and in complete control of their faculties, while at the same time not experiencing any unnecessary thinking activity. Realising that this is very similar to what people describe when they are in flow states, we started to investigate whether or not this connection was actually real. Our findings so far have indicated that by using the meditative techniques outlined in this book, practitioners – even novices – appear to be tapping into this flow state more or less at will.

An anecdote

In a guest lecture I gave at the Australian Institute of Sport on the psychological benefits of meditation, I hinted at the idea that mental silence may essentially be a flow state. At the end of the lecture, the audience took part in a 15 minute meditation session. One of the participants decided to try to put the practice into action shortly after this, during his daily swim. He later contacted me with his own description of mental silence and its impact on his swimming performance:

> *When I entered the water, having taken part in the 'mental silence' exercise only 10 minutes before, I had the sensation of feeling more buoyant than usual. I felt I was really floating high in the water and it felt easier to swim ... Now, this could have been due to not swimming the day before as I went for a long run instead, or auto-suggestion of some kind, having only just completed the meditation exercise, but I thought that it was worth reporting. I will certainly try the mental silence exercise again prior to swimming to see if the sensation is replicated.*
>
> **Ken Black, Sports Development Consultant**

Case study: The cyclist

At about the time that I delivered my lecture at the Australian Institute of Sport, a corporate trainer and experienced meditator colleague of mine, who has a special interest in competitive cycling, told me about his experience. He was training an elite cyclist who had competed in the Tour de France and held a number of junior world championship titles. He was using the same meditation strategies described here, with his main focus on mental silence rather than the spiritual and metaphysical aspects of the technique, and said that he had achieved some remarkable results with the athlete that he was coaching.

The cyclist's experience of what he described as 'the right headspace' matched the fundamental features of flow, and he felt that meditation not only replicated the experience when he was not cycling, it made it easier for him to achieve when he was cycling. Here's an excerpt from my discussion with him.

> *I've performed really challenging skills, or skills that I would normally consider very challenging and they're effortless when you're in the zone. Time just seems to tick by and you just seem to be floating through this experience, through this journey, and you're just in an objective state. You're reacting to the outside influences that are coming at you and you're just reacting spontaneously and objectively and that's when the best results have come, I've found, consistently in my professional sporting career.*
>
> *I think that state of 'the zone' and the meditation are very closely linked. When I practise the meditation, I'm very aware of my body and of that present moment, and there's no thoughts in my head. And that's the same when you're competing, or when you're performing well. Your senses are really heightened and you're very alert. I think practising meditation off the bike is a similar state to being in the zone, in a really passive way. You do the physical practice in training leading up to the event, and the meditation is like the mental practice for getting in that zone at the event.*

The connection between the two phenomena that this cyclist points out is intriguing. It seems that meditation – especially mental silence and therefore Sahaja yoga – offers athletes, and others, the ability to tap into an optimal performance state, or flow, at will.

Recognising the need for more research, we conducted three exploratory studies to help us bring the relationship between mental silence – meditation – and flow into clearer focus.

Flow and mental silence in novice meditators

In this first study we assessed the experience of 450 adults who had never meditated before. We gave them around 30 minutes of hands-on practical instruction in Sahaja yoga meditation. Immediately after the meditation session we asked the participants to rate the degree to which they experienced silencing of the mind. In addition we used a test developed by Susan Jackson at the University of Queensland[11] to assess their experience of the key features of flow during the same meditation session.

In this way we established that there was a close correlation between flow and mental silence; as the meditators became more mentally silent, their flow experience increased. Those meditators who experienced a state of complete silence also tended to score the maximum for flow.

So, it was clear that meditation and flow are closely related, and that this similarity could be scientifically verified. Moreover, the relationship between flow and mental silence was particularly strong. Was it possible to increase the flow experience with meditation training?

Next we looked at the impact of meditation on flow experienced by twenty-five senior managers in a multinational finance company's head office in Sydney. The importance of flow in the workplace is increasingly recognised. Employees who experience flow are more likely to find their work satisfying and are less likely to leave their jobs. They are also more likely to be productive and to engage with their organisation to advance its interests. This means higher morale and a more positive workplace culture. So, naturally, workplaces everywhere are looking for ways and means to increase the flow experience for their staff.

While it is logical to structure roles and tasks in such a way that people can achieve a level of engagement that facilitates the flow experience, it might be even more valuable if a worker could establish that experience independently of their task. This way, they could apply that peak performance state to whatever they are doing. Meditation has the potential to achieve this in workplaces, thereby reducing stress and improving productivity at the same time.

We trained the managers in meditation daily for two weeks. Each session lasted for 30 minutes. The first week involved simple meditation while the second week involved the addition of footsoaking (see pages 178–9 for details on how to do this). The sessions were held in the company's meeting rooms and were facilitated by a group of instructors with experience in teaching a simplified and secularised version of Sahaja yoga suitable for the workplace.

An important component of the strategy was the emphasis on the meditative experience of mental silence for stress management and as a performance enhancement strategy, since it facilitated the internal conditions for flow. The decision-makers were attracted to this idea but, like most good managers, they wanted evidence. So we incorporated a flow assessment to determine if meditation was, in fact, triggering flow-like experiences, and whether or not it might have the potential to increase those experiences.

After the first session of meditation the participants' flow scores were high, registering at about 72% of the maximum possible score for flow experience. In three further sessions, totalling about one hour of training, an improvement in flow occurred, bringing them to an average score of 84% of the maximum possible flow experience. So the initial flow levels were quite high but they improved substantially with brief practice.

Participants described how they were able to take that calm but focused state back into their daily work, with noticeable improvements in their perception of their performance. Again the correlation between flow and mental silence was substantial, and as the managers' ability to tap into mental silence improved, so did their ability to experience flow. The participants rated this series of training sessions as one of the best in-house professional development opportunities they had ever undertaken.

The third set of evidence has already been described in Chapter 11 where we assessed the impact of meditation on flow in a group of fifty senior high school students. To recap, we found that the flow experience of the meditation class was 50% greater compared to the class they had just prior. This finding gave us a glimpse at the potential for meditation in the creation of positive learning environments in schools.

In conclusion

What conclusions can we draw from these observations? First, that flow may be facilitated by manipulating the person's own internal environment towards mental silence. Second, the results of the explorations described here suggest that flow may be learnt using methods that are relatively independent of the external environment in which the person finds themselves or the task that they may be doing. Third, even a single session of meditation is sufficient to give a good flow experience, and brief additional training increases the flow experience substantially.

The studies so far have provided insights into the crossover between flow and meditation, with wide-ranging implications for those decision-makers in organisations looking for strategies that may provide sustainable ways to enhance performance.

Admittedly, these are just small field studies and they are unable to answer many important questions about whether or not this effect is specific to Sahaja yoga, or mental silence. However, when considered within the context of the other research detailed in this and other chapters, it is reasonable to conclude that mental silence is a flow state and that Sahaja yoga meditation is, therefore, a way of facilitating the flow experience. I would estimate that other approaches to meditation probably bring about flow-like experiences too since they also involve calmness combined with focused attention, but I think that the unique emphasis on developing the mental silence state is likely to make Sahaja yoga more effective. Nevertheless, this must be subjected to more thorough scientific research. Watch this space.

The equivalence between meditation and flow suggested to me that even those who are not directly looking for a meditative experience may actually be reaching it through other means. Most people learn how to trigger flow by trial and error. At one end of the spectrum their flow experience is just focused attention, but at the other, higher-quality end, flow is indistinguishable from the mental silence state and, thus, *is* meditation. It seems that people are looking, consciously or unconsciously, for ways to participate in the meditative experience and sometimes finding it, stumbling upon it, by engaging in intense tasks.

The possibility of accidental meditators, haphazardly tapping into optimal consciousness, suggests that there is an instinctive drive within us that seeks out places, situations and opportunities to push us closer to the meditative experience and the ideal state of being.

In the East, meditation, yoga and related practices have evolved to satisfy that instinctive seeking. Popular culture in the West has given rise to a variety of activities ranging from extreme sports, hobbies, art and entertainment – more than perhaps any other culture in the present or past. I have often wondered what drives the development of and participation in many of these activities. Is it just the pursuit of entertainment? I realise now that, despite the superficial differences between them, these activities can be understood as strategies aimed at triggering flow, at satisfying a deep urge to touch upon the optimal state of being. It seems that flow, like meditation, is a universal experience and that every culture has within it certain practices aimed at facilitating the attainment of optimal consciousness.

Implications

This intersection between Eastern and Western psychology has a number of exciting implications.

The Western discovery of flow and related phenomena and the realisation that it is a key contributor to human psychological fulfilment is fascinating because although the discovery occurred independently of the Eastern meditative tradition, it directly corresponds with it. This suggests to me that many people in one way or another are seeking some kind of optimal consciousness, an ideal state of being, and that mental silence is a central feature of that state.

For some reason Eastern culture, especially that of India, has given rise to clearly defined, socially and culturally validated pathways by which flow, optimal consciousness and the ideal state of being can be achieved. The field of positive psychology, and mental health generally, has therefore much to gain from close study of this aspect of ancient Eastern traditional culture. Western researchers looking for standardised strategies to trigger flow can gain a great deal from studying the yoga tradition since it can enable practitioners to tap into flow states on demand.

One of the most significant influences on Western culture is Sigmund Freud's idea that humans are primarily driven by instinctive subconscious and mundane desires for things such as sex and food. Yet the Western ideas of flow and peak experience, as well as the ancient Eastern ideas of meditation, demonstrate that there is another powerful instinct driving us toward sublime experience and the profound happiness associated with the state of optimal being.

The American constitution states that every individual has a right to pursue happiness. This has become a foundation concept of what is now known as 'the happiness movement'. Embraced by millions of people around the world, it has led to an abundance of books, gurus, television shows and other paraphernalia to help us achieve the 'happiness' goal. Yet scientific evidence shows we are less happy and more stressed than ever before. Could the American social philosopher Eric Hoffer be right when he said that, 'The search for happiness is one of the chief sources of unhappiness'?[12] It seems that somewhere in our pursuit of happiness, we have missed an important point – that happiness can't be achieved in a vacuum, but must come about as a by-product of being engaged with life.

This is why the notion of flow and the growing research into its effects is particularly significant – those who experience flow and peak experiences more regularly also have more lasting and meaningful happiness. Therefore, rather than being overly concerned with achieving happiness, we should become primarily concerned with achieving flow. From flow and peak experiences positive moods and feelings naturally follow within the context of a fruitful and productive life. The ancient methods of meditation and particularly mental silence are emerging as an effective and reliable way of finding the happiness of flow on a daily basis. Our research shows that Sahaja yoga meditation and the mental silence experience it elicits is one way that you can reliably and regularly 'catch' happiness. Moreover, it is something that, once learnt, can be shared with others, giving them the ability to catch it too.

> *There is a benevolent force flowing through all reality. When you are aligned with that force, you move forward with tremendous power.*
>
> Lao Tse

Words from meditators

> *I used to go through many difficult situations in my head while doing household jobs. It did not make work easy and I could not concentrate, dealing with all these bad feelings. Nowadays, since learning to meditate, my thoughts are much lighter, and often I am thoughtless. I am able to first finish one thing and then start another one, planning better and concentrating on what I am doing at the present moment and not thinking about what is to be done next.*
>
> Lenka, Finland

When I was twenty-eight years old, I learnt to meditate. Soon after, I enrolled in a part-time Masters programme in Mechanical Engineering while working full-time in a very demanding job. Being in the state of thoughtless awareness refreshed and rejuvenated me, enabled me to absorb lectures and reduced the stress of balancing my career and studies. I also found that my memory improved and I felt somehow 'guided' internally to the important aspects of whatever I needed to do. This allowed me to minimise my time and maximise my effectiveness in my work, studies and even in my life in general.

I was born with partial facial paralysis and have an 'undeveloped' left ear. The facial paralysis made the whole left side of my face droop, and I was not able to close my left eye properly – a problem that created endless problems of irritation. After about a year of meditation, the paralysis very gradually reduced. I was able to move more parts of my face and even my left eye could be closed more completely. This improvement still continues to this day.

Latha, Malaysia

PART VII
THE BRAIN IN MEDITATION

13
Brain, mind and non-mind

The highest activities of consciousness have their origins in physical occurrences of the brain, just as the loveliest melodies are not too sublime to be expressed by notes.

W. Somerset Maugham[1]

In 1990, the *Journal of the American Medical Association* (*JAMA*), one of the most influential medical journals in the world, published news of a curious discovery. An American physician, Dr Frank Lynn Meshberger, was touring the Sistine Chapel in the Vatican when he noticed something uncanny about the image popularly called *Creation*, one of the world's most iconic paintings.[2] Painted by Michelangelo in 1512 CE, it represents God reaching out from the heavens to touch Adam, and Adam reaching out from earth to touch God. The strangely shaped arrangement of drapery that surrounds God Almighty

and a cluster of other divine beings including a female –
widely thought to be Eve, Sophia, the Virgin Mary or the
Holy Spirit – and eleven other cherub-like children, was not
an arbitrary shape but, in fact, something very specific that
perhaps only a medico could have recognised so easily. When
Meshberger traced the outlines of the picture his hunch was
confirmed: the shape is an exact outline of the human brain,
accurately indicating its major internal structures in cross-
section (see figure below). He described his discovery in a
scholarly article that intrigued the editors of *JAMA* so much
that they approved it for publication.[3]

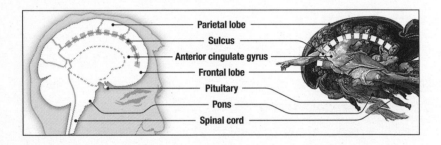

Michelangelo is not the only Renaissance painter to conceal an
image of the human brain in his art. Raphael's *Transfiguration* and
Gerard David's *Transfiguration of Christ* are two other examples.
However, what is particularly significant about Michelangelo's
image is that it is much more than just a painting with an image
of the brain carefully hidden inside. Close examination reveals
that its composition is so detailed and specifically contextualised
that it amounts to a commentary on the politics of the Catholic
Church and its control over philosophical thought and the nature
of human spirituality. Also, it is quite possibly a hypothesis
concerning the mechanisms in the brain by which human beings
experience higher states of consciousness.

The amazing discovery of the brain hidden in Michelangelo's *Creation* has many parallels with themes in this book: the idea that profound truths, such as the existence of mental silence, are often hidden in plain sight; the idea that higher states of awareness must necessarily involve biological events in the brain; and the idea that the state of optimal being or meditative awareness is more about an internal experience, a 'happening' rather than an intellectual concept or religious dogma.

In the appendix we look at many of the other coincidences in Michelangelo's painting in all their intriguing detail. In this chapter we explore the relationship between the mental silence experience and the brain.

Introducing the brain

The brain is as fascinating as it is poorly understood. Much of the challenge in trying to understand it arises from the fact that it is a sophisticated biological technology far surpassing anything that humans have yet created. The brain's basic building block is the cell or neuron, of which there are several billion. These neurons are interconnected in a dense, microscopic, three-dimensional array that involves at least ten trillion connections. The array uses a combination of electrical and chemical signals transmitted along microscopically thin channels that, if connected end to end, would total several hundred thousand kilometres.

Each second the brain produces millions of signals arranged across a variety of complex circuits and regions. Nature has created a super-computer inside the head of every person and animal that processes massive amounts of information every second, using only glucose for fuel. Our modern technology can't even hope to reproduce that level of subtle complexity, let alone fully comprehend it. Brain science is undergoing rapid growth and development, leading to many new insights and understandings about how the brain works. Two of these emerging areas are particularly relevant to the mental silence phenomenon that we have explored in this book: neuroplasticity and brain imaging.

Neuroplasticity

The phenomenon of neuroplasticity is an important way of understanding the brain that may help explain how meditation, and particularly mental silence, might influence it, and, consequently, the meditator's behaviour, health and wellbeing. It might also help to explain many of the results from the studies that we have described in previous chapters.

Until recently it was thought that the human brain developed until about mid-adolescence, after which time its circuits became locked together and that was how the brain was thought to stay for the rest of our lives. Now it is understood that the brain is continuously developing.[4] During childhood to early adulthood the brain's circuits undergo constant and extensive rearrangement as new experiences accrue, intellectual and emotional skills are acquired, hormones are released and growth occurs. Even once the brain has finished its major developmental processes, it continues to respond and change until the end of our life. Hence the idea of it being plastic, like plasticine, rather than rigid like concrete. This notion has some important ramifications for everyday life, and meditation in particular.

To appreciate the idea of neuroplasticity we need to understand some basic ideas about how thoughts and memories form in the brain. When we have a thought, idea, memory or emotion it occurs as a result of certain activity in the brain, at the level of the neurons and their interconnections, called synapses. For example, select a thought you might have had recently – that thought is represented in the brain by a circuit of neurons that have joined up with each other. When an electrical signal is transmitted around that circuit the thought is generated in our awareness. The synapses are reinforced every time the circuit fires. Now, if we never have that thought again those neurons rapidly lose their connection with each other, such that if the circuit doesn't fire again, the reason for the circuit to remain in existence subsides and the circuit dissolves within a few seconds. If, however, we have that thought several times, the circuit becomes reinforced and persists for much longer because the synapses are strengthened with each firing of the circuit. If the circuit is fired regularly the interconnections between the neurons can become long lasting, staying for weeks, months, years, or even a lifetime.

The wiring together of certain brain areas to create automatic units can occur on an even larger scale. Say we smell a rose and enjoy the experience of that fragrance – immediately our brain starts to connect the parts that are involved in that complex event: the colour red (perhaps); the image of the flower; the smell; the tactile sensation of the stem; the emotional content, which may be romantic love, spiritual devotion, a person or a place. Each of these factors activates a different part of the brain. If the same experience happens repeatedly, even only a few times, the brain starts connecting those areas together – 'areas that fire together wire together', say brain scientists – in such a way that after a number of repetitions the wiring together is so effective that if just one part of that complex experience is triggered (say, the fragrance) all the other associated experiences can be triggered as well. It's a kind of information-processing shortcut that helps the brain to work more efficiently. If the experience doesn't happen again for a long time these interconnections will disassemble themselves and the associations between those experiential factors are lost. Hence the other term that brain scientists use: 'Use it or lose it.'

Now apply this idea to patterns of thought and experiences that are not good for us, that cause us stress, make us have pessimistic feelings towards ourselves or others, or lead us to behave unconstructively. Certain negative thought patterns may have started out as an idle thought, but as we ruminated on them the brain circuit supporting that thought was reinforced, making it easier to have that thought again and again until it became very difficult to get rid of. Eventually, it became a habitual way of thinking – ultimately shaping our perception and behaviour. Similarly, our brain might have wired together certain negative thoughts and feelings with certain places, people or experiences. Those now fire together in a way that traps us into a complex habit of unconstructive or negative thoughts, feelings and behaviours.

Within this context, the benefits of mental silence become immediately obvious. The state of mental silence provides the opportunity to interrupt those negative-thinking patterns. By interrupting them the constant reinforcement of that negative wiring pattern is reduced, allowing those dysfunctional brain circuits to fade, and giving the meditator an opportunity to break free of the negative-thinking habits that those circuits created.

Changing negative mind habits

The ancient Greek sage and philosopher Epictetus once said, 'People are disturbed not by things but by the views which they take of them.' Some thousands of years later, psychologists realised the potential of this connection. David Burns, a professor of psychology at Stanford University, who is widely credited with the popularisation of cognitive behavioural therapy (CBT), said: 'By learning to change your thoughts, you can change the way you feel.'[5] The basic recognition that our mind has developed habits that result in things being interpreted either negatively or positively – which then influences the way we feel about them – seems like common sense. For psychologists, though, it was revolutionary, as many people are not even conscious of the fact that their mental habits are responsible for much of the way they deal with reality.

Neuroplasticity provides an even deeper level of understanding of this concept because it explains that these 'mind habits' are the result of certain brain regions wiring together to create 'dysfunctional brain circuits'. Strategies aimed at changing the way the mind perceives and reacts, hence changing those dysfunctional circuits, can lead to better results for many people.

CBT and positive-thinking strategies are based on the idea that some of those unwanted wiring patterns can be disassembled by recognising the pattern with which they are connected and then actively preventing the thoughts, or avoiding the events that trigger the whole circuit. The principle of plasticity underpins the method of CBT, which seeks to stop entrenched negative-thinking patterns and create and foster positive patterns. CBT is a remarkably effective, common-sense idea that is now widely recommended as first-line therapy for mild to moderate depression, for example.

As recognition of the usefulness of CBT has grown, so has the idea that encouraging positive thinking in general might also be beneficial. This is how the positive-thinking movement began and has mushroomed over the last two decades, spawning a plethora of books, courses, lectures and gurus. Yet when the hard science is taken to positive-thinking strategies, very little seems to happen at a measurable level. In fact there is now a growing realisation that while it is scientifically verifiable that negative thoughts and feelings are bad for you, forcing oneself to have positive thoughts and feelings doesn't seem to have the opposite effect. There are many health professionals who describe how they are often called upon to deal with the fallout of the positive-thinking fad. What many of these professionals observe is that forcing oneself to 'think positive' will not eliminate negative feelings.

Typically, a patient finds that despite their best efforts to make themselves think positively, they are unable to do so, or they discover that the course of their physical illness – or whatever problem they have set out to deal with using positive thinking – has not changed. Rather than realising the limitations of enforced positive thinking, the patient blames him or herself, which only magnifies the mental dimension of the problem. The frustration of failure sets up even more negative-thought and feeling cycles.

In other situations, people can misuse the concept of positive thinking to avoid facing unpleasant realities that are nevertheless essential to be faced and dealt with. In these situations positive thinking becomes a way of avoiding reality. The whole 'think positive' paradigm for many has thus degenerated into a destructive process of either self-blame or denial. This is not to say that there is not a role for positive thinking, but it is important to recognise the significant limitations of trying to change our thinking using thinking.

There are some situations in which the circuits are so deeply wired that our brain is simply unable to rewire itself, and the mind habits become so deeply entrenched that it's not possible to change the patterns using either positive thinking or CBT. Because deeply ingrained negative thought, emotion or behaviour patterns are often so persistent that they are very difficult to shut off, they constantly reinforce the dysfunctional wiring that supports them. It's probably the same reason CBT can be remarkably effective in people with mild to moderate disorders but seems to be less effective when dealing with more severe conditions.

This is where the experience of mental silence becomes particularly relevant. When our mind becomes overwhelmed with the burden of many different but more or less dysfunctional thinking patterns, a period of mental silence acts as a circuit-breaker, and could quite possibly be the best way to stop those negative-thinking circuits. It may even allow CBT and related strategies to work better. Meditation can provide the kind of downtime necessary for the disassembling of those entrenched neural circuits that have been built up around, and which perpetuate, each set of negative thoughts. So, when we find that positive thinking is not working it may be best to try a dose of *non-thinking*.

This new perspective may help explain the findings from a number of the studies described in previous chapters of this book. For example, in the work-stress study described in

Chapter 8 we observed substantially greater improvements in stress and related symptoms in those who practised the mental silence approach to meditation, compared to a non mental-silence approach such as relaxation. We also observed that those in the mental-silence group showed a significant change in the way they reacted to their work environment, whereas those in the non mental-silence group did not. Could this change in perception be due to the un-wiring of negative-thought habits and the re-establishment of more constructive ones – 'a positive rewiring' as a result of mental silence influencing the brain via neuroplasticity?

The children in our school-based programmes described in Chapter 10 did not receive any instruction from us on how to change the way they thought about themselves, stressful situations such as exams or how they related with others, and yet they reported improvements in all these areas. Could these changes have come about as a result of mental silence facilitating a spontaneous positive rewiring to allow more constructive feelings, thoughts and behaviour?

Similarly, it helps us understand why Golosheykin's study of long-term meditators (described in Chapter 8) who watched stressful video clips did not react as negatively as non-meditators. Could the meditation have facilitated a rewiring that reduced the likelihood of a negative reaction to the stressor?

This is your brain in meditation

What can the science of brain imaging tell us about what is happening in the brain in the state of meditation? Despite the fact that it is early days in this field of research, there are facts worth knowing about the brain and meditation. There are also a number of caveats that will help you critically appraise the next brain imaging 'discovery' that makes it onto the nightly news,[6] which I describe in some detail at www.beyondthemind.com.

Things that happen in the brain with or without mental silence

The research tells us that the most prominent brain functions involved in meditation are the mechanisms that manage our attention, regulate the effect of relaxation and modulate mood.[7] For example, when a meditator moves their attention away from external distractions and focuses it on an object or mantra, networks of neurons in the frontal and parietal lobes are activated. If the meditator brings their attention inside by focusing on their breath or an internal body state, they will also activate the anterior cingulate gyrus (which is part of the limbic system) as well as the insula. Meditation techniques that involve focus on an emotion also activate interconnections between the frontal lobes and the limbic system (the emotional core of the brain). Researchers have concluded that the frontal lobes and the interconnections between the frontal lobes and limbic system are thus a particularly important part of the meditative mechanism.

The sense of relaxation that occurs during most meditative practices appears to involve similar regions of the brain in addition to structures such as the amygdala, which is a centre in the limbic system involved in the experience of fear (and hence the fight-or-flight response – see www.beyondthemind. com for more about this) and parts of the thalamus, which is involved in physical regulation of the body. This makes sense since relaxation can only occur when the emotion of fear is reduced, and it is associated with specific events in the physical body such as the reduction of blood pressure, reduced activation of muscles, decreased heart rate and all the other features of the relaxation response that were described in Chapter 8.

The improved mood that most meditators report as a result of meditation also appears to be related to changes in activation of certain brain structures. It is well known, for example, that the left frontal lobe tends to deal with positive feelings – what we would describe as happiness – while the right lobe seems to deal with negative feelings. When the right lobe is more active than the left, we tend to have more negative feelings than positive. These emotions are generated as a result of interactions between the frontal lobes and the limbic system. Several studies have shown that during meditation there are increases in those parts of the brain that deal with positive feelings, namely, the left frontal lobe and its interconnections with the limbic system. Other studies have also shown increases in neurotransmitter chemicals such as serotonin, endorphins, dopamine and even melatonin in the brain and bloodstream that are associated with positive mood, many of which are produced in the limbic system.

Mental silence and the brain

With regard to mental silence, there are a small number of good quality studies, mostly looking at the mental silence experience triggered by Sahaja yoga, that provide important and fascinating clues into the nature of mental silence and how it might be differentiated from the non mental-silence approaches to meditation.

To appreciate the implications of these findings we need to understand the function of two important areas of the brain: the frontal lobes, located in the area of the forehead above the eyebrows, and the limbic system which is deep inside the centre of the brain. Generally speaking, these two areas function and interact to influence our behaviour, emotions, thinking, and what we're going to do with our life. Together they have a profound influence on our personality, who we are and how we feel. The other parts of the brain are the parietal lobes, at the top of the head, which primarily deal with the physical body; the occipital lobes at the back of the head that deal mostly with vision; and the temporal lobes, above the ears, which deal with auditory information.

The limbic system is, from an evolutionary point of view, an ancient structure that is found in both humans and lower animals, and is associated with survival instincts and emotions. The instinct to nurture our young, for example, or defend territory, are functions of the limbic system. The limbic system – and, in fact, emotion generally – has been studied by scientists with an inordinate interest in negative emotions such as fear, anger, anxiety and despair. However, researchers have only recently come to acknowledge that equally if not more important are the positive emotions such as happiness and love – since, after all, it is these emotions that we all aspire to achieve. The bias toward negative emotion is partly because the brain sciences emerged from the study of animals, mental illness (rather than mental wellness) and partly, I believe, because scientists seem to find it easier to identify negative feelings rather than positive ones. Whether or not this is a reflection of reality or a reflection of our culture is itself an important question.

Emotions originate from the limbic system but the nature of these emotions, either positive or negative, is strongly influenced by the frontal lobes, which communicate with the limbic system through a set of important fronto-limbic communication loops.

The frontal lobes are more or less the 'front portion' of the brain, the most important part of which is the pre-frontal lobe. The pre-frontal lobes are considered to be the newest and most evolved part of the human brain. Only a few animals – dolphins are the best example – have a similar, although more limited, version of the structure. Our pre-frontal lobes appear to give us the ability to experience human happiness and enjoyment of life. They also seem to be responsible for other important positive human qualities such as idealism, joy, our ability to concentrate, creativity, and our ability to think abstractly. The frontal lobes and the limbic system work in tandem to influence our experience. To put it simply, the frontal lobes interpret situations and events and then communicate that interpretation through the fronto-limbic loops to the limbic system, which then produces the appropriate emotion.

Now, with this knowledge, we might be able to better appreciate what's happening during the practice of Sahaja yoga, and hence the experience of mental silence.

A series of EEG-based studies conducted by Aftanas and Golosheykin provide the majority of good quality and useful data with regard to mental silence and Sahaja yoga.[8] In these studies, the brain activation patterns observed in association with this approach to meditation revealed a consistent pattern. These patterns were symmetrical rather than asymmetrical, involving the front and midline areas of the brain, suggesting a powerful interaction between the frontal lobes and the limbic system. The studies are described in more detail opposite.

Two groups of meditators were studied: novices (less than six months' practice) and advanced (three to seven years of practice). The meditators were each asked to meditate while wearing a set of EEG leads arranged inside a special cap which was designed to pick up the tiny electrical signals produced by the brain. Combining the EEG signals and using some sophisticated computing, they were able to produce two-dimensional maps of the electrical changes in the brain as the meditator entered into and remained in the state of meditation, similar to those shown in the images below.

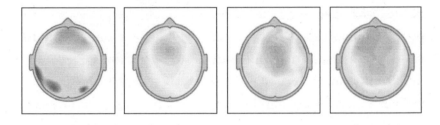

EEG changes as meditation progresses from onset to established meditative state

The study required the meditators to sit quietly for some time, then to commence meditation. Their brain activity was assessed before, during and after meditation. Each meditator was also asked to give a rating of their meditative experience.

As expected, the long-term meditators reported feeling a more positive mood, that is, happiness, and more mental silence than the novices. What was fascinating was that this subjective experience was reflected in the electrical activity of their brains. The long-term meditators had more theta and alpha activity than the novices, distributed evenly across the central parts of both the left and right frontal lobes.

In fact, there was a strong positive correlation between their ratings of happiness and the amount of theta activity in the midline of the brain across the two lobes. Similarly, their subjective rating of meditation had a strong, mathematical correlation with theta activity in the middle frontal and central brain regions. Theta activity in the frontal brain is thought to occur as a result of signals from the limbic system, anterior cingulate gyrus and prefrontal cortex. Other research has shown that this theta activity is associated with both emotional processing and focused attention.

In addition, the powerful relationship between positive mood and the electrical changes in the brain is strong evidence of specific involvement of the limbic system such that the brain regions that mediate positive emotions are more active, presumably by changing the way that the frontal lobes communicate with the limbic system. There thus appears to be a complex, symmetrical interaction between the frontal and limbic parts of the brain, presumably using the fronto-limbic communication loops mentioned earlier.

Importantly, the strength of these electrical changes seems to correlate very closely with two important factors. First, whether or not the meditator was advanced or a beginner. Advanced meditators had much more pronounced changes. Second, the degree of subjective meditation experience, especially positive mood, reported by the meditator – the deeper the experience the more profound the electrical changes in the brain. Very few other studies of meditation and the brain have been able to make such a connection between the subjective experience of meditation and objectively measured brain activation patterns. Another key feature of the findings was the remarkable degree of symmetry in activation across both sides of the brain. These findings point to these changes being crucial and specific to the mental silence experience. Studies of non mental-silence meditation do not appear to have shown the same patterns or relationships with the meditative experience. Brain studies of mindfulness, for example, appear to create an asymmetrical activation with an emphasis on left frontal lobe activation.

The fact that the subjective experience of Sahaja yoga meditation correlates closely with the objectively measured changes in the brain can be interpreted as biological evidence in support of the mental silence definition of meditation. This indicates that it is not just describing a conceptual framework but, in fact, a physiological reality that occurs during the meditative state.

It seems reasonable to conclude that the short-term dimension of mental silence is related to the alpha and theta activation patterns over the frontal and parietal surface of the brain giving rise to a sense of inner silence and positive mood. However, as we saw earlier in this chapter, the long-term impacts of mental silence may well arise as a result of neuroplastic effects that facilitate the elimination of negative thinking and emotional habits, and more complex dysfunctional neural networks associated with dysfunctional and maladaptive behaviours and negative 'mind habits'. Could the short-term effects of meditation, the alpha and theta activity, and all the biological activity associated with it, represent a brain state that somehow allows the long-term 'positive rewiring' to occur?

The molecules of silence

A final piece of evidence regarding the connection between the experience of meditation, the brain, positive mood and health comes from two small but fascinating studies assessing the levels of endorphins in the blood stream of meditators. Endorphins are a group of the body's own mood-enhancing chemicals. They are released by the brain and seem to act both on the brain's own emotion centres as well as on the body. Studies have shown that they are released in association with the emotion of love, during sport and eating chocolate, for example. Professor Ram Mishra, a neuro-pharmacologist from McMasters University in Canada, found that Sahaja yoga meditators had higher levels of endorphins after a single meditation session.[9] Jane Harte, an Australian researcher, made a similar finding when she studied meditators, some of whom used Sahaja yoga and some whom didn't.[10] Endorphins are thought to play an important role in pain reduction and mood elevation, and may even affect the immune system, which might explain some of the improvements in physical and mental health that we observed in the various studies described in this book. The degree to which mental silence is particularly associated with these or other blood-borne, naturally produced mood enhancers is yet to be studied more specifically.

The final frontier

There is a popular saying in neuroscience: 'The mind is what the brain does for a living.' But is this true? Certainly, from a Western scientific perspective the mind appears to be located in the brain. However, this book may have helped you to see that the capabilities of our brain that occur beyond the mind are equally important. We have seen that mental silence – what we might call the 'non-mind' function of the brain – is associated with specific benefits for physical and mental health as well as performance. So it may be more accurate to say that while one function of the brain is to 'do' the mind, another important function is its potential to 'do' the non-mind. The two functions just happen to share a certain amount of biological real estate.

Throughout this book the evidence and experiences have all conveyed one message: that meditation is not about modifying, editing or slowing the thoughts; it is about *stopping them altogether at will*. Not mindfulness but *mind-emptiness*. The experience of complete inner silence enables us to master the mind and the mental content that it creates.

Our awareness, no longer cluttered by unnecessary thinking, becomes capable of experiencing ourselves and our world more richly and with more joy. Meditation is not just about reducing stress, learning to relax or even improving mental or physical health. It is about unlocking our potential for higher, more dynamic awareness and performance. We have seen that although knowledge of how to trigger and cultivate mental silence has its origins in the ancient East, it is in fact a universal phenomenon frequently associated with the attainment of the optimal state of being. In the East this optimal state is called Sahaja, a state in which the body, the psyche and the soul find a synergistic integration to achieve complete fulfilment of their human potential. In the West, Carl Jung described the same concept as individuation and Abraham Maslow called it self-actualisation. Regardless of the cultural label, it is the realisation of the potential for wisdom and insight that exists in all of us, a potential that is unlocked whenever we go beyond the normal limitations of the human mind and its thinking activity.

Our modern scientific data concerning this state of being provides an important new dimension to this ancient understanding. It confirms that the meditative state, the state of mental silence, is not a clever philosophical concept or intellectual exercise but a discrete and specific experience, a state of awareness or a level of consciousness. In the state beyond the mind, our research shows that the positive impacts on mental and physical wellbeing may well be associated with specific, possibly unique, patterns of physiological activity in the body and brain.

The ancient tradition tells us that when we learn to silence the mind, that is when we have mastered it. As the mind is relegated to its rightful place as faithful servant, not only does our psyche change but so too does our entire being. The research in this book is the beginning of a completely new scientific journey: the exploration and understanding of that crucial dimension of human experience and capability that exists beyond the mind.

In Western culture, I continue to be fascinated by Michelangelo's fresco, in which he brilliantly concealed an image of the human brain, along with a profound philosophical message. To me, his fresco has come to symbolise what we have uncovered in our exploration of the mental silence phenomenon: optimal consciousness, the state beyond the mind, is not about a different way of thinking so much as a different way of using the human brain – a different way of being. Michelangelo's hidden image of the brain in *Creation* was not just a representation of God creating man but also a representation of the internal phenomena associated with the attainment of each individual's ultimate potential – a metaphorical snapshot of the brain in the midst of the meditative, peak experience, the neurobiology of mental silence and the ideal state of being, the Sahaja state.

Over the course of this book we have examined the scientific and cultural evidence for the phenomenon that is mental silence – a central feature of what might be called the optimal state of being. Our research has shown that virtually everyone has the potential to attain the experience, and that the techniques in this book are effective for the majority of people. Now it's up to you to verify this for yourself. If you achieve mental silence then please do show the people you love and care for how they can do it too. In my opinion, the ability to experience the state of mental silence is a priceless gift. Once you 'get it' it will become a life skill that will last forever.

The ultimate mystery of being is beyond all categories of thought …

Joseph Campbell[11]

This section has been prepared in consultation with a group of very experienced Sahaja yoga instructors. Together, we have compiled some answers to the most frequently asked questions.

Does it matter if I've never done meditation before?

Absolutely not. Most people who try this type of meditation are complete beginners who successfully achieve the desired stillness of mind during their first few sessions. In fact, our research has shown that people with no prior meditation experience seem to achieve the state of mental silence more quickly than those who have practised other techniques. This may seem counterintuitive; however, the difference is probably because it takes time for experienced meditators to disentangle themselves from ingrained habits, to 'un-learn'.

I've done other meditations previously – is this the same?

The reason this book exists is precisely because the mental silence experience is very different from that which occurs in other approaches to meditation. Importantly, our research demonstrates that this difference has real and practical significance. Sahaja yoga is easily learnt regardless of the individual's age, background or educational status. The fact that it is taught free of charge maximises accessibility of the benefits.

Why is it free?

This is an interesting question. It relates to the philosophical and spiritual roots of the meditation tradition in which it is recognised that meditation should be taught on an altruistic basis. The Buddha did not charge for his teachings, for example. This universal principle is relevant even today and so the founder of

Sahaja yoga, Shri Mataji, was emphatic that access to the skills and experience relating to it should be accessible to anyone regardless of their financial status or place in society. In keeping with these principles, Sahaja yoga is a not-for-profit community service, with no paid positions, conducted entirely by volunteer practitioners in their free time. Those who have been helped, help others. Sahaja yoga instruction is funded by voluntary donations from regular practitioners.

Can I add this to the mix of other meditations and New Age therapies I currently practise?

Our experience, both in the research programme and elsewhere, is that mixing the different practices often dilutes all of them and as a result the meditator misses the benefits altogether. Just as we would not consume every medicine in a pharmacy at once, so too it is more sensible to systematically trial and evaluate individual strategies until you find the one that gives you the best experience of mental silence. Rather than combining Sahaja yoga with other techniques, we suggest that you do it exclusively for 21 days, as a personal experiment, to determine if it works for you.

Are there any food exclusions? Do vegetarians have better results?

Diet is entirely a personal choice. Some people may decide they are more suited to one style of eating or another. In general, our experience has been that eating 'light and healthy' enhances meditative focus. We have found that people who have a richer, fatty diet (whether vegetarian or not) generally seem to find it more difficult to manage and sustain their attention, which has a negative effect on the quality of meditation. There is a broad misperception that somehow vegetarianism confers special benefits on the consciousness of those who practise it, or that it is somehow essential for successful meditation. Our research indicates that vegetarians and non-vegetarians are equally capable of experiencing mental silence.

Does it matter if I do / don't have any religious beliefs?

We have taught thousands of people from many different cultural and religious backgrounds how to meditate. Sahaja yoga meditation is freely available to everyone in over a hundred countries. It gives people the experience of peaceful meditation, irrespective of their belief system, race, gender, age or status. Participants in our research programme had a wide variety of religious and cultural perspectives but few found that these prevented them from practising or experiencing mental silence. In many ways the experience of inner silence might be described as a common thread that can be found in all religious traditions. However, it is important to point out that while the practice of meditation does not require anyone to give up their religious beliefs, we have found that those who hold fundamentalist religious beliefs - regardless of the denomination - sometimes feel that meditation is contrary to their values.

Do I have to sit cross-legged on the floor?

It doesn't matter whether you choose to sit on a chair, a cushion or the floor to practise meditation. Just sit comfortably so you are not distracted while meditating. If your legs are aching or you are experiencing some other physical discomfort, this can be unnecessarily distracting and thus make it more difficult to maintain your attention in the silence, so it is better to take a practical approach and adopt a position that suits you. Having said that, lying down is not always the best position to meditate in because it becomes tempting to drift off to sleep. On the other side of the coin, do not adopt a rigid or prolonged posture of any kind, since extreme physical effort is also not conducive to the meditative experience.

How long does it take to see a result?

It depends on the individual. Many people feel the peaceful silence immediately, some need a little more time practising the meditation techniques before having the desired effect. Keep meditating and let it work out. Don't try to convince yourself that it's happening; just wait for it to happen. My experience, as mentioned in Chapter 1, was that despite enjoying the meditation, it was some weeks before I had my first deep meditative experience. In our research we found that about 10-20% of people experienced mental silence quite profoundly the first or second time that they tried the practice, but with regular practice the majority of people did get the experience.

I felt very silent - how do I repeat it?

To repeat and strengthen that incredible feeling of touching the silence, keep meditating daily, using the affirmations to help settle your thinking. To go beyond thoughts, put your attention above your head, where you may have felt the cool sensation. You can also do clearing techniques such as footsoaking. Attending Sahaja yoga meditation classes in your local area can also be useful to pick up practical tips, and many people find the experience of group meditation particularly enjoyable.

Have I failed if I can't maintain the silence for long?

No, that's fine. Many people have brief periods of silence at first, and gradually extend and maintain the experience as they learn to master it.

I keep thinking.

Experiment with what works best for you, whether that is affirmations or particular techniques such as footsoaking. Don't be hard on yourself or expect perfection while you meditate. Forgive everyone, including yourself. Don't think about any particular person or circumstance, just feel the release of forgiveness, letting go of any hold the past has on you. Above all, have patience and a bit of persistence.

While meditating I felt some sensations on my hands and / or above my head – what were they?

Many regular Sahaja yoga meditators describe feeling cool – and sometimes warm – sensations on the hands and above the head. They describe it as feeling like a cool breeze. Professor Umesh Rai assessed skin temperature changes that occurred concomitant to these reports and found that regular meditators did manifest skin temperature reduction on the palms of the hands during meditation, and that as meditators became more experienced the drop in skin temperature became more profound. We observed a similar phenomenon in our preliminary research, and also found that the degree of temperature drop was directly related to the depth of inner silence that the meditator experienced (see page 137). However, while the sensation is not imaginary, it is difficult to explain how it happens from a scientific point of view. Given, though, that the skin temperature changes appear to be positively correlated with the experience of mental silence, it would be a reasonable assumption that feeling coolness on the hands is a good sign.

Sahaja yoga practitioners - and the founder of Sahaja yoga, Shri Mataji - have described this sensation as a spiritual energy corresponding to the *Kundalini* itself and the activation of the energy centres. I'll leave it to you to decide about which explanation you prefer. The most important thing to keep in mind is that you are experiencing mental silence.

I feel very peaceful when meditating, but don't feel anything on my hands or head.

Just enjoy the peace. The most important thing to keep in mind is that you are experiencing the state of mental silence. You may find that the skin temperature changes with further practice.

What should I use as a focus for my meditation?

We have frequently been asked about what is an effective focal point for this meditation. There is no one specific answer, as it may be different in varying situations. For example, at work or the beach, you might close your eyes and use some of the techniques to simply take your attention inwards, then above your head. When you have more time you might set up a meditation area at home. Many people use a candle flame, incense or pleasant music as a means of bringing the focus of their attention away from distracting thoughts and closer to the present moment. Focusing the attention internally, by paying attention to the movement of the breath or the general 'feeling within', is also useful. Ideally our attention should be directed at the space between the thoughts, or at the point at the top of the head or just above the top of the head.

Many Sahaja yoga practitioners have found it very useful to use a photo of the founder of Sahaja yoga, Shri Mataji, to assist in focusing their attention. This is quite an Eastern idea and there is no real way to understand this scientifically, so, like everything else in this book, I will leave it to you to decide through your own experience. I suggest that you experiment with each of the strategies above and choose whichever seems to help you experience mental silence the best.

When using a visual focus, whether it is a candle, the photo, a naturescape or something else, it is important not to use it in an extreme way. For example, don't stare at it without blinking or gaze at it for long periods of time. Just use it as a way of gathering your attention to one point and then, once your attention is focused, close your eyes and bring your attention from the focal point to within yourself. If your attention wanders when your eyes are closed, open your eyes, re-establish your attention on the focal point and then close your eyes again and bring your attention within and so on.

Can meditation cure diseases?

While we have observed remarkable results with the use of meditation and, indeed, our research does indicate that it is useful for improving physical wellbeing, we must recommend that you be cautious if you wish to use it to help you with a physical illness. You should be cautious both in the way that you use it and in your expectation of what kind of results may occur. Most importantly, you should not stop your normal treatments for the illness, and we strongly recommend that you consult your supervising health professional before you commence. This is not because meditation is dangerous, but we feel that it is important to understand that our experience shows it to be a remarkably effective meditation technique that, as a peripheral effect, has some physical benefits. It is not, however, intended to be a medical treatment.

With regard to mental illness, again, you should only consider trying meditation if your supervising mental health professional agrees that it may be beneficial. This goes for any kind of meditation, not just Sahaja yoga. If you have a serious mental illness that involves severe symptoms, such as psychosis or extreme feelings to harm yourself or others, then we do not recommend meditation of any kind. Do not stop any medication that you may be taking for your mental health condition unless your mental health professional expressly permits it.

Since meditating, my sense of wellness has significantly improved – do I still need to use my medical treatments?

We *do not* recommend that you stop any treatment unless your supervising health professional approves. Please consult with him or her and follow their advice.

How do I show my family / friends how to meditate?

First, it's important that you become familiar with the experience of mental silence. Once you are confident that you know what it is, then you can show others. There are many ways to assist your friends, family and loved ones to get the experience. You can sit down with them and read out the affirmations from the basic sequence on page 170. You can play audio or a video from the website (www.beyondthemind.com) and go through it together. You can send them a copy of this book, or lend them your copy. Once you have shown a few people, you will find that the affirmations are quite easy to remember and you will be able to recall them any time that the opportunity arises and someone wants to try it out.

Personally, I feel the most effective thing we can do for our society is to make this skill as widely available as possible, and as more and more people learn it, we will find that the individual balance that they achieve will lead to us having a more balanced society.

How do I learn more – are there classes and websites?

In a world where stress and lifestyle imbalance has a major impact on our health and wellbeing, Sahaja yoga practitioners adhere to a guiding philosophy of sharing the benefits of this simple method, and have provided free meditation classes as a community service in Australia since 1981. There are currently free weekly classes in 125 Australian locations, plus courses and one-day workshops. Beginners are welcome and everything is explained. There are also classes happening in more than 100 other countries around the world, all free of charge. For online meditations, podcasts, radio programme details, or to subscribe for workshops, news and events, refer to www.beyondthemind.com.

What happens at the free community-based classes and who attends?

There may be group meditations, explanatory sessions, information on how to maximise your experience and recorded lectures by the founder, Shri Mataji, explaining how Sahaja yoga meditation works. Attendees are ordinary people of all ages, from family groups to business professionals.

Does meditating with others enhance the experience?

Definitely, yes. People frequently report that they have pleasant meditations by themselves, but enjoy a stronger experience when meditating collectively.

Any tips on staying 'balanced' at work or in stressful meetings?

Try to establish a regular pattern of meditation, which will give you a better framework with which to deal with stress generally. Ideally, meditation should become a part of your daily lifestyle so that you meditate for about 5 to 10 minutes before leaving home for the day. That experience of inner silence should be carried with you for as long as possible while you deal with your various daily tasks. See how long you can maintain it during each day. When you feel that your sense of silence, calm or peacefulness needs replenishing try closing your eyes and taking a minute to do some of the brief meditations described in this book.

When you get back home, before sleeping, try meditating again. If the day has been particularly hectic, stressful or demanding, do the footsoaking as well. Once you have re-established the silence, go to bed and see if you can maintain that experience while sleeping by gently keeping your attention at the top of your head as you drift off to sleep. You should find that your sleep becomes more refreshing as a result.

Will consuming alcohol, cigarettes or drugs have an impact on my meditation?

Very simply, our experience would lead us to say that the answer is 'yes'. Our research with novice meditators has shown that people who have recently consumed alcohol, or who are regular consumers of alcohol, have a lower-quality experience of mental silence compared to those who consume less or none at all. Why is this? Presumably because alcohol and most other drugs exert their effects on the brain by impairing brain cell function. Meditation, however, relies on the optimal functioning of the brain and so it seems logical that any substance that impairs brain function is likely to reduce our ability to experience mental silence. Again, I suggest that you take an experimental approach and observe the quality of your meditations in relation to the times at which you have consumed alcohol or other substances. If you find that there is a relationship between consumption of alcohol and lower quality of meditation, for example, then it would seem sensible to reduce consumption. However, there is no dogmatic requirement with regard to this issue. Once again, allow your own experience of mental silence to shape your lifestyle choices.

What should I aim for when meditating?

You should be aiming to experience the five essential features of the meditation experience described on pages 100-1.

—

Sahaja yoga meditation is a paradox in that there are different ways to approach it, each with the aim of reaching the end result: finding the silence of being in the present moment. We all seek the peace that thoughtless awareness can offer. Behind Sahaja yoga are theoretical and practical features – philosophy, science, philanthropy, a 'universal' spiritual element, medical aspects, clinically proven benefits and an undeniable history of giving participants a deeply calm meditative experience. Yet whether you wish to approach it in a scholarly fashion, or know nothing about meditation and simply want to sit down and try it, the results are the same – it takes you beyond the mind into the stillness of mental silence.

Appendix:
The Michelangelo Code

Brain scientists spend much of their time assessing the workings of the brain, as it performs small, well-defined tasks, in the hope that such experiments will ultimately help them understand how the brain performs more common but highly complex functions. Not just functions that involve, say, mental arithmetic or reading a sentence, but functions that involve much more of the brain, such as creativity, problem solving and even the meditative experience.

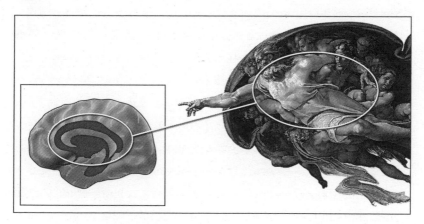

The God figure is placed in the limbic area of the brain

There are many layers of meaning in *Creation* and some fascinating coincidences worth exploring in detail. The most pertinent to this book is the profound commentary on the connection between spirituality and the brain. As a result of some odd coincidences this theme extends beyond just the anatomy of the brain into a field that has come to be known among modern researchers as the 'neural correlates of consciousness'.

Creation is one of a series of beautiful frescoes that adorn the walls of the Sistine Chapel, the chapel where the leaders of the Catholic Church meet as the Papal Conclave to elect each pope. For almost 2000 years it has been ground zero of one of the most influential institutions in Western civilisation. Despite the brilliance of the frescoes that he painted, Michelangelo did not regard himself as a painter. He took on this particular job, it seems, because he was coerced to do so by Pope Julius II.

Obviously, the image of the brain hidden inside Michelangelo's representation of the moment when God created man was no accident, so why hide it? At this time the Church was the most powerful organisation in Europe, if not the world. It controlled every aspect of life from international politics to individual thought. The Church was vehemently opposed to the study of the human body and anatomical dissection was taboo. Nevertheless, many Renaissance artists did secret dissections to learn more about the shape and structure of the body in order to enhance the realism of their artistic work. Often, their study of anatomy would extend into a study of how physical structure related to living function. How was it that the brain was responsible for the mind? And, the inevitable question, where in the body did the soul reside? These were dangerous questions at a time when the Church controlled all such areas of inquiry and discourse.

Some Renaissance artists, in acts of studied rebellion, incorporated images of the human brain into their paintings. Their patrons were usually devout Catholics, often Church leaders, who were none the wiser that their money had been used to create beautiful pictures complete with secretly embedded images defying the authority of the Church. It's no surprise, since the Renaissance period was all about the rise of humanism and was thus fundamentally at loggerheads with any organisation that might want to stifle exploration and expression of human potential.

Creation could be seen not only as subversive art but also as a commentary on the connection between consciousness and the brain. Amazingly, this level of meaning is filled by a series of coincidental convergences between certain details of Michelangelo's image and modern brain science. It's not only the anatomy that is remarkably accurate.

Frank Lynn Meshberger notes a number of unexpected but remarkably significant coincidences between the specific composition of the painting and specific functions (not just structures) of the brain. Functions that modern science has come to discover but were not known at the time of Michelangelo:

> *Below the right arm of God is a sad angel in an area of the brain that is sometimes activated on PET scans when someone experiences a sad thought. God is superimposed over the limbic system, the emotional center of the brain and possibly the anatomical counterpart of the human soul. God's right arm extends to the prefrontal cortex, the most creative and most uniquely human region of the brain.*[1]

It is certainly feasible for Michelangelo to have represented physical structures in his painting since he was well versed in human anatomy. However, it is not so easy to explain how he predicted the functional significance of structures such as the limbic system and the prefrontal cortex. Meshberger identified the only cherub whose face appears to be profoundly unhappy, perhaps even crying. More recent brain imaging studies provide further confirmation that this is one of the areas of the brain that is involved in severe prolonged depression. Intrigued by Meshberger's observations, I have been able to identify several more such coincidences, all of which can be verified by cross-referencing with published scientific research:

1. Meshberger already established that the God figure very closely corresponds to the location and shape of the limbic system. Earlier in this book we explored the important role that the limbic system plays in the generation of emotion and its potential role in the experience of meditation, especially the deeper states of meditation. More recent brain imaging research indicates that it is a special part of the limbic system, called the anterior cingulate cortex, that is probably the most significant contributor to the meditation experience.[2] Strangely enough, the exact location of the God figure's torso and shoulder, and even his very posture, seem to correspond to the location and shape of the anterior cingulate cortex.

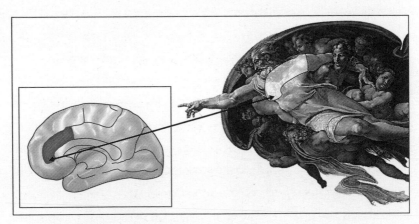

The anterior cingulate gyrus corresponds to the head, chest and shoulder of the God figure.

2. We also know that the anterior cingulate cortex plays a role in supporting attentional focus. We can see that the right arm of the God figure extends out from his head and shoulders (the location that precisely corresponds to the anterior cingulate cortex), through the front of the brain to reach out to Adam, thereby creating the famous near touching of God's and Adam's fingers. The gaze of God and Adam is locked, their attention clearly focused along the axis of this physical gesture. Thus, the very action of the God figure, with his attention so directly fixated on Adam, directly reflects the physiological function of the brain structure that his body has been positioned in. In fact, the entire composition of this painting seems to direct the viewer's attention as well. The painting seems to represent diagrammatically, metaphorically and experientially the process of focusing and directing attention.

3. Neuroimaging studies have demonstrated that the frontal lobes of the brain, where the major aspects of personality are said to reside, interact with the emotional centres in the limbic system along specific fronto-limbic loops.[3] You will also recall that the brain studies of Sahaja yoga meditation, for example, demonstrate that the meditative experience of mental silence involves a communication loop between the frontal lobes of the brain and the limbic system. Looking at the God figure, we can see that God's right arm extends out from the area that corresponds to the limbic system's

anterior cingulate cortex, through the frontal lobes of the brain to the prefrontal cortex. God's right arm therefore appears to diagrammatically and metaphorically correspond to the location and function of the fronto-limbic loops, presumably within the context of how humans might connect with the divine or higher consciousness.

4. About thirty years ago, neuropsychologists discovered that the left and right halves of the human brain operate in many ways like two distinct entities that communicate using a thick bundle of nerve fibres that cross between them, called the corpus callosum.[4] They discovered that the left brain preferred to deal with analytical, planning and calculation activities, while the right brain was the lateral thinker, preferring images, emotions and more intuitive behaviour. As a result, the right side of the brain is often described as being more feminine in nature, whereas the left side of the brain is more masculine. Looking closely at the image, you will see that the male God figure is located more towards the left side whereas the female figure is located more towards the right side.

5. Golosheykin's neuroimaging studies[5] demonstrated that during meditation there is an area of alpha and theta activity at the midline front of the brain and also in the midline parietal area (top) of the brain. By coincidence, the arm of the God figure reaches out to Adam through the midline front of the brain – one of the areas where alpha/theta activity was observed to occur during meditation – and the top of the God

figure's head touches the same area that corresponds to the midline parietal area of the brain – the other area in which the alpha/theta activity occurred.

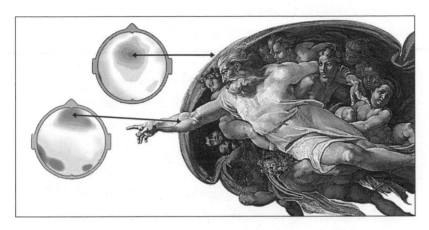

Areas of increased alpha theta activity in the frontal and parietal areas of the brain and corresponding locations in the fresco.

There is no rational explanation for these fascinating coincidences, and yet whether he knew it or not, Michelangelo's painting amounts to a visual metaphor for a hypothesis explaining the biological underpinnings of meditation. He has supplanted the idea of blind faith with the idea of a neurophysiological event. In this context, and given all that has been discussed in previous chapters of this book, we might speculate further by suggesting that in the iconic image of God's finger reaching out to Adam's, the small space that was purposely left between them may be a metaphor for the space between the thoughts, the dimension of meditative experience that the ancient tradition says is, in fact, the place where the human awareness connects with a higher principle.

I am not suggesting that Michelangelo was a brain scientist nor that he knowingly composed this work to portray these neurophysiological functions. I am proposing, however, that this is an example of how insights generated by artistic intuition can lead to discoveries about nature in the same way that scientific insight does. Perhaps the 'eureka' moments of scientific discovery and the process of artistic creation are very similar as far as brain function is concerned. This is all the more fascinating when we consider that Csikszentmihalyi's initial research into flow was based on experiences described by visual artists and the creative process. Flow, you will recall, is itself frequently associated with higher creativity and insight. Similarly, we have seen how meditation and peak experience are associated with their own kinds of profound perceptions. Michelangelo's artistic intuition led him to represent aspects of reality that he could not have consciously known about. Yet that creative insight was so profound that it delivered a level of detailed knowledge that required a further 500 years of scientific progress for us to appreciate.

It is said that Michelangelo would become so engrossed in his fresco that he would paint for days without stopping for food or sleep, to the point of passing out. Many of the greatest scientists, including Albert Einstein, described the profoundly important role that intuition played in their scientific discoveries. I propose that both scientific and artistic intuition occur when tapping into insights that arise in the state beyond the mind. Perhaps the scientist, artist and mystic are all striving to activate the same structures and function of the brain.

Five hundred years ago, in one of the strangest coincidences of art and science, Michelangelo concealed a message that closely reflects the ancient understandings of Eastern meditation hidden inside one of the most iconic pictures of Western Christianity. It subverts the authority of organised religion in favour of personal spiritual consciousness while at the same time describing the very mechanisms in the brain by which higher consciousness might come about. Michelangelo's painting, with all its hidden meanings, is in effect a proposal to humanity that artistic inspiration, scientific insight and yogic mystical experience may in fact all be the product of the same higher consciousness. It is a pictorial representation of the spectacular capabilities that reside within the human brain. Capabilities that, I propose, are awakened in association with the mental silence experience.

Let us be silent that we may hear the whispers of the Gods.
Ralph Waldo Emerson[6]

Endnotes

CHAPTER ONE: THE ANTS

1.   Umesh Rai, *Medical Science Enlightened: New Insight into Vibratory Awareness for Holistic Health Care*, New Delhi: Life Eternal Trust, London, 2005. – Deepak Chugh, *Effect of Sahaja Yoga Practice on the Patients of Psychosomatic Diseases*, Delhi University, 1987, p. 51. – U.C Rai, S. Setji & S.H. Singh, 'Some effects of Sahaja yoga and its role in the prevention of stress disorders', *Journal of International Medical Sciences Academy*, vol. 2, no. 1, 1988, pp 19–23. – U. Panjwani, H.L. Gupta, S.H. Singh, W. Selvamurthy & U.C. Rai, 'Effect of Sahaja yoga practice on stress management in patients of epilepsy', *Indian Journal of Physiology and Pharmacology*, vol. 39, no. 2, 1995, pp 111–116. – H.L. Gupta, U. Dudani, S.H. Singh, S.G. Surange & W. Selvamurthy, 'Sahaja yoga in the management of intractable epileptics', *Journal of the Association of Physicians of India*, vol. 39, no. 8, 1991, p. 649. – U. Panjwani et al. 'Effect of Sahaja yoga practice on stress management in patients of epilepsy', op. cit, pp 111–116. – U. Panjwani, W. Selvamurthy, S.H. Singh, H.L. Gupta, S. Mukhopadhyay, & L. Thakur, 'Effect of Sahaja yoga meditation on auditory evoked potentials (AEP) and visual contrast sensitivity (VCS) in epileptics', *Applied Psychophysiology and Biofeedback*, vol. 25, no. 1, 2000, pp 1–12. – U. Panjwani, W. Selvamurthy, S.H. Singh, H.L. Gupta, L. Thakur & U.C Rai, 'Effect of Sahaja yoga practice on seizure control & EEG changes in patients of epilepsy', *Indian Journal of Medical Research*, vol. 103, 1996, pp 165–172.

CHAPTER TWO: THE PATH TO RESEARCH

1.   Thomas Carlyle, *Sartor Resatus*, Taylor & Francis, 1926.
2.   R. Manocha, G. Marks, P. Kenchington, D. Peters & C. Salome, 'Sahaja yoga in the management of moderate to severe asthma: A randomised controlled trial', *Thorax*, vol. 52, no. 2, 2002, pp110–115.
3.   Guy Claxton, *Hare Brain, Tortoise Mind: How Intelligence Increases When You Think Less*, Harper Collins, New York, 1999.
4.   Mihaly Csikszentmihalyi, *Flow: The Psychology of Optima Experience*, HarperCollins Publishers, New York, 2008. – Abraham Maslow, *Religions, Values and Peak-Experiences*, Penguin Arkana, 1994.

CHAPTER THREE: DEFINING MEDITATION

1.   Boorstin, quoted by Edward Bond in *Washington Post*, 29 January, 1984.
2.   Herbert Benson, *The Relaxation Response*, HarperCollins Publishers, New York, 2001.
3.   Maria Ospina, Kenneth Bond, Mohammad Karkhaneh, Lisa Tjosvold, Ben Vandermeer, Yuanyuan Liang, Liza Bialy, Nicola Hooton, Nina Buscemi,

Donna Dryden & Terry Klassen, 'Meditation practices for health: State of the research', *University of Alberta*, vol. 155, 2007, pp 1–263.

4.   Ramesh Manocha, 'Does meditation have a specific effect? A systematic experimental evaluation of a mental silence orientated definition', University of New South Wales, Sydney, 2008.

5.   Georg Feuerstein, 'Yoga and Meditation (Dhyana)', *Santosha.com*, 2006, <www.santosha.com/moksha/meditation1.html>.

6.   Stephen Mitchell (trans.), 'Tao Te Ching', Mindfully.org, <www.mindfully. org/Tao-Te-Ching-Lao-tzu.htm>.

7.   E. Ernst, 'A historical perspective on the placebo', *Clinical medicine*, vol. 8, no. 1, 2008, pp 9–10.

8.   Benson Herbert & Richard Friedman, 'Harnessing the power of the placebo effect and renaming it "remembered wellness"', *Annual Review of Medicine*, vol. 47, 1996, pp193–99.

9.   S. Hollon & K. Ponniah, 'A review of empirically supported psychological therapies for mood disorders in adults', *Depress Anxiety*, vol. 27, no. 10, 2012, pp 891–932.

CHAPTER FOUR: SPECIFIC EFFECTS - UNDERSTANDING THE EVIDENCE

1.   Kahlil Gibran, *A Tear and a Smile*, Knopf Doubleday Publishing Group, 1950.

2.   Ramesh Manocha, 'Does meditation have a specific effect? A systematic experimental evaluation of a mental silence orientated definition', University of New South Wales, Sydney, 2008.

3.   Maria Ospina, Kenneth Bond, Mohammad Karkhaneh, Lisa Tjosvold, Ben Vandermeer, Yuanyuan Liang, Liza Bialy, Nicola Hooton, Nina Buscemi, Donna Dryden & Terry Klassen, 'Meditation practices for health: State of the research', *University of Alberta*, vol. 155, 2007, pp 1–263.

4.   Ramesh Manocha, Deborah Black & Leigh Wilson, 'Quality of life and functional health status of long-term meditators', *Evidence-Based Complementary and Alternative Medicine*, 2012.

5.   R. Manocha, D. Black & B. Semmar, (2007). 'A pilot study of a mental silence form of meditation for perimenopausal women.' *Journal of Clinical Psychology in Medical Settings*, 14(3):266–273.

6.   L. Harrison, R. Manocha & K. Rubia, 'Sahaja yoga meditation as a family treatment programme for children with attention deficit-hyperactivity disorder', *Clinical Child Psychology and Psychiatry*, vol. 9, no. 4, 2004, pp 479–497.

7.   R. Manocha, G. Marks, P. Kenchington, D. Peters & C. Salome, 'Sahaja yoga in the management of moderate to severe asthma: A randomised controlled trial', *Thorax*, vol. 52, no. 2, 2002, pp110–115.

8.   R. Manocha, D. Black, J. Sarris & C. Stough, 'A randomized, controlled trial of meditation for work stress, anxiety and depressed mood in full-time workers', *Evidence-Based Complementary and Alternative Medicine*, 2011.

9.   Mihaly Csikszentmihalyi, *Flow: The Psychology of Optimal Experience*, HarperCollins Publishers, New York, 2008.

10.   Susan Jackson & Mihaly Csikszentmihalyi, *Flow in Sports: The Keys to Optimal Experiences and Performances*, Human Kinetics, Champaign, 1999.

CHAPTER FIVE: MENTAL SILENCE - A UNIQUE DISCOVERY

1.   'The complete site on Mahatma Gandhi', *Gandhi Research Foundation*, <www.mkgandhi.org/>.
2.   Carl Jung & Richard Wilhelm (trans.), *The Secret of the Golden Flower: A Chinese Book of Life*, Houghton Miffl in Harcourt, New York, 1970.
3.   Ramesh Manocha, 'Intervention Insights: meditation, mindfulness and mind-emptiness', *Acta Neuropsychiatrica*, vol. 23, no. 1, 2011, pp 46–47. – Ramesh Manocha, 'Why Mediatation?', *Australian Family Physician*, vol. 29, no. 12, 2000, pp 1135–1338.
4.   Ramesh Manocha, Deborah Black & Leigh Wilson, 'Quality of life and functional health status of long-term meditators', *Evidence-Based Complementary and Alternative Medicine*, 2012.

CHAPTER SIX: THE ANCIENT PARADIGM

1.   Rene Descartes, *The method, meditations and Philosophy of Descartes: Translated from the original texts, with a new introductory essay, historical and critical by John Veitch and a special introduction by Frank Sewall*, Tudor Publishing Co, New York, 1901.
2.   Georg Feuerstein, 'Yoga and Meditation (Dhyana)', Santosha.com, 2006, <www.santosha.com/moksha/meditation1.html>.
3.   Juan Mascaro, *The Bhagavad Gita*, Penguin Books, Baltimore, 1962.
4.   Juan Mascaro, *The Upanishads*, Penguin Books, Baltimore, 1965.
5.   Ibid
6.   Chester Messenger (trans.), 'Yoga Sutras of Patanjali', *The Reluctant Messenger*, <www.reluctant-messenger.com/yoga-sutras. htm>.
7.   Stephen Mitchell (trans.), 'Tao Te Ching', *Mindfully.org*, <www.mindfully.org/Tao-Te-Ching-Lao-tzu.htm>.
8.   Chuang Tzu, Solala Towler (trans.), *The Inner Chapters: The Classic Taoist Text*, Watkins, 2010.
9.   Yoshito S. Hakedas (trans.), 'The awakening of the faith in Mahayana', Columbia University Press, 1967, <http://www.acharia.org/downloads/the_awakening_of_faith_in_mahayana_english.pdf>.
10.   Surendranath Dasgupta, *A History of Indian Philosophy*, vol. 1, Cambridge University Press, Cambridge, 1963.
11.   Carl Jung & Richard Wilhelm (trans.), *The Secret of the Golden Flower: A Chinese Book of Life*, Houghton Miffl in Harcourt, New York, 1970.
12.   J. Noyce, *Seeking and finding*, Noyce Publishing, 2006.
13.   'Contemplative Meditation', The Cloud of Unknowing, <contemplativemeditation.weebly.com/the-cloud-of-unknowing.html>
14.   Saint John of the Cross, Kieran Kavanaugh (trans.) & Otilio Rodriquez (trans.), *The Collected Works of John of the Cross*, ICS Publications, Washington, 1991.
15.   'Psalm 62:5', *Biblos.com: Search, Read, Study*, <http://bible.cc/psalms/62-5.htm>.
16.   'Psalm 62:5', *Biblos.com: Search, Read, Study*, <http://bible.cc/psalms/62-5.htm>.
17.   'Revelations 8:1', *Biblos.com: Search, Read, Study*, <http://bible.cc/revelation/8-1.htm>.
18.   Victor Sogen Hori, Steve Heine (ed.) & Dale S. Wright (ed.), *The Koan: Texts and Contexts in Zen Buddhism*, Oxford University Press, Oxford, 2000.

19. Hu Ming Ching & Richard Wilhelm (ed.), 'Scripture of wisdom and life', *Hui-ming Ching*, <http://www.taodirectory.co.uk/phocadownload/huiming.pdf>.

20. Arthur Osborne (ed.), *The Teachings of Ramana Maharshi in His Own Words*, 5th ed., Tiruvannamalai/Sri Ramanasramam, India,1988.

21. S. Cohen, *Reflections: On Talks with Sri Ramana Maharshi*, 5th ed., Sri Ramanasramam, India, 2006.

22. Henri Cartier-Bresson in Piers Moore Ede, *All Kinds of Magic: A Quest for Meaning in a Material World*, Bloomsbury Publishing, London, 2010.

23. J. S. Neki, 'Sahaja: an Indian ideal of mental health', *Psychiatry*, vol. 38, no. 1, 1975, pp 1–10.

24. S. Cohen, *Reflections: On Talks with Sri Ramana Maharshi*, 5th ed., Sri Ramanasramam, India, 2006.

25. Ibid.

26. Nigel Powell (ed.), *Meditation: The Joy of Spiritual Self Knowledge through Sahaja Yoga Meditation*, Corvalis Publishing, London, 2005.

27. Her Holiness Shri Mataji Nirmala Devi, *Meta Modern Era*, 3rd edition, Vishwa Nirmala Dharma, 1997.

28. William Wordsworth, *The Complete Poetical Works*, Macmillan and Co, London, 1888.

29. Baseball player Satchel Paige (1906–1982) is credited for saying this, although no date for his having said this is given. It can also be found in Winnie the Pooh (pub 1926) by A.A. Milne (1882–1956), or *The House at Pooh Corner* (pub 1928) also by A.A. Milne, Hoff, Benjamin, Egmont Books Ltd, London, 2003.

30. Jonathan Hales, *Star Wars: Episode II – Attack of the Clones*, directed by George Lucas, spoken by Yoda, 2002.

31. L. Wright, 'Meditation: myths and misconceptions', *Alternative Therapies in Health and Medicine*, vol. 7, no. 2, 2001, p 96.

CHAPTER SEVEN: A THOUGHT EXPERIMENT THAT ENDS IN SILENCE

1. Paul Moliken (ed.), *Transcendentalism: Essential Essays of Emerson & Thoreau*, Prestwick House, 2008.

2. William James, 'The varieties of religious experience: A study in human nature', *Gifford lectures: University of Edinburgh*, 1901–1902, <http://www2.hn.psu.edu/faculty/jmanis/wjames/Varieties-Rel-Exp.pdf>

3. Juan Mascaro, *The Upanishads*, Penguin Books, Baltimore, 1965.

4. 'Foreword to Aldous Huxley's "Brave New World"', *mrtom.com*, <http://www.mrtom.com/quotes/huxley_essay.htm>.

CHAPTER EIGHT: STRESS – THE NOISE IN THE MIND

1. Aldous Huxley, *The Perennial Philosophy: An Interpretation of the Great Mystics, East and West*, Harper Perennial Modern Classics, 2009.

2. 'Stress in America Findings', *American Psychological Association*, 9 November 2010, <www.apa.org/news/press/releases/stress/national-report.pdf>.

3. 'Gallup Wellbeing', *Gallup.com*, <www.gallup.com/poll/wellbeing.aspx>.

4. J. Helliwell (ed.), Richard Layard (ed.) & Jeffery Sachs (ed.), 'World Happiness Report', *Columbia University*, New York, 2012.

5. 'Stress in America: Our Health at Risk', *American Psychological Association*, 11 January 2012, <www.apa.org/news/press/releases/stress/2011/fi nal-2011. pdf>. – Colin Mackay, Rosanna Cousins, Peter Kelly, Steve Lee & Ron McCaig, 'Management standards and work-related stress in the UK: Policy background and science', *Work and Stress*, vol. 18, no. 2, 2004, pp 91–112.

6. H. J. Eysenck, 'Personality, stress and cancer: predicition and prophylaxis', *Journal of Med Psychology*, vol. 61, pt. 1, 1988, pp 57–75.

7. M. Kalia, 'Assessing the economic impact of stress – the modern day hidden epidemic', *Metabolism*, vol. 51, no. 6, suppl. 1, 2002, pp 49–53 – *The American Institute of Stress*, <http://www.stress.org>.

8. Clive Hamilton & Richard Denniss, *Affluenza*, Allen & Unwin, 2006.

9. Helena Britt, Graeme C. Miller, Joan Henderson & Clare Bayrum, 'Patient-based substudies from BEACH: abstracts and research tools 1999-2006', *Australian GP Statistics and Classification Centre*, 2007.

10. J. Manuso, *Testimony to the president's commission on mental health*, US Government Printing Office, Washington, 1978.

11. Jane Dixon, Bob Douglas & Richard Eckersley, *The Social Origins of Health and Well-being*, Cambridge University Press, Cambridge, 2001 – Richard Eckersley, *Measuring Progress: Is life Getting Better?*, CSIRO Publishing, Collingwood, 1998.

12. Hans Selye, *The Stress of Life*, McGraw-Hill, New York, 1956.

13. Cary Cooper & Philip Dewe, *Stress: A Brief History*, Wiley-Blackwell, Malden, 2004.

14. L. Aftanas & S. Golosheykin, 'Impact of regular meditation practice on EEG activity at rest and during evoked negative emotions', *International Journal of Neuroscience*, vol. 115, no. 6, 2005, pp 893–909.

15. 'Conditions of Work Digest: Preventing Stress at Work', *International Labour Office*, Geneva, 1992.

16. M. Kalia, 'Assessing the economic impact of stress – the modern day hidden epidemic', *Metabolism*, vol. 51, no. 6, suppl. 1, 2002, pp 49–53 – *The American Institute of Stress*, <http://www.stress.org>.

17. 'The Cost of Workplace Stress in Australia', *Medibank Private*, August 2008, <www.medibank.com.au/client/documents/pdfs/the-cost-of-workplace-stress.pdf>.

18. J. Jones, C. Huxtable, J. Hodhson, M. Price, 'Self-reported work related illness in 2001/2: Results from a household survey', *HSE*, 2003, pp 207–33.

19. 'Self-reported work-related illness and workplace injuries in 2006/07: Results from the Labour Force Survey', *HSE*, 2008. – R.Z. Goetzel, D.R. Anderson, R.W. Whitmer, R.J. Ozminkowski, R.L. Dunn, J. Wasserman, 'The relationship between modifiable health risks and health care expenditures: An analysis of the multi-employer HERO health risk and cost database', *Journal of Occupational and Environmental Medicine*, vol. 40, no. 10, 1998, pp 843-54.

20. Stress in America Findings, *American Psychological Association*, 9 November 2010, <www.apa.org/news/press/releases/stress/national-report.pdf>

21. James Bright, Angela Clow, Angela & Fiona Jones, *Stress: Myth, Theory and Research*, Prentice Hall, Harrow, 2001.

22.   Ramesh Manocha, 'Can meditation reduce work stress?', *OHS Alert*, February 2009.

23.   Ramesh Manocha, Amy Gordon, Deborah Black, Gin Malhi, 'Using meditation for less stress and better wellbeing: A seminar for GPs', *Australian Family Physician*, vol. 38, no. 2, 2009, pp 369–464.

24.   DHS: The Kessler Psychological Distress Scale (K10). In: Services, DoH, editor: Centre for Population Studies in Epidemiology, 2002:1–2.

25.   Susan Schneider, Maurizio Zollo, Ramesh Manocha, 'Developing Socially Responsible Behaviour in Managers: Experimental Evaluation of Traditional Vs. Innovative (Meditation) Learning Approaches', *Journal of Corporate Citizenship*, 2011. – Donal Crilly, Susan Schneider, Maurizio Zollo, 'Psychological antecedents to socially responsible behaviour', *European Management Review*, vol. 5, no. 3, 2011, pp 175–190.

26.   R. Manocha, D. Black, J. Sarris & C. Stough, 'A randomized, controlled trial of meditation for work stress, anxiety and depressed mood in full-time workers', *Evidence-Based Complementary and Alternative Medicine*, 2011.

27.   Ramesh Manocha, 'Does meditation have a specific effect? A systematic experimental evaluation of a mental silence orientated definition', *University of New South Wales*, Sydney, 2008.

28.   David Holmes, 'To meditate or rest? The answer is rest', *American Psychologist*, vol. 40, no. 6, 1985, pp 728–31.

29.   R. Manocha, D. Black, J. Ryan, C. Stough & D. Spiro, 'Changing definitions of meditation: Physiological corollorary', *Journal of the International Society of Life Sciences*, vol. 28, no. 1, 2010.

30.   H. Benson, F. Frankel, R. Apfel, M. Daniels, H. Schniewind, J. Nemiah, P. Sifneos, K. Crassweller, M. Greenwood, J. Kotch, P. Arns & B. Rosner, 'Treatment of anxiety: a comparison of the usefulness of self-hypnosis and a meditate relaxation technique: An Overview', *Psychotherapy and Psychosomatics*, vol. 30, no. 3–4, 1978, pp. 229–42. – David Holmes, *The influence of meditation versus rest on physiological arousal: A second examination*, Clarendon Press, Oxford, 1987, pp. 81–103. – Herbert Benson, *The Relaxation Response*, HarperCollins Publishers, New York, 2001.

31.   'Sri Granth', <*SriGranth.org*, www.srigranth.org/servlet/gurbani. gurbani?S=y>

32.   Juan Mascaro, *The Dhammapada: The Path of Perfection*, Penguin Books, Harmondsworth, 1973.

33.   John Noyce, *Seeking and Finding: a sourcebook of historical texts on Kundalini, yoga, realization, Sahaja and nirvikalpa-samadhi*, Noyce publishing, 2006.

CHAPTER NINE: BEYOND THE MIND-BODY CONNECTION

1.   Alan Watkins, *Mind-body Medicine: A Clinician's Guide to Psychoneuroimmunology*, Elsevier Health Sciences, London, 1997.

2.   James Le Fanu, *The Rise and Fall of Modern Medicine*, Carroll & Graf Publishers, New York, 2000.

3.   H.L. Gupta, U. Dudani, S.H. Singh, S.G. Surange & W. Selvamurthy, 'Sahaja yoga in the management of intractable epileptics', *Journal of the Association of Physicians of India*, vol. 39, no. 8, 1991, p. 649. – U. Panjwani,

H.L. Gupta, S.H. Singh, W. Selvamurthy & U.C. Rai, 'Effect of Sahaja yoga practice on stress management in patients of epilepsy', *Indian Journal of Physiology and Pharmacology*, vol. 39, no. 2, 1995, pp 111–116. – U. Panjwani, H.L. Gupta, S.H. Singh, W. Selvamurthy & U.C. Rai, 'Effect of Sahaja yoga practice on stress management in patients of epilepsy', ibid. – U. Panjwani, W. Selvamurthy, S.H. Singh, H.L. Gupta, S. Mukhopadhyay, & L. Thakur, 'Effect of Sahaja yoga meditation on auditory evoked potentials (AEP) and visual contrast sensitivity (VCS) in epileptics', *Applied Psychophysiology and Biofeedback*, vol. 25, no. 1, 2000, pp 1–12. – U. Panjwani, W. Selvamurthy, S.H. Singh, H.L. Gupta, L. Thakur & U.C Rai, 'Effect of Sahaja yoga practice on seizure control & EEG changes in patients of epilepsy', *Indian Journal of Medical Research*, vol. 103, 1996, pp 165–172.

4.   J.E. Rossouw, G.L. Anderson, R.L. Prentice, et al, 'Risks and benefits of estrogen plus progestin in healthy postmenopausal women: principal results from the Women's Health Initiative randomized controlled trial', *JAMA*, vol. 288, no. 3, 2002, pp 321–33. – G.L. Anderson, R.T. Chlebowski, J.E. Rossouw, et al, 'Prior hormone therapy and breast cancer risk in the Women's Health Initiative randomized trial of estrogen plus progestin', *Maturitas*, vol. 55, no. 2, 2006, pp 103–15. – J.V. Porch, I.M. Lee, N.R. Cook, K.M. Rexrode & J.E. Burin, 'Estrogen-progestin replacement therapy and breast cancer risk: the Women's Health Study (United States)', *Cancer Causes Control*, vol. 13, no. 9, 2002, pp 847-54.

5.   Jamie L. Habib, (2012). 'Misreporting and Poorly Presented Results Shrouded Benefits of HRT', *OBGY.net*. <http://hcp.obgyn.net/menopause/content/article/1760982/2081471>.

6.   R. Manocha, D. Black & B. Semmar, (2007). 'A pilot study of a mental silence form of meditation for perimenopausal women.' *Journal of Clinical Psychology in Medical Settings*, 14(3):266–273.

7.   Helen Tobler, 'A meditative approach to menopause', *The Weekend Australian*, 13 July 2002.

8.   Deepak Chugh, *Effect of Sahaja Yoga Practice on the Patients of Psychosomatic Diseases*, Delhi University, 1987, p. 51. – Umesh Rai, *Medical Science Enlightened: New Insight into Vibratory Awareness for Holistic Health Care*, New Delhi: Life Eternal Trust, London, 2005 – U.C Rai, S. Setji & S.H. Singh, 'Some effects of Sahaja yoga and its role in the prevention of stress disorders', *Journal of International Medical Sciences Academy*, vol. 2, no. 1, 1988, pp 19–23. – U. C. Rai & B. Wells, 'Role of Sahaja yoga in asthma', *XVI World Congress on diseases of the chest*, Boston, 1989. – R. Manocha, G. Marks, P. Kenchington, D. Peters & C. Salome, 'Sahaja yoga in the management of moderate to severe asthma: A randomised controlled trial', *Thorax*, vol. 52, no. 2, 2002, pp110–115.

9.   R. Manocha, G. Marks, P. Kenchington, D. Peters & C. Salome, 'Sahaja yoga in the management of moderate to severe asthma: A randomised controlled trial', *Thorax*, vol. 52, no. 2, 2002, pp110–115.

10. Ramesh Manocha, Deborah Black & Leigh Wilson, 'Quality of life and functional health status of long-term meditators', *Evidence-Based Complementary and Alternative Medicine*, 2012.

11.   'National Survey of mental health and wellbeing: Summary of results, 2007', *Australian Bureau of Statistics*, 2008, <www.abs.gov. au/AUSSTATS/ abs@.nsf/Lookup/4326.0Explanatory%20Notes12007?OpenDocument>

12.   Janice Meisenhelder & Emily Chandler, 'Frequency of prayer and functional health in Presbyterian pastors', *Journal for the scientific study of religion*, vol. 40, no. 2, 2001, pp 323–29.

13.   Palta, Anuradha, 'Sahaja yoga and quality of life: An empirical study.' *Journal of Indian Psychology*, vol. 27, no. 1–2, Jan–Jul 2009, pp 21–34.

14.   J. Balk, M. Brooks, S. Chung & U.C. Rai, 'Effect of Sahaja yoga meditation on quality of life, anxiety, and blood pressure control', *Journal of Alternative Complement Medicine*, vol. 18, no. 6, 2012, pp 589–96.

15.   Richard Eckersley, 'Teaching happiness: hope or hype?', Unpublished article based on keynote address to the First Australian Positive Psychology in Education Symposium, *Sydney University*, May 2009.

CHAPTER TEN: YOUNG MINDS

1.   C. Blanco, M. Okuda, C. Wright, D.S. Hasin, B.F. Grant, S.M. Liu & M. Olfson, 'Mental health of college students and their non-college-attending peers: results from the National Epidemiologic Study on Alcohol and Related Conditions', *Arch Gen Psychiatry*, Vol. 64, no. 12, 2008, pp 1429-37.

2.   'Mental illness facts and statistics', *Responseability.org*, 2008, <www. responseability.org/site/index.cfm?display=134882#19>.

3.   Jean Twenge, Brittany Gentile, C. DeWall, Debbie Ma, Katherine Lacefi eld & David Schurtz, 'Birth cohort increases in psychopathology among young Americans, 1938–2007: A cross-temporal meta-analysis of the MMPI', *Clinical Psychology Review* , vol. 30, no. 2, 2919, pp 145-54. – Keith Campbell & Jean Twenge, *The Narcissism Epidemic: Living in the Age of Entitlement*, Free Press, New York, 2009. – Jean Twenge, *Generation Me: Why Today's Young Americans Are More Confident, Assertive, Entitled – And More Miserable Than Ever Before*, Simon and Schuster Free Press, New York, 2007.

4.   Maurice Sendak, *Where the Wild things Are*, HarperCollins, 1988.

5.   Maggie Hamilton, *What's Happening to Our Girls?*, Penguin Books Australia, Hawthorn, 2009. – Richard Eckersley, 'Troubled youth: an island of misery in an ocean of happiness, or the tip of an iceberg of suffering?', *Early Intervention in Psychiatry*, vol. 5, suppl. 1, 2011, pp 6-11. – Richard Eckersley, 'Progress, culture and young people's wellbeing', In A. Furlong (ed.), *Handbook of Youth and Young Adulthood: New Perspectives and Agendas*, Routledge, London, 2009, pp 353-360. – Richard Eckersley, 'Values and visions - youth and the failure of modern western culture', *Youth Studies Australia*, vol. 27, no. 3, 2008, pp 10-19. – Richard Eckersley, 'Failing a generation: The impact of culture on the health and well-being of youth', *Journal of Paediatrics and Child Health*, vol. 29, suppl. 1, 1993, pp S16-S19.

6.   Andrew Fuller, 'From Surviving to thriving in the 21st century', *Home Economics Institute of Australia*, 2001, <www.deewr.gov.au/Schooling/Programs/ REDI/Documents/Research/from_surviving_to_thriving_pdf.pdf>.

7.   C. Lesesne, A. Abramowitz, R. Perou & E. Brann, 'Attention deficit/ hyperactivity disorder: A public health research agenda', *Centers for Disease*

Control and Prevention, 2000, <www.cdc.gov/ncbddd/adhd/dadphra.htm>. – Russell Barkley, *Attention-deficit hyperactivity disorder: A handbook for diagnosis and treatment*, 2nd ed., The Guilford press, New York, 1998. – K. Kelleher, G. Childs & J. Harman, 'Healthcare costs for children with attention deficit/ hyperactivity disorder', *The Economics of Neuroscience*, vol. 3, 2001, pp 60-63. – C. Leibson, S. Katusic, W. Babaresi, J. Ransom & P. O'Brien, 'Use and costs of medical care for children and adolescents with and without attention-deficit/hyperactivity disorder', *JAMA*, vol. 285, 2001, pp 60–6.

8. L. Harrison, R. Manocha & K. Rubia, 'Sahaja yoga meditation as a family treatment programme for children with attention deficit-hyperactivity disorder', *Clinical Child Psychology and Psychiatry*, vol. 9, no. 4, 2004, pp 479–497.

CHAPTER ELEVEN: MEDITATION IN THE CLASSROOM

1. Baseball player Satchel Paige (1906–1982) is credited for saying this, although no date for his having said this is given. It can also be found in Winnie the Pooh (pub 1926) by A.A. Milne (1882–1956), or *The House at Pooh Corner* (pub 1928) also by A.A. Milne, Hoff, Benjamin, Egmont Books Ltd, London, 2003.
2. *Mission Australia*, <https://www.missionaustralia.com.au/document-downloads>.
3. Mihaly Csikszentmihalyi, 'Motivating People to Learn', *Edutopia*, 4 November 2002, <www.edutopia.org/mihaly-csikszentmihalyi-motivatingpeople-learn>.
4. 'Work-related mental disorders in Australia', *Australian Safety and Compensation Council: Australian Government*, 2006, <www.safeworkaustralia. gov.au/sites/SWA/ AboutSafeWorkAustralia/WhatWeDo/Publications/ Documents/416/Workrelated_Mental_Disorders_Australia.pdf>.
5. C. Murray & A. Lopez, 'The global burden of disease: A comprehensive assessment of mortality and disability from diseases, injuries and risk factors in 1990 and projected to 2020', *Harvard School of Public Health*, 1st ed., 1996. – C. Mathers & D. Loncar, 'Projections of global mortality and burden of disease from 2002 to 2030', *PLOS Med*, vol. 3. no. 11, 2006.
6. 'National Survey of mental health and wellbeing: Summary of results, 2007', *Australian Bureau of Statistics*, 2008, <www.abs.gov.au/AUSSTATS/ abs@.nsf/Lookup/4326.0Explanatory%20Notes12007?OpenDocument>.
7. Ramesh Manocha, 'Does Meditation Have a Specific Effect? A Systematic Experimental Evaluation of a Mental Silence Orientated Definition', *University of New South Wales*, 2008.
8. W. Hackl, 'Die Auswirkungen von Sahaja Yoga auf das Drogenkonsumverhalten' ('The effect of Sahaja yoga on drug consumption'), *Doctoral thesis submitted to the University of Vienna*, 1995.
9. D. Morgan, 'Sahaja Yoga: An ancient path to modern mental health?' *Transpersonal Psychology Review*, vol. 4, no. 4, 2000, pp 41–49.

CHAPTER TWELVE: MEDITATION AND FLOW

1. Foshontohannanow, 'Ayrton Senna on Monte Carlo Grand Prix, 3/14/1988', *YouTube*, 17 January 2012, <www.youtube.com/ watch?v=aXbgs5fuISw>.

2. Pandey, Manish, 'Ayrton Senna: The faith of the man who could drive on water', *Huffington Post*, 8 January 2011, <www.huffingtonpost.com/manish-pandey/ayrton-senna_b_909096.html>.
3. Robert Pele, *My Life and the Beautiful Game: The Autobiography of Soccer's Greatest Star*, Skyhorse Publishing Inc., 2007.
4. Mihaly Csikszentmihalyi, *Flow: The Psychology of Optimal Experience*, HarperCollins Publishers, New York, 2008.
5. Abraham Maslow, *Religions, Values and Peak-Experiences*, Penguin Arkana, 1994.
6. Mihaly Csikszentmihalyi, *Flow: The Psychology of Optimal Experience*, HarperCollins Publishers, New York, 2008.
7. Andrew Garcia, 'Mental State Called Flow', <http://c2.com/cgi/wiki?MentalStateCalledFlow>.
8. Abraham Maslow, *Religions, Values and Peak-Experiences*, Penguin Arkana, 1994.
9. Susan Jackson & Mihaly Csikszentmihalyi, *Flow in Sports: The Keys to Optimal Experiences and Performances*, Human Kinetics, Champaign, 1999.
10. Clyde Brolin, *Overdrive: Formula 1 in the Zone*, Vatersay Books, Bourn, 2010.
11. Susan Jackson & Robert Eklund, *The Flow Scales Manual*, Fitness Information Technology, 2004. – Susan Jackson, Robert Eklund & A.J. Martin, *The FLOW Manual*, Mind Garden Inc. <www.mindgarden.com>.
12. Eric Hoffer, *The Passionate State of Mind: And Other Aphorisms*, Hopewell Publications, Titusville, 2006.

CHAPTER THIRTEEN: BRAIN, MIND AND NON-MIND

1. W. Maugham & A. Somerset, *Writer's Notebook*, Vintage, 2009.
2. Frank Meshberger, 'An interpretation of Michelangelo's Creation of Adam based on neuroanatomy, *Wellcorps International*, 2011, <www.wellcorps.com/fi les/TheCreation.pdf>.
3. Frank Meshberger, 'An interpretation of Michelangelo's Creation of Adam based on neuroanatomy', *JAMA*, vol. 264, no. 14, 1990, pp 1837–1841.
4. Norman Doidge, *The Brain That Changes Itself: Stories of Personal Triumph from the Frontiers of Brain Science*, Penguin Books, London, 2008.
5. David Burns, *The Feeling Good Handbook*, Penguin Books, 2000.
6. Deena Weisberdg, Frank Keil, Joshua Goodstein, Elizabeth Rawson & Jeremy Gray, 'The seductive allure of neuroscience explanations', *Journal of Cognitive Neuroscience*, vol. 20, no. 3, 2008, pp 470-477 – Rebecca Goldin & Cindy Merrick, 'Neuroscience of Neurobabble?', *STATS*, 2012, <www.stats.org/stories/2012/Neuroscience_Or_Neurobabble_jul16_12.html>.
7. D. Lehmann, P. Faber, S. Tei, R. Pascual-Marqui, P. Milz & K. Kochi, 'Reduced functional connectivity between cortical sources in five meditation traditions detected with lagged coherence using EEG tomography', *Neuroimage*, vol. 60, no. 2, 2012, pp 1574–86. – John Shaw, *The Brain's Alpha Rhythms and the Mind: A Review of Classical and Modern Studies of the Aplhga Rhythm Component of the Electroencephalogram with Commentaries on Associated Neuroscience and Neuropsychology*, Elsevier Science B.V., Amsterdam, 2003. – Evian Gordon (ed.), *Integrative Neuroscience: Bringing Together Biological, Psychological and Clinical Models of the Human Brain*, CRC Press, Amsterdam, 2005.

8. L. Aftanas & S. Golocheikine, 'Human anterior and frontal midline theta and lower alpha reflect emotionally positive state and internalized attention: high-resolution EEG investigation of meditation', *Neuroscience Letters*, vol. 310, no. 1, 2001, pp.57–60. – L. Aftanas & S. Golocheikine, 'Linear and non-linear concomitants of altered state of consciousness during meditation: high resolution EEG investigation', *International Journal of Psychophysiology*, vol. 45, no. 1-2, 2002, pp 158–1158. – L. Aftanas & S. Golocheikine, 'Non-linear dynamic complexity of the human EEG during meditation', *Neuroscience Letters*, vol. 330, no. 2, 2002, pp 143–146. – L. Aftanas & S. Golocheikine, 'Changes in cortical activity in altered states of consciousness: the study of meditation by high-resolution EEG', *Journal of Human Physiology*, vol. 29, no. 3, 2003, pp 143–151.
9. Ram Mishra, Cia Barlas & A. Pradham, 'Effect of meditation on plasma beta-endorphins in humans', 1993.
10. J.L. Harte, G.H. Eifert & R. Smith, 'The effects of running on beta-endorphin, corticotropin-releasing hormone and cortisol in plasma, and on mood', *Biology and Psychology*, vol. 30, no. 3, 1995, pp 251-65.
11. Tom Collins, 'Reflections: Thoughts on myth, spirit, and our times. An interview with Joseph Campbell, by Tom Collins', *Context Institute*, no. 12, 1997.

APPENDIX: THE MICHELANGELO CODE

1. Frank Meshberger, 'An interpretation of Michelangelo's Creation of Adam based on neuroanatomy', *JAMA*, vol. 264, no. 14, 1990, pp 1837–1841.
2. B. Cahn & J. Polich, 'Meditation states and traits: EEG, ERP, and neuroimaging studies', *Psychology Bull*, vol. 132, no. 2, 2006, pp 180–211.
3. K. Rubia, 'The neurobiology of Meditation and its clinical effectiveness in psychiatric disorders', *Journal of Biological Psychology*, vol. 82, no. 1, 2009, pp 1–11.
4. Michael Gazzaniga, R. Ivry, R & G. Mangun, *Fundamentals of Cognitive Neuroscience*, WW Norton, 1998.
5. L. Aftanas & S. Golocheikine, 'Non-linear dynamic complexity of the human EEG during meditation', *Neuroscience Letters*, vol. 330, no. 2, 2002, pp 143–146. – L. Aftanas & S. Golocheikine, 'Changes in cortical activity in altered states of consciousness: the study of meditation by high-resolution EEG', *Journal of Human Physiology*, vol. 29, no. 3, 2003,pp 143–151.
6. Paul Moliken (ed.), *Transcendentalism: Essential Essays of Emerson & Thoreau*, Prestwick House, 2008.

Resources

BOOKS

Benson, Herbert, *The Relaxation Response*, HarperCollins Publishers, New York, 2001.

Blackmore, Susan, *Consciousness: An Introduction*, 2nd edition, Hodder Education, London, 2010.

Bright, James, Clow, Angela and Jones, Fiona, *Stress: Myth, Theory and Research*, Prentice Hall, Harrow, 2001.

Brolin, Clyde, *Overdrive: Formula 1 in the Zone*, Vatersay Books, Bourn, 2010.

Bucke, Richard, *Cosmic Consciousness: A Study in the Evolution of the Human Mind*, Innes & Sons, Philadelphia, 1905.

Campbell, Keith and Twenge, Jean, *The Narcissism Epidemic: Living in the Age of Entitlement*, Free Press, New York, 2009.

Cleary, Thomas, *The Secret of the Golden Flower: The Classic Chinese Book of Life*, HarperCollins Publishers, San Francisco, 1991.

Cooper, Cary and Dewe, Philip, *Stress: A Brief History*, Wiley-Blackwell, Malden, 2004.

Csikszentmihalyi, Mihaly, *Flow: The Psychology of Optimal Experience*, HarperCollins Publishers, New York, 2008.

Denniss, Clive and Hamilton, Clive, *Affluenza: When Too Much is Never Enough*, Allen & Unwin, Crows Nest, 2006.

Devi, Her Holiness Mataji Shri Nirmala, *Meta Modern Era*, 3rd edition, Vishwa Nirmala Dharma, 1997.

Dixon, Jane, Douglas, Bob and Eckersley, Richard, *The Social Origins of Health and Well-being*, Cambridge University Press, Cambridge, 2001

Doidge, Norman, *The Brain That Changes Itself: Stories of Personal Triumph from the Frontiers of Brain Science*, Penguin Books, London, 2008.

Eckersley, Richard, *Measuring Progress: Is life Getting Better?*, CSIRO Publishing, Collingwood, 1998.

Eckersley, Richard, *Well & Good: Morality, Meaning and Happiness*, Text Publishing, Melbourne, 2005.

Gladwell, Malcolm, *Blink: The Power of Thinking Without Thinking*, Penguin Books Limited, London, 2006.

Gordon, Evian (ed.), *Integrative Neuroscience: Bringing Together Biological, Psychological and Clinical Models of the Human Brain*, CRC Press, Amsterdam, 2005.

Hamilton, Maggie, *What's Happening to Our Boys?*, Penguin Books Australia, Hawthorn, 2010.

Hamilton, Maggie, *What's Happening to Our Girls?*, Penguin Books Australia, Hawthorn, 2009.

Jackson, Susan, and Mihaly Csikszentmihalyi, *Flow in Sports: The Keys to Optimal Experiences and Performances*, Human Kinetics, Champaign, 1999.

Le Fanu, James, *The Rise and Fall of Modern Medicine*, Carroll & Graf Publishers, New York, 2000.

Levin, Jeff, *God, Faith and Health: Exploring the Spirituality-Healing Connection*, John Wiley & Sons, New York, 2002.

Mascaro, Juan, *The Bhagavad Gita*, Penguin Books, Baltimore, 1962.

Mascaro, Juan, *The Dhammapada: The Path of Perfection*, Penguin Books, Harmondsworth, 1973.

Mascaro, Juan, *The Upanishads*, Penguin Books, Baltimore, 1965.

Powell, Nigel (ed.), *Meditation: The Joy of Spiritual Self Knowledge through Sahaja Yoga Meditation*, Corvalis Publishing, London, 2005.

Rai, Umesh, *Medical Science Enlightened: New Insight into Vibratory Awareness for Holistic Health Care*, New Delhi: Life Eternal Trust, London, 1993.

Shaw, John, *The Brain's Alpha Rhythms and the Mind: A Review of Classical and Modern Studies of the Aplhga Rhythm Component of the Electroencephalogram with Commentaries on Associated Neuroscience and Neuropsychology*, Elsevier Science B.V., Amsterdam, 2003.

Turek, Greg, *A Seeker's Journey: Searching for Clues to Life's Meaning*, Fast Books, Glebe, 1995.

Twenge, Jean, *Generation Me: Why Today's Young Americans Are More Confident, Assertive, Entitled – And More Miserable Than Ever Before*, Free Press, New York, 2006.

Watkins, Alan, *Mind-Body Medicine: A Clinician's Guide to Psychoneuroimmunology*, Elsevier Health Sciences, London, 1997.

Wilber, Ken, *Quantum questions: Mystical Writings of the World's Greatest Physicists*, Shambhala, Colorado, 1984.

PEER-REVIEWED PAPERS

Aftanas, L.I. & Golosheykin, S.A. (2003). 'Changes in cortical activity in altered states of consciousness: the study of meditation by high resolution EEG.' *Journal of Human Physiology*, 29(2):143–151.

Aftanas, L.I. & Golosheykin, S.A. (2001). 'Human anterior and frontal midline theta and lower alpha refl ect emotionally positive state and internalized attention: high-resolution EEG investigation of meditation.' *Neuroscience Letters*, 310(1):57– 60.

Aftanas, L.I. & Golosheykin, S.A. (2005). 'Impact of regular meditation practice on EEG activity at rest and during evoked negative emotions.' *International Journal of Neuroscience*, 115(6):893–909.

Aftanas, L.I. & Golosheykin, S.A. (2002). 'Linear and non-linear concomitants of altered state of consciousness during meditation: high resolution EEG investigation.' *International Journal of Psychophysiology*, 45(1–2):158–1158.

Aftanas, L.I. & Golosheykin, S.A. (2002). 'Non-linear dynamic complexity of the human EEG during meditation.' *Neuroscience Letters*, 330(2):143–146.

Balk, J., Brooks, M., Chung, S. & Rai, U.C. (2012). 'Effect of Sahaja yoga meditation on quality of life, anxiety, and blood pressure control.' *Journal of Alternative Complement Medicine*, 18(6):589–96.

Chrilli, Schneider, Zollo. (2011) 'The psychological antecedents to socially responsible behaviour.' *European Management Review*, 5(3):175-190.

Gupta, H.L., Dudani, U., Singh, S.H., Surange, S.G. & Selvamurthy, W. (1991). 'Sahaja yoga in the management of intractable epileptics.' *Journal of the Association of Physicians of India*, 39(8):649.

Hackl, W. (1995). 'Die Auswirkungen von Sahaja Yoga auf das Drogenkonsumverhalten.' ('The effect of Sahaja yoga on drug consumption.') *Doctoral thesis submitted to the University of Vienna.*

Harrison, L.J., Manocha, R. & Rubia, K. (2004). 'Sahaja yoga meditation as a family treatment programme for children with attention deficit-hyperactivity disorder.' *Clinical Child Psychology and Psychiatry*, 9(4):479–497.

James, William. (1901–1902). 'The varieties of religious experience: a study in human nature.' *Gifford lectures: University of Edinburgh*, <http://www2.hn.psu.edu/faculty/jmanis/wjames/Varieties-Rel-Exp.pdf>

Lehmann D., Faber, P.L., Tei, S., Pascual-Marqui, R.D., Milz, P. & Kochi, K. (2012). 'Reduced functional connectivity between cortical sources in five meditation traditions detected with lagged coherence using EEG tomography.' *Neuroimage*, 60(2):1574–86.

Manocha, R., 'Intervention insights: Meditation, mindfulness and mind-emptiness.' *Acta Neuropsychiatrica*, 23(1):46–47.

Manocha, R. (2000). 'Why meditation?' *Australian Family Physician*; 29(12):1135–1138.

Manocha, R., Black, D., Ryan, J., Stough, C. & Spiro, D. (2010). 'Changing definitions of meditation: Physiological corollorary.' *Journal of the International Society of Life Sciences*, 28(1).

Manocha, R., Black, D., Sarris, J. & Stough, C. (2011). 'A randomised, controlled trial of meditation for work stress, anxiety and depressed mood in full-time workers.' *Evidence-based Complementary and Alternative Medicine*, 960583.

Manocha, R., Black, D. & Wilson, L. (2012). 'Quality of life and functional health status of long-term mediators.' *Evidence-based Complementary and Alternative Medicine*, 350674.

Manocha, R., Gordon, A., Black, D., Malhi, G. & Seidler, R. (2009). 'Using meditation for less stress and better wellbeing – Evaluation of a seminar for GPs.' *Australian Family Physician*, 38(6):369–464.

Manocha, R., Marks, G.B., Kenchington, P., Peters, D. & Salome, C. M. (2002). 'Sahaja yoga in the management of moderate to severe asthma: a randomised controlled trial.' *Thorax*, 57(2):110–115.

Manocha, R., Semmar, B. & Black, D. (2007). 'A pilot study of a mental silence form of meditation for perimenopausal women.' *Journal of Clinical Psychology in Medical Settings*, 14(3):266–273.

Mishra, R. (2001). 'Analysis of yoga: implications of Sahaja Yoga in treatment of mental and neurological disorders.' *The World Assembly for Mental Health: Respecting Diversity in a Changing World, The 28th Congress of the World Federation for Mental Health*, Vancouver, Canada.

Morgan, D. (2000). 'Sahaja yoga: An ancient path to modern mental health?' *Transpersonal Psychology Review*, 4(4):41–49.

Palta, Anuradha. (2009). 'Sahaja yoga and quality of life: An empirical study.' *Journal of Indian Psychology*, 27(1–2):21–34.

Panjwani, U., Gupta, H.L., Singh, S.H., Selvamurthy, W. & Rai, U.C. (1995).
    'Effect of Sahaja yoga practice on stress management in patients of epilepsy.'
    Indian Journal of Physiology and Pharmacology, 39(2):111–116.

Panjwani, U., Selvamurthy, W., Singh, S.H., Gupta, H.L., Mukhopadhyay, S.
    & Thakur, L. (2000). 'Effect of Sahaja yoga meditation on auditory evoked
    potentials (AEP) and visual contrast sensitivity (VCS) in epileptics.' *Applied
    Psychophysiology and Biofeedback*, 25(1):1–12.

Panjwani, U., Selvamurthy, W., Singh, S.H., Gupta, H.L., Thakur, L. & Rai,
    U.C. (1996). 'Effect of Sahaja yoga practice on seizure control & EEG
    changes in patients of epilepsy.' *Indian Journal of Medical Research*, 103:165–172.

Rubia, K. (2009). 'The neurobiology of meditation and its clinical effectiveness
    in psychiatric disorders.' *Journal of Biological Psychology*, 82(1):1–11. Epub 2009,
    Apr 23.

Schneider, S., Zollo, M. & Manocha, R. (2011). 'Developing socially responsible
    behaviour in managers: Experimental evaluation of traditional vs. innovative
    (meditation) learning approaches.' *Journal of Corporate Citizenship*.

Acknowledgements

My thanks go to the following institutions for their help: The School of Women's and Children's Health and the Faculty of Medicine, University of New South Wales, who demonstrated infinite patience in their support of my doctoral thesis, much of which is described in this book. The Trainee Scholarship and Research Fund, Royal Australian College of General Practitioners; the Barry Wren Trust, Royal Hospital for Women; the Australian Headache Society; The Sydney Menopause Centre; Natural Therapies Unit, The Prince of Wales Hospital; Sydney Hospital; Swinburne University; Neuropsychology Unit; Brain Sciences Institute; The Woolcock Institute, The Department of Psychiatry, University of Sydney.

There are many Sahaja yoga practitioners who deserve acknowledgement for their selfless participation as instructors and the support they gave to various projects. Some of them are named here: Peter Kenchington, Robert Hutcheon, Greg Turek, Harish and Jan Rajak, Alice Bhasale, Neil Avoledo, Prue Page, Deborah Keetley, Sunil and Aarti Sivarajah, Shanti Gosh, Justin Tiptaft, Celeste Jones, Richard Kennett, Max Lieberman, David Morgan, Dr Bohdan and Mrs Brigitte Shehovych, Brian Bell, Paul Keetley, Hauke Horn, Peter Aerfeldt, Sandeep and Gabby Mane, Raymond Hampton, Kim Pearce, Liallyn Fitzpatrick, Ione Docherty, Robert Henshaw, Bruce Ridge, Keiran McPhail, Priya Rapyal, Sheetu Arora, Annaliese Donoghue, Guy and Lene Jeffrey, Sue Nickson, Rita Skipper, Leanne Lingard, Cathy Beaven, Andrei Ratiu, Anil Sattarshetty, Andrew Rohowyj, Peter Hewitson, Christine

Clear, Chris Kyriacou, Hari Gaikwad and Sno Bonneau and many more. They heroically tolerated the various impositions that my research and my imperfect management style have imposed on them over the past many years.

Thanks to all those who provided moral support, encouragement and inspiration. And everyone and anyone who may have tolerated instances of bizarre and impetuous behaviour of the author, arising from the demands of the research or manuscript writing.

As far as other individuals go, I must first thank my wife and children, who have selflessly supported and tolerated the coexistence of this research work since we first met. On many occasions my wife has gone above and beyond the call of duty, made considerable sacrifices, with little acknowledgement, to support something she felt would be of benefit to others. Everybody needs a couple of completely uncritical fans. My children are the best fan club anyone could hope for.

Thanks to Associate Professor John Eden, who supported this research programme for ten years, and Professor Deborah Black, who supervised the original doctoral thesis along with John. I feel deeply indebted to the many researchers who worked with my team and me, especially: Professor Guy Marks, Professor Con Stough, Professor Gurjinder Malhi. To Professor Umesh Rai and his pioneering work done in India and Dr Sandeep and Dr Madhur Rai who now selflessly continue his vision. Mr John Noyce, of Noyce Publishing, and Linda Williams for their help in rounding up the various quotations and meditators' experiences. And, the students who worked with me on various projects, particularly Dr Amy Gordon, Kabir Sattarshetty, Shanti Gosh, Sheetu Arora, Tristan Boyd and Nicholas Scali. The talented Brian Bell,

John and Judy Dobbie, Gloria Webb, Michael Fogarty, Greg Turek, Peter Gesovic, David Morgan and Keiran McPhail and others who provided me with their unvarnished opinions, feedback and assistance with the manuscript.

I am most grateful to Bernadette Foley for her wisdom in commissioning this book, despite my lack of experience with such things, and to Kate Stevens for her remarkable patience and professionalism.

Most importantly, my deepest gratitude is offered to Shri Mataji Nirmala Devi, founder of Sahaja yoga, who encouraged fair, thorough and genuinely scientific evaluation without precondition on the outcomes. Her unique contribution to the modern understanding of meditation has made this book possible. She permitted research on the technique on the proviso that no part of it be commercialised or distorted, and I hope that this book and the research that it describes is true to this request. Her selfless dedication to making meditation skills available to the public without charge is consistent with the ancient tradition of meditation and continues to be a source of great inspiration. The distinguished career of Shri Mataji's husband, Sir CP Srivastava, in international administration, management and academics was also a great example for me. My humble gratitude to their daughters, Kalpana and Sadhana.

Finally, I offer my humble thanks to all the great and authentic sages, seers, gurus, prophets, saints, gnostics, mystics, avatars, rishis and yogis from all cultures, societies, civilisations, religions and epochs whose experiences of mental silence and contribution to the meditative experience created the foundation upon which this book is based. I hope that in at least some very small way this book contributes to the fulfilment of their vision of benevolence for humanity.

Index